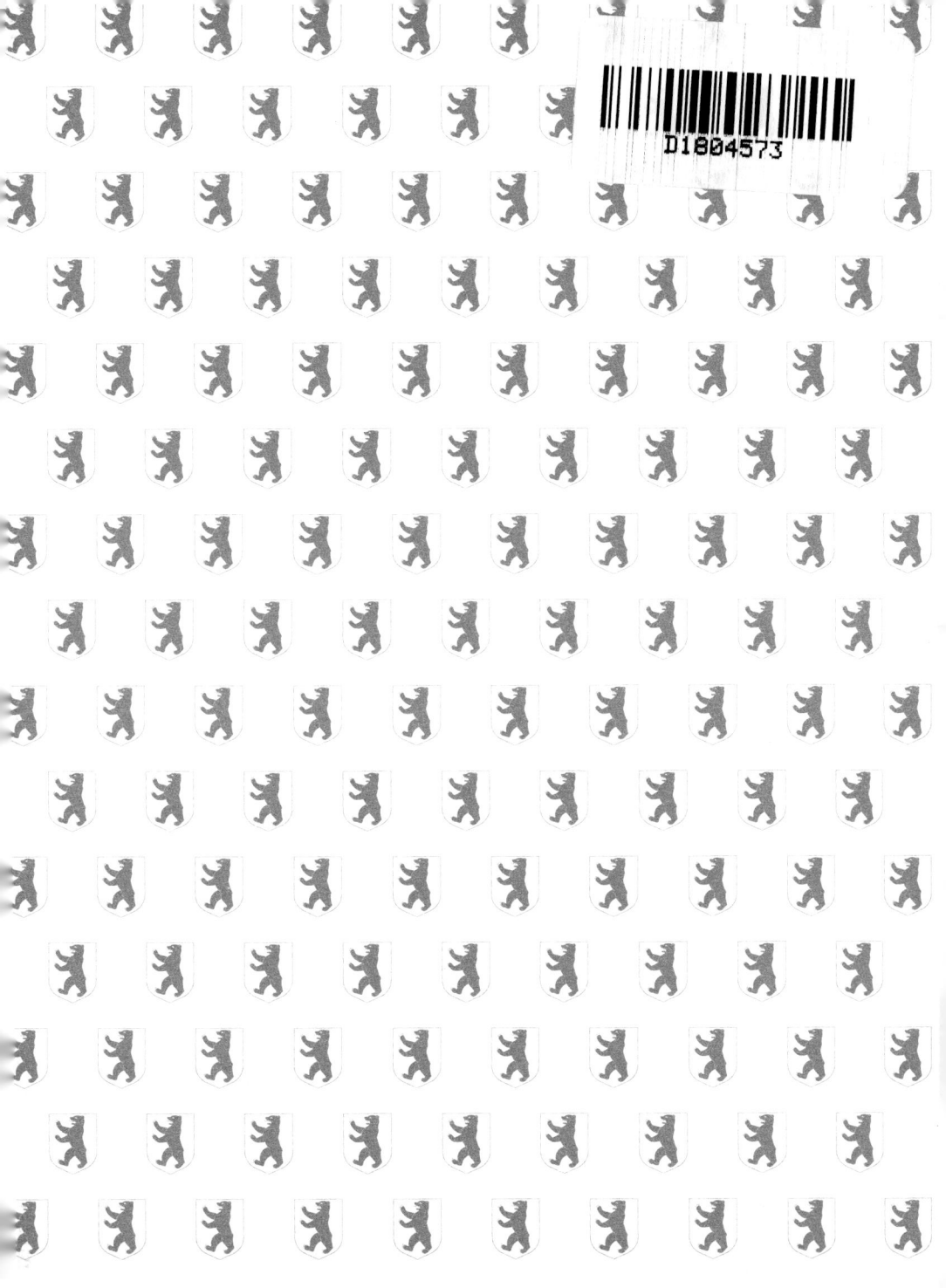

+++ Die Bildchronik +++ The Illustrated History +++

BERLIN

Bibliographische Information der Deutschen Bibliothek
Die Deutsche Bibliothek verzeichnet diese Publikation in der
Deutschen Nationalbibliographie; detaillierte bibliographische
Daten sind im Internet über http://dnb.ddb.de abrufbar.

Bildredaktion und Texte: MediText, Stuttgart;
DuMont monte Verlag, Köln; Ursula Härtling
Übersetzung ins Englische:
First Edition Translations Ltd., Cambridge
Korrektorat der englischen Texte: Jardi Mullinax, Köln
Abbildungsnachweis:
(163, 327) Christo und Jeanne-Claude: Verhüllter Reichstag,
Berlin 1971-95, Foto: Wolfgang Volz, © Christo
Alle übrigen Abbildungen: akg-images, Berlin
(141) Otto Dix © VG Bild-Kunst, Bonn 2003

akg-images
Berlin London Paris

Reproduktion: PPP Pre Print Partner, Köln
Druck und buchbinderische Verarbeitung:
Druckerei APPL, Wemding

© 2003 DuMont monte Verlag GmbH & Co. KG, Köln
Originalausgabe
Alle Rechte vorbehalten
Printed in Germany

ISBN 3-8320-8811-3

Picture research and text: MediText, Stuttgart;
DuMont monte Verlag, Cologne; Ursula Härtling
English translation: First Edition Translations Ltd., Cambridge
English copyediting: Jardi Mullinax, Cologne

Photographs:
(163, 327) Christo and Jeanne-Claude: Wrapped Reichstag,
Berlin 1971-95, Photo: Wolfgang Volz, © Christo
All other photographs: akg-images, Berlin
(141) Otto Dix © VG Bild-Kunst, Bonn 2003

akg-images
Berlin London Paris

Reproduction: PPP Pre Print Partner, Cologne
Printing and binding: APPL, Wemding

© 2003 DuMont monte Verlag GmbH & Co. KG, Cologne
All rights reserved

Printed in Germany

ISBN 3-8320-8811-3

INHALT / CONTENTS

Alles Berlin	**8**	All about Berlin
Auf Sand gebaut	**14**	Built on sand
Residenzstadt Berlin	**26**	Berlin becomes a royal residence
Zeit der Revolutionen	**44**	A time of revolutions
Glanz und Elend der Gründerzeit	**78**	Splendour and poverty of the early years
Vom Ersten Weltkrieg ins Dritte Reich	**96**	From First World War to Third Reich
Die Zentrale der NS-Macht	**154**	Nerve centre of Nazi power
Neubeginn in Ost und West	**204**	New beginnings in East and West
Die geteilte Stadt	**264**	The divided city
1989 – die Welt blickt auf Berlin	**308**	1989 – the eyes of the world are on Berlin
Die neue Hauptstadt	**322**	The new capital
Chronik	**354**	Chronology

ALLES BERLIN

ALL ABOUT BERLIN

Das Völkchen besitzt viel Selbstvertrauen, ist mit Witz und Ironie gesegnet und nicht sparsam mit diesen Gaben. (Johann Wolfgang von Goethe, 1749-1832) | Berlin ist mehr ein Weltteil als eine Stadt. (Jean Paul, 1763-1825) | Die Umgegend von Berlin ist ein Sandmeer. Wer dort eine Stadt erbaut hat, muss vom Teufel geplagt gewesen sein. (Stendhal, 1783-1842) | Berlin ist gar keine Stadt, sondern Berlin gibt bloß den Ort dazu her, wo sich eine Menge Menschen, und zwar darunter viele Menschen von Geist, versammeln, denen der Ort ganz gleichgültig ist. (Heinrich Heine, 1797-1856) | Du bist varickt, mein Kind, / Du musst nach Berlin, / Wo die Varickten sind, / Da jehörst Du hin. (Franz von Suppé, 1819-1895) | Vor Gott sind eigentlich alle Menschen Berliner. (Theodor Fontane, 1819–1898) | Der Berliner Westen, diese elegante Kleinstadt, in welcher alle Leute wohnen, die etwas können, etwas sind und etwas haben und sich dreimal soviel einbilden, als sie können, sind und haben. (Alfred Kerr, 1867-1948) | Der Horizont des Berliners ist längst nicht so groß wie seine Stadt. (Kurt Tucholsky, 1890-1935) | Berlin wird eines Tages die Hauptstadt der Welt sein. (Adolf Hitler, 1889-1945) | Berlin bleibt doch Berlin. (Bruno Balz, 1902-1988) | Wer Berlin zur neuen Hauptstadt macht, schafft geistig ein neues Preußen. (Konrad Adenauer, 1876-1967) | Ich bin ein Berliner! (John F. Kenne-

Seite 8/9: Dem deutschen Volke: Das neue Reichstagsgebäude von Sir Norman Foster

The people are very self-confident; they are blessed with wit and irony and do not keep these gifts to themselves (Johann Wolfgang von Goethe, 1749-1832). | Berlin is more a small world than a city (Jean Paul, 1763-1825). | Berlin's surroundings are a sea of sand. Whoever built a city there must have been mad (Stendhal, 1783-1842). | Berlin is not a city; it is simply the place where many spirited people, completely indifferent to it, choose to gather (Heinrich Heine, 1797-1856). | You are mad, my dear; / You need to go to Berlin. / The city of the mad, / That is where you belong (Franz von Suppé, 1819-1895). | Before God, all people are Berliners (Theodor Fontane, 1819-1898). | Western Berlin, this small and elegant town, inhabited by all those who can achieve something, are something, and have something, and think three times as highly of themselves as to what in fact they can achieve, who they are, and what they have (Alfred Kerr, 1867 - 1948). | The Berliner's horizon is not nearly as wide as his city's (Kurt Tucholsky, 1890-1935). | One day, Berlin will be the capital of the world (Adolf Hitler (1889-1945). | Berlin will always be Berlin (Bruno Balz, 1902-1988). | Whoever makes Berlin the new capital, creates a new Prussia in his mind (Konrad Adenauer, 1876-1967). | Ich bin ein Berliner! (John F. Kennedy, 1917-1963). | West Berlin is the bunion of the Western Allies that needs to be stepped on from time to

dy, 1917-1963) | Westberlin ist das Hühnerauge der Westmächte, auf das man von Zeit zu Zeit kräftig treten muss. (Nikita Sergejewitsch Chruschtschow, 1894-1971) | Ein fruchtbares Gelände für sumpfige Typen, seit 750 Jahren. (Wolfgang Neuß, 1923-1989) | Mal sehn, was im Dschungel läuft, Musik ist heiß, das Neonlicht strahlt. Irgendjemand hat mir 'nen Gin bezahlt, die Tanzfläche kocht, hier trifft sich die Scene, ich fühl' mich gut, ich steh' auf Berlin! (Ideal, 1980) | Germania Tod in Berlin (Heiner Müller, 1929-1995) | Was im Laboratorium Berlin nicht gelingt, das wird auch in ganz Deutschland nicht gelingen. (Roman Herzog, *1934) | Du lächelst / Ich bin glücklich / Wir haben viel vor / Berlin liebt Dich (Surrogat, 2000) | Schluss mit lustig, die Tristesse allemande hat uns wieder. Berlin, das kulturelle Großlabor, macht dicht. (Der Spiegel, 2002) | Wir Berliner haben uns daran gewöhnt, dass Hilfe immer von oben und von außen kam. (Gregor Gysi, *1948) | Das grundlegende Problem liegt darin, dass sich Berlin auf einen Schlag neu erfinden wollte. Statt einen Raum zu bewohnen und die Stadt allmählich aus den Lebensformen der Menschen zu entwickeln, hat man einen Plan aufgestellt. (Richard Sennett, *1943) | Wie würden Sie sich das neue Berlin und das damit verbundene Staatsbild wünschen? - Schön ruhig in der Ecke. Nicht auffällig - und nicht angeberisch (Günter Behnisch, *1922) | Diese Stadt ist eine nationale Projektionsfläche. (Christina Weiss, *1953) |

time (Nikita Sergeyevtch Khrushchev, 1894-1971). | A prosperous terrain for dodgy guys, and it has been like this for 750 years (Wolfgang Neuß, 1923-1989). | Let's find out what goes on in the jungle. The music is hot, the neon lights are bright. Someone paid for my gin, the dance floor is heaving, this is where the in-crowd meets, I feel great, I love Berlin! (Ideal,1980). | Germania – death in Berlin (Heiner Müller, 1929-1995). | Anything that fails in the laboratory of Berlin will fail in Germany as a whole (Roman Herzog, *1934). | You are smiling / I am happy / We have many plans / Berlin loves you (Surrogat, 2000). | The fun is over, welcome back 'tristesse allemande'. Berlin, the big cultural laboratory, is closing down (Der Spiegel, 2002). | We Berliners have become accustomed to help that comes from above and from outside (Gregor Gysi, *1948). | The basic problem is that Berlin wanted to reinvent itself in one go. Instead of living in an area and developing the town gradually based on the life style of its inhabitants, they drew up a plan (Richard Sennett, *1943). | What would you want the new Berlin and associated state to be like? Very quiet; remaining on the sidelines. Not conspicuous; not showing off (Günter Behnisch, *1922). | This city is the projection screen of the nation (Christina Weiss, *1953). |

Pages 8/9: To the German people: The restored Reichstag building, designed by Sir Norman Foster.

Ein Bär geht mit der Zeit:
Wappenentwurf von Sigmund von Weech 1934,
plastisches Detail von Eduard Lürssen
an der Karl-Liebknecht-Brücke
und auf Banknoten der Inflation 1919-1923.

BERLIN BLEIBT BÄRLIN

Berlin ist schon kurz nach der Stadtgründung 1237 auf den Bär gekommen. Das älteste bekannte Siegel mit zwei aufrecht gehenden Bären stammt von 1280. Darauf ist zu lesen: »Sigillum burgensium de berlin sum« – »Ich bin das Siegel der Bürger von Berlin«.

Über die Jahrhunderte wurde der Bär zum allgegenwärtigen Wappentier. Im Stadtwappen von 1701 stand er noch unter dem preußischen und märkischen Adler, später wurde er allein dargestellt. Sigmund von Weech entwarf 1934 einen Berliner Bären, der nach Kriegsende zum Ostberliner Stadtwappen wurde. Für die Westberliner schuf Otto Neubecker 1954 einen eigenen Bären, der 1990 zum Landeswappen für das wiedervereinigte Berlin avancierte.

Der Bär symbolisiert die Freiheit und Unabhängigkeit Berlins. Unklar ist allerdings, ob der Bär der Stadt den Namen gegeben hat. Egal wie er in die Stadtgeschichte geriet, die Berliner lieben ihren Bär. Einen Tag nach dem 700-jährigen Stadtjubiläum 1937 stand in der »BZ am Mittag«: (...) so bitten wir uns nachträglich ein Geburtstagsgeschenk aus, einen richtigen lebendigen, brummenden, tanzenden, schönen Petz.« Zwei Jahre später bezogen Lotte, Jule, Urs und Vreni den Bärenzwinger im Köllnischen Park. Der heute amtierende Stadtbär heißt Tilo.

A bear through the changing times: Coat-of-arms design by Sigmund von Weech, 1934, sculptural detail by Eduard Lürssen on the Karl-Liebknecht Bridge, and banknotes issued during the 1919-1923 inflation.

BERLIN REMAINS 'BEARLIN'

Berlin came up with the symbol of the bear shortly after the founding of the city in 1237. The oldest known seal, showing two bears walking on their hind legs, dates from 1280. The text reads: 'Sigillum burgensium de berlin sum' ('I am the seal of the citizens of Berlin').

Over the centuries, the bear became the ubiquitous heraldic beast. In the city coat of arms of 1701, it was still to be seen beneath the eagle of Prussia and Brandenburg. Later it appeared alone. In 1934 Sigmund von Weech designed a Berlin bear, which became the coat of arms of East Berlin after the end of the war. Otto Neubecker created a bear especially for the West Berliners in 1954, which was promoted to the coat of arms of the reunited Berlin when it became a federal state in 1990.

The bear symbolizes the freedom and independence of Berlin. It is not clear, however, whether the bear gave the city its name. No matter how it became a part of the city's history, the Berliners love their bear. One day after the seven hundredth anniversary of the city in 1937, the newspaper 'BZ am Mittag' carried the following: '... so we are giving ourselves a belated birthday present, a real live, growling, dancing, beautiful Bruin'. Two years later, Lotte, Jule, Urs, and Vreni moved into the bear-pit in the Köllnischer Park. The current holder of the office of city bear is called Tilo.

AUF SAND GEBAUT

BUILT ON SAND

Berlin ist – verglichen mit anderen europäischen Städten – eine junge Stadt. Von ihren ersten Anfängen ist wenig überliefert, da schwere Brände wichtige Dokumente aus der Gründungszeit vernichtet haben.

Die Stadt entwickelte sich Ende des 12. Jahrhunderts aus zwei verkehrstechnisch günstig gelegenen Kaufmannssiedlungen zu beiden Seiten der Spree. Am 28. Oktober 1237 wird das auf der Spreeinsel gelegene Cölln zum ersten Mal urkundlich erwähnt, 1244 Berlin.

Vor allem Berlin war ein wichtiger Knotenpunkt des Fernhandels, konnte Zölle erheben und besaß Stapel- und Niederlagerechte.

Die Schwestergemeinden kooperierten: ab 1307 gründeten sie eine Union und bauten eine gemeinsame Verwaltung auf. 1342 wurde erstmals ein gemeinsames Rathaus erwähnt.

Die Doppelstadt Berlin/Cölln wuchs durch Spreeübergänge und befestigt von einer Stadtmauer mehr und mehr zusammen. Das erweiterte Stadtgebiet umfasste damals insgesamt 70 Hektar.

Als die Hohenzollern, die seit dem 15. Jahrhundert die Mark Brandenburg beherrschten, 1440 unter Kurfürst Friedrich II. hier ihre Residenzstadt erbauen wollten, regte sich großer Widerstand, weil die Berliner um ihre städtischen Privilegien

Seite 14/15:
Berlin und Cölln zur Zeit des Großen Kurfürsten Friedrich Wilhelm. Stich um 1652 von Kaspar Merian aus der berühmten Kupferstecherfamilie.

Berlin is a young city in comparison to others in Europe. Very little evidence of its earliest beginnings has survived, as terrible fires completely destroyed important documents dating from its foundation.

Berlin developed in the late twelfth century from two trading settlements on both sides of the Spree, which were favourably situated with regard to the trade routes. Cölln, which stands on the island in the Spree, is first mentioned on 28 October 1237, and Berlin in 1244.

Berlin, in particular, was an important centre for long-distance trade; the citizens were allowed to levy customs duties, and had rights to store and trade in staple goods. The two communities worked together. In 1307 they founded a union and set up a common administration. The first mention of a common town hall dates from 1342. The twin cities of Berlin/Cölln grew together more and more as bridges were built over the Spree, and a city wall was built to fortify them. At that time, the extended city covered a total area of 70 hectares.

When the Hohenzollerns, who had ruled the Mark of Brandenburg since the fifteenth century, wanted to set up their royal seat here in 1440 under Elector Friedrich II, the idea met with great opposition because the Berliners feared for their civic privileges. In 1443, the sovereign had the foundation stone of his residence laid on the bank of the Spree. The stronghold was intended to undermine the autonomy of the two refractory towns.

fürchteten. Am Ufer der Spree ließ der Regent 1443 den Grundstein des späteren Stadtschlosses legen, die »Zwingburg« sollte die Autonomie der beiden renitenten Städte untergraben. Schließlich wurde Berlin zur Haupt- und Residenzstadt: 1470 erklärten die Brandenburgischen Fürsten Berlin zu ihrem Regierungssitz.

Im Zuge der Reformation wurde Berlin 1539 zu einer protestantischen Hochburg. Zu Beginn des 17. Jahrhunderts zählte die kurfürstliche Residenzstadt 10.000 Einwohner. Doch dann wurde der Dreißigjährige Krieg (1618-1648) für Berlin zu einer schrecklichen Zäsur: fast die Hälfte aller Einwohner starb. 1640 übernahm Friedrich Wilhelm, der »Große Kurfürst«, die Herrschaft. Er regierte nach zentralistischen und absolutistischen Grundsätzen. Seine Regierungszeit dauerte fast fünfzig Jahre, in denen die Bevölkerungszahl wieder auf 20.000 Menschen anwuchs. Dazu trugen viele Glaubensflüchtlinge bei: 1671 siedelten sich in Berlin jüdische Familien an, die aus Wien vertrieben worden waren, und gründeten die erste jüdische Gemeinde. Gut zehn Jahre später, 1685, fanden 6.000 protestantische Hugenotten, die aus Frankreich geflohen waren, Zuflucht in der Stadt. Beide Gruppen sollten das Gesicht Berlins entscheidend mitprägen.

Wenig später regten sich in Berlin auch die ersten Anfänge wissenschaftlichen Lebens. Am 11. Juli 1700 gründete Gottfried Wilhelm Leibniz die kurfürstlich-brandenburgische »Societät der Wissenschaften«. Aus dieser Institution entstand die spätere Akademie der Wissenschaften.

In the end, Berlin became the capital and the royal seat. In 1470, the ruler of Brandenburg declared Berlin to be the seat of the government.

In 1539, during the Reformation, Berlin became a Protestant stronghold. At the beginning of the seventeenth century, the royal capital had ten thousand inhabitants, but then the "Thirty Years" War (1618-1648) marked a dreadful turning point for Berlin, when almost half its population died. In 1640, Friedrich Wilhelm, the 'Great Elector', assumed power and ruled according to centralist and absolutist principles. His reign lasted almost fifty years, during which the population climbed back to twenty thousand. Many religious refugees contributed to this increase. In 1671, Jewish families who had been expelled from Vienna settled in Berlin and founded the first Jewish community. Some ten years later, in 1685, six thousand Protestant Hugenots, who had fled from France, found shelter in the city. Both groups were to leave a crucial mark on the face of Berlin.

Not long afterwards, the first stirrings of scientific life also began in Berlin. On 11 July 1700, Gottfried Wilhelm Leibniz founded the royal Brandenburg 'Societät der Wissenschaften' ('Society of Science'). This institution later gave birth to the Academy of Science.

Pages 14/15: Berlin and Cölln at the time of the Great Elector Friedrich Wilhelm. Copperplate engraving by Kaspar Merian, one of the famous families of copper engravers, dated around 1652.

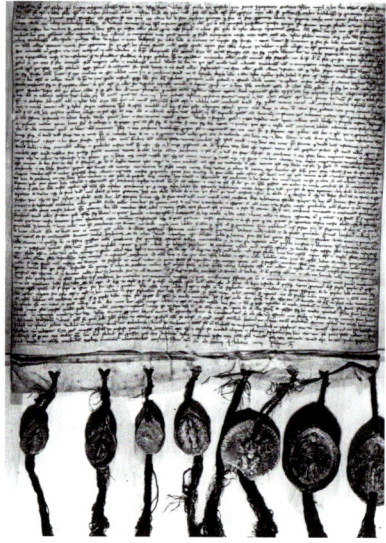
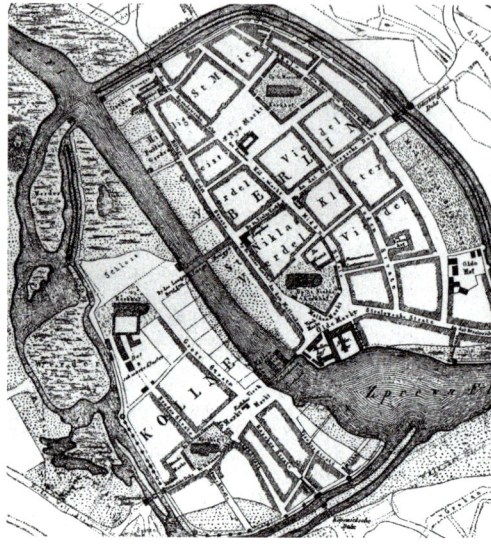

Erste urkundliche Erwähnung der Stadt Cölln vom 28. Oktober 1237. Diese Pionierstadt in den Sümpfen der Spree und Berlin (hier eine Karte von 1250), eine Handelsstadt auf dem Festland, die sechs Jahre später in einer Urkunde genannt wird, schließen sich um 1307 zusammen, um gegen raubende Ritter gewappnet zu sein. Das Berliner Stadtbuch enthält eine Aufzeichnung des Berliner Stadtrechts.

First recorded mention of Cölln dating from 28 October 1237. This pioneering town in the marshes of the Spree and Berlin (shown here on a map from 1250), a trading town built on terra firma, the first documented mention of which was six years later, joined forces around 1307 in order to protect themselves against marauding knights. Berlin's municipal records contain a copy of the city's charter.

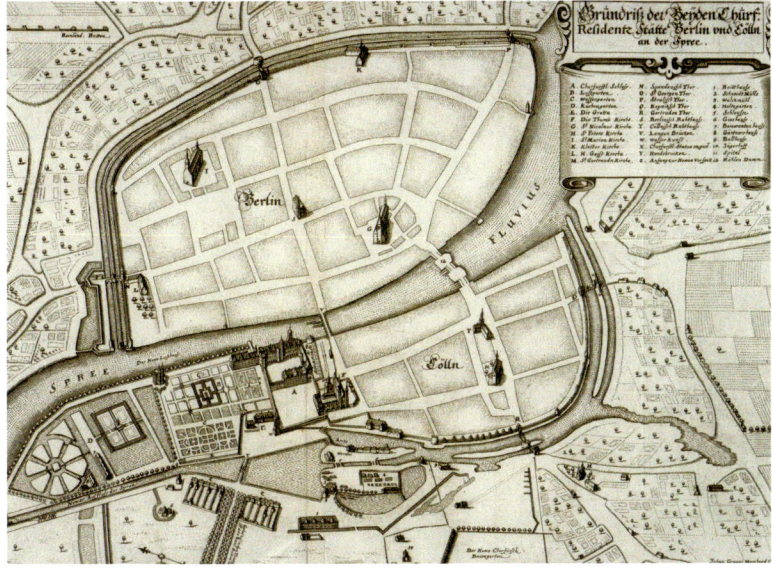

Berlin im Jahr 1413. Belehnung des Johann von Torgau mit Steglitz, Zossen und anderen Ortschaften durch Friedrich VI., Burggraf von Nürnberg und Statthalter des Markgrafen von Brandenburg.
Fresko von Müller-Münster, 1896.

Berlin in 1413: Johann von Torgau is invested with the lands of Steglitz, Zossen, and other estates by Friedrich VI, Burgrave of Nuremberg and governor of the Margrave of Brandenburg.
Fresco by Müller-Münster, 1896.

Grundriss von Berlin und Cölln.
Kupferstich von Johann Georg Memhardt, 1650/51.

Plan of Berlin and Cölln. Copper engraving by Johann Georg Memhardt, 1650/51.

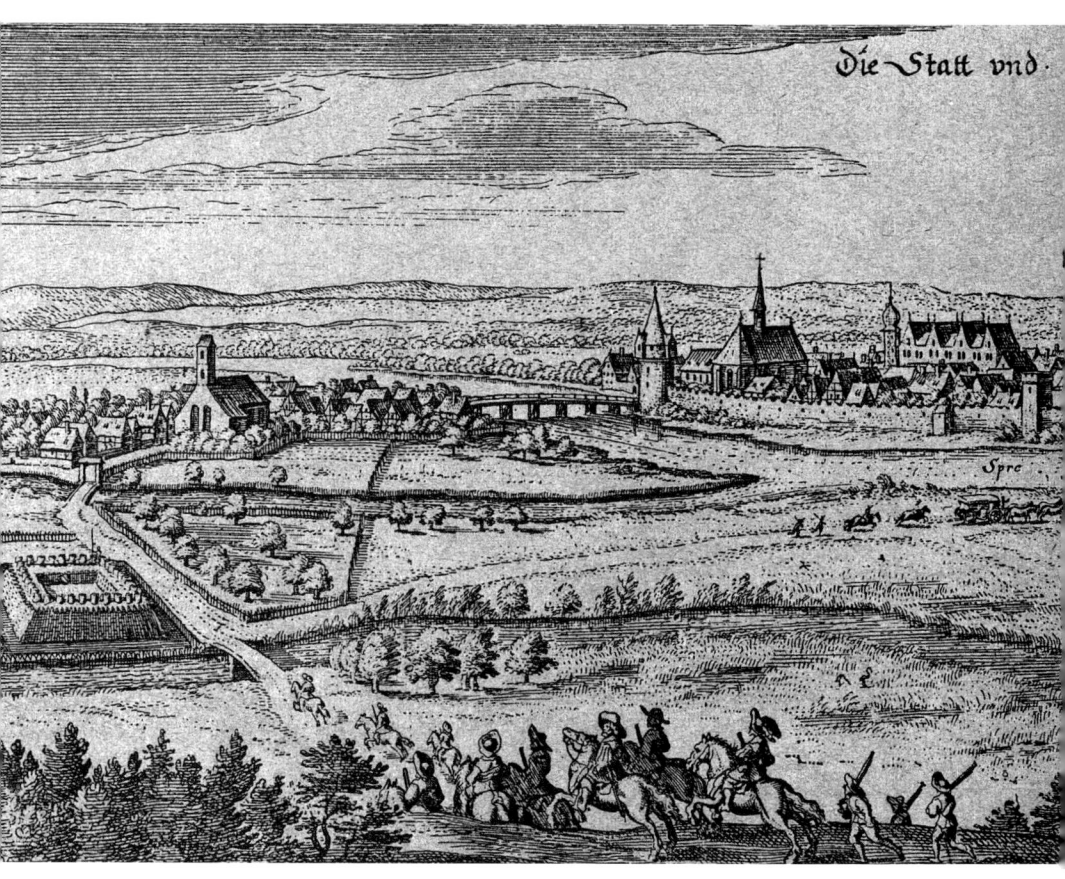

»Die Statt und Vestung Spandaw«. Spandau, ursprünglich Burg an der Handelsstraße nach Magdeburg, hatte 1232 die Stadtrechte erhalten. Ab 1560 wurde mit dem Bau der Zitadelle begonnen, bis Ende des 19. Jahrhunderts herrschte Festungszwang. Erst 1920 erfolgte die Eingemeindung nach Groß-Berlin. Kupferstich von Matthäus Merian (1593-1650), um 1640.

'The town and fortress of Spandau'. Spandau, originally a castle on the trade route to Magdeburg, had its town status conferred in 1232. Building work on the citadel began in 1560 and its fortress status persisted until the end of the nineteenth century. It was not amalgamated into Greater Berlin until 1920. Copperplate engraving by Matthäus Merian (1593-1650), dated around 1640.

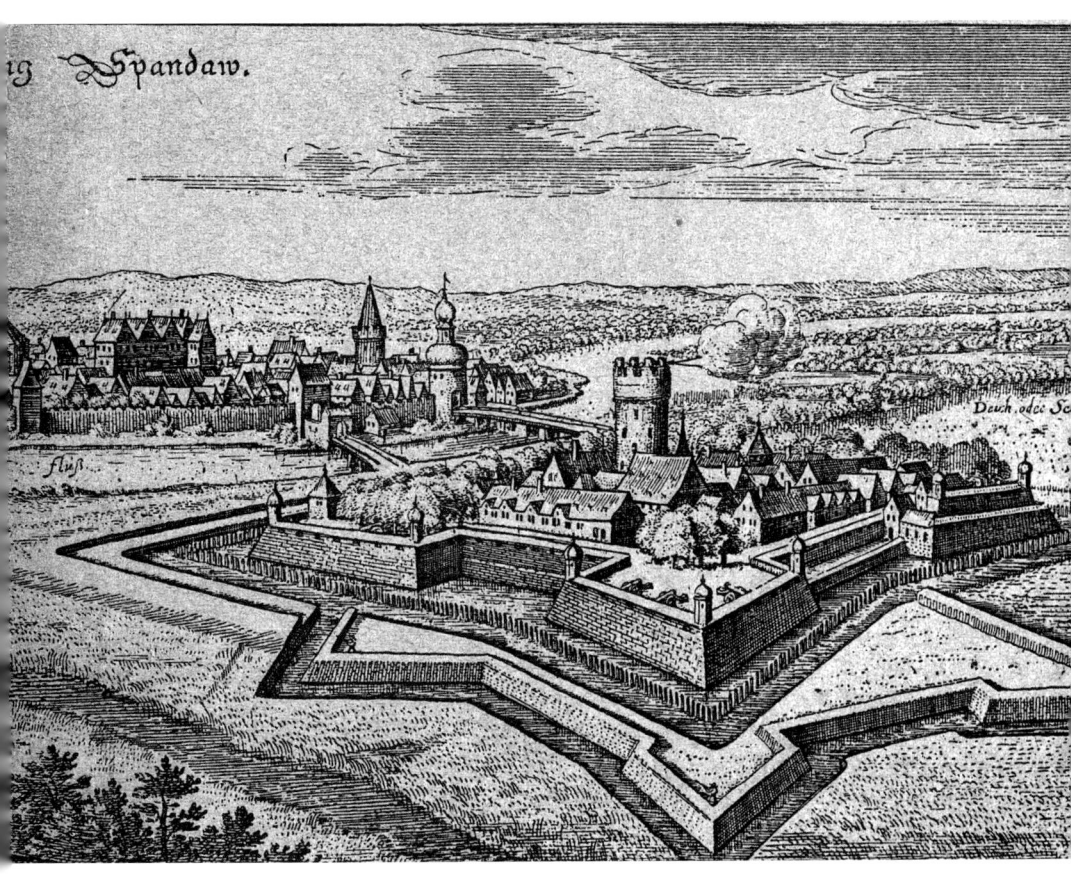

Nach dem Ende des Dreißigjährigen Krieges benötigt das Land des Großen Kurfürsten Friedrich Wilhelm dringend Arbeitskräfte, um die Wirtschaft wieder anzukurbeln. Durch seine Heirat mit Louise von Oranien kommen Holländer ins Land, aber auch zahlreiche Glaubensflüchtlinge: Hugenotten aus Frankreich, Protestanten und Juden aus Österreich. Hier ein Reiterstandbild von Andreas Schlüter.

In the aftermath of the Thirty Years' War, Great Elector Friedrich Wilhelm's land was desperately in need of workers to get the economy back on its feet. His marriage to Louise of Orange led to an influx of Dutch people, as well as religious refugees: Huguenots from France, Protestants and Jews from Austria. Here is an equestrian statue by Andreas Schlüter.

Aufnahme der aus Frankreich geflohenen Hugenotten in Berlin durch den Großen Kurfürsten am 8. November 1685. Relief.

The Great Elector receiving Huguenot refugees in Berlin on 8 November 1685. Relief.

Prunksarg des 1688 gestorbenen Großen Kurfürsten in der Hohenzollerngruft des Berliner Doms. Foto, 1890.

The ornate sarcophagus of the Great Elector, who died in 1688, in the Hohenzollern crypt of Berlin Cathedral. Photo, 1890.

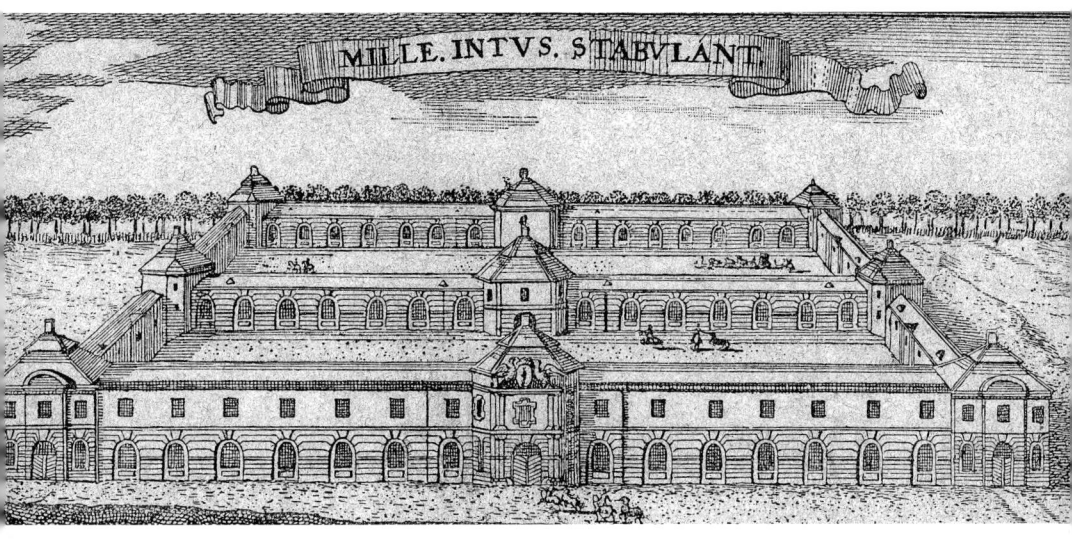

Der Philosoph Gottfried Wilhelm Leibniz (1646-1716) bei der Kurfürstin von Brandenburg, Sophie Charlotte, nach der das Charlottenburger Schloss benannt wurde. Bei diesem Besuch entstand die Idee zur Gründung der Akademie der Wissenschaften, die im Jahr 1700 unter der Bezeichnung »Churfürstlich Brandenburgische Societät der Wissenschaften« realisiert wurde und deren erster Präsident Leibniz war. Die Einrichtung fand »Unter den Linden« in dem von Johann Arnold Nehring 1687/88 erbauten Marstall ein Zuhause.

The philosopher Gottfried Wilhelm Leibniz (1646-1716) with the Electress of Brandenburg, Sophie Charlotte, after whom the Charlottenburg Palace was named. It was during this meeting that the idea of founding an Academy of Sciences was born. This plan eventually reached fruition in 1700 when the 'Churfürstlich Brandenburgische Societät der Wissenschaften' (Electoral Brandenburg Society of Sciences) was established, with Leibniz as its first president. The academy found a home in the Royal Stables building on Unter den Linden, built by Johann Arnold Nehring 1687/88.

RESIDENZSTADT BERLIN

BERLIN BECOMES A ROYAL RESIDENCE

Das 18. Jahrhundert war gekennzeichnet vom Aufstieg Preußens zur europäischen Macht. 1701 krönte sich Kurfürst Friedrich III. als Friedrich I. zum »König in Preußen«. Damit wurde Berlin zur königlichen Residenz, und wie in allen Residenzstädten mussten repräsentative Gebäude entstehen, die der königlichen Herrschaft prachtvollen Ausdruck verleihen sollten. So setzte gleich eine rege Bautätigkeit ein. Schon ab Ende des 17. Jahrhunderts war mit dem Bau von Friedrichsstadt und Schloss Lietzenburg (das spätere Charlottenburg) begonnen worden. 1698 begann auch der Bau des Friedrichshospitals, 1701 wurden die Grundsteine des Deutschen und des Französischen Doms gelegt. Unter der Herrschaft Friedrichs I. wurde 1706 auch das imposante Zeughaus des Barockbaumeisters Andreas Schlüter fertiggestellt. Das Stadtschloss, das schon seit dem 15. Jahrhundert die Mitte Berlins markierte, und um dessen Rekonstruktion gerade eine erregte Diskussion geführt wird, ließ Friedrich I. prunkvoll ausstatten. Dieser enorme Aufwand für repräsentative Bauten und die Förderung von Kultur und Wissenschaft hinterließen im Staatshaushalt jedoch Lücken, die nur mit höheren Steuern gefüllt werden konnten.

Sein Nachfolger, Friedrich Wilhelm I., der 1713 den Thron bestieg und als »Soldatenkönig« Geschichte machte, war aus ande-

The eighteenth century was characterized by the rise of Prussia to become a European power. In 1701, Prince Elector Friedrich II was crowned Friedrich I, King of Prussia. Berlin became the royal residence and, as in all royal residential cities, imposing buildings had to be built to give splendid expression to the power of the monarchy. Thus, a frantic spate of building activity immediately began. Construction of Friedrichsstadt and the Lietzenburg Palace (which later became Charlottenburg Palace) commenced as early as the end of the seventeenth century. The year 1698 saw work begin on the Friedrichs hospital, the Zeughaus was built between 1695 and 1706, and in 1701 the foundation stones of the German and French cathedrals were laid. The reign of Friedrich I also saw the completion of the imposing armory designed by the baroque architect, Andreas Schlüter. The Stadtschloss, which had marked the center of Berlin since the fifteenth century and reconstruction of which is even now the subject of lively debate, was sumptuously furnished by the king. This enormous expenditure on imposing buildings and the promotion of culture and science did, however, make holes in the state budget, holes that could only be filled by increased taxes.

Seite 26/27: Schloss Köpenick wurde 1677-1681 unter dem Architekten Rutger von Langerfeld für Friedrich I. von Preußen errichtet. Es ist ein Kleinod barocker Architektur.

Pages 26/27: Schloss Köpenick, designed by architect Rutger von Langerfeld, was built between 1677-1681 for Friedrich I of Prussia. It is a jewel of Baroque architecture.

rem Holz. Er investierte in die Armee. Kunst und Kultur, Eleganz und Prunk verabscheute er. Er war ein durch und durch asketischer Mensch, der Wissenschaft und Technik förderte, wenn sie dem Staat praktischen Nutzen versprachen. So begründete er 1710 die Charité, die zum führenden Krankenhaus Europas wurde.

Erst der Sohn des »Soldatenkönigs«, Friedrich der Große (1740-1786) förderte wieder die Künste und ließ bedeutende Bauwerke errichten. Sein Freund, der Architekt Georg Wenzeslaus von Knobelsdorff, schuf verschiedene Gebäude in einem Stil, für den später der Begriff »Friderizianisches Rokoko« geprägt wurde. Glänzendes Beispiel dieser weniger verspielten preußischen Variante des Rokoko wurde Schloss Sanssouci in Potsdam. Auch die Preußische Staatsoper Unter den Linden (1741-43) ist ein Werk Knobelsdorffs.

Der Nachfolger Friedrichs des Großen, König Friedrich Wilhelm II. (1744-97), war ein Lebemann, der sein Volk mit Zensurmaßnahmen unterdrückte, doch auch er förderte die Kultur. Er ließ Mozart und Beethoven in Berlin musizieren, und im »Königlichen Nationaltheater« wurden Schiller und Lessing inszeniert. Unter der Regierung Friedrich Wilhelms II. wurde 1791 das berühmteste Bauwerk Berlins, das Brandenburger Tor des Architekten C. G. Langhans eingeweiht, das bis heute Wahrzeichen der Stadt geblieben ist und nach aufwändiger Restauration Ende 2002 wieder zur Besichtigung frei gegeben wurde.

His successor, Friedrich Wilhelm I, who came to the throne in 1713 and went down in history as the 'soldier king', was altogether a different kettle of fish. He invested in the army. He loathed art and culture, elegance and splendour. He was thoroughly ascetic, only encouraging science and technology if they were of practical use to the state. Thus, in 1711 he founded the Charité, which became one of Europe's leading hospitals.

It was not until the 'soldier king' was succeeded by his son, Frederick the Great (1740-1786) that once again the arts were promoted and important buildings erected. His friend, the architect Georg Wenzeslaus von Knobelsdorff, created various buildings in a style for which the term 'Frederickan Rococo' was later coined. Schloss Sanssouci in Potsdam was a splendid example of this less elaborate, Prussian variation of rococo. The Preußische Staatsoper (1741-43) is another of Knobelsdorff's works.

Frederick the Great's successor, King Friedrich Wilhelm IIs (1744-97), was a bon vivant who oppressed his people through the imposition of strict measures, but even he promoted culture. He had Mozart and Beethoven make music in Berlin, and Schiller and Lessing were performed at the Königliches Nationaltheater. It was during the reign of Friedrich Wilhelm II that the most famous construction in Berlin was officially opened in 1791: the Brandenburg Gate, designed by the architect C G Langhans, which is still the emblem of Berlin. After restoration work, it was reopened to visitors at the end of 2002.

Wappen aus dem Siegel der durch Patent vom 17.1.1709 vereinigten Magistrate, verliehen durch Reskript vom 6.2.1710. Das Wappen enthält den schwarzen Adler von Preußen, den roten Adler von Brandenburg und den nunmehr vollkommen aufrechten Berliner Bären. Diese Embleme kamen in den Wappen der damals vereinigten Magistrate (Berlin, Cölln, Friedrichswerder, Dorotheenstadt und Französische Gemeinde) sowie der Bürgerschaften von Königstadt und Friedrichstadt bereits vor.
Auf dem Schilde der Kurhut - die Königskrone stand nur Königsberg zu.
Siegel mit diesem Wappen wurden auch noch nach 1839 weitergeführt.

Nachdem sich Kurfürst Friedrich III., der wegen seines Buckels »der schiefe Fritz« genannt wurde, 1701 zum König Preußens erklärt hatte, erhielt die Stadt 1709 ihr Wappen und 1710 endlich ihren Namen: Berlin. Der als prunksüchtig bekannte Monarch begann mit riesigen Bauvorhaben.

Oben: Das Friedrichshospital, ein Waisen-, Irren- und Arbeitshaus, wurde 1698-1727 von Martin Grünberg und Philipp Gerlach erbaut. Links der militärische Getreidespeicher, im Hintergrund die Oberspree. Radierung von Johann David Schleuen d.Ä. (1711-1771), um 1749.

After Elector Friedrich III, nicknamed 'crooked Fritz' on account of his hump, proclaimed himself the king of Prussia in 1701, the city received its coat of arms in 1709 and was officially named 'Berlin' in 1710. The King, who was known for his love of ostentation, instigated ambitious building projects.

Pictured above is the Friedrichshospital, a combined orphanage, lunatic asylum, and workhouse, built between 1698-1727 by Martin Grünberg and Philipp Gerlach. To the left is the military grain silo, with the Upper Spree in the background. Etching by Johann David Schleuen (1711-1771) from around 1749.

Prospect des Königl: Zeughauses zu Berlin

Das Zeughaus gehörte neben dem Stadtschloss zu den monumentalen Prachtbauten Friedrichs I. von Preußen. Es wurde 1695-1706 von Nering, Grünberg und Schlüter Unter den Linden erbaut.
Ansicht links mit Alter Wache und Stadtschloss. Auf der rechten Seite das Stadtschloss.

After the Palace, the Zeughaus (arsenal) is one of the most monumentally splendid buildings of the reign of Friedrich I of Prussia. It was built between 1695-1706 on Unter den Linden by Nering, Grünberg, and Schlüter. The view on the left is with the Alte Wache (Royal Guard) and Palace and, on the right, the Palace.

Nachdem der erste Preußenkönig 1713 verstorben war, übernahm Friedrich Wilhelm I. das Amt. Durch eine strenge Sparpolitik sanierte er den Haushalt. Seine Leidenschaft galt vor allem zwei Dingen: seiner Armee und einer ordentlichen Stadt. So inspizierte er persönlich die Neubauten in der Friedrichstadt und ließ das Invalidenhaus planen. Bekannt ist die Vorliebe des »Soldatenkönigs« für die »Langen Kerls«. Am 30. April 1732 ziehen aus Salzburg vertriebene Protestanten in Berlin ein.

After the death of the first king of Prussia in 1713, Friedrich Wilhelm I assumed the reins of monarchy. As a result of drastic economic measures, he managed to put the economy back on an even keel. His two passions were his army and an orderly city. He initiated the construction of new buildings in Friedrichstadt, for example, and had plans drawn up for the Invalidenhaus (home for the disabled). The 'Soldier King's' special fondness for 'die Langen Kerls', his unit of high-born bodyguard soldiers, is well documented. On 30 April 1732, persecuted Protestant refugees from Salzburg began arriving in Berlin.

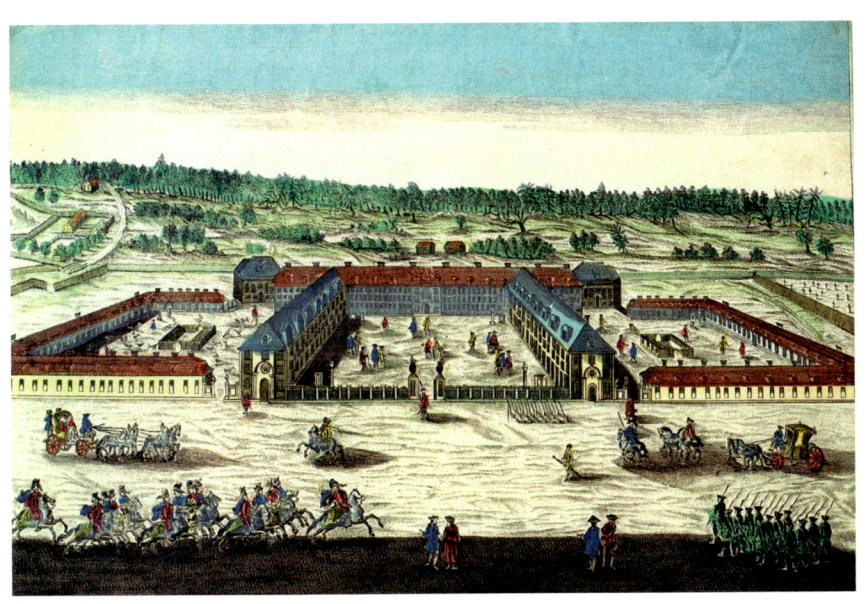

CHARITÉ

Der Preußenkönig Friedrich I. ließ 1710 ein Quarantäne-Haus für die drohende Pestepidemie errichten und legte so den Grundstein für das heutige Universitätsklinikum in Friedrich-Wilhelm-Stadt. Die Pest verschonte Berlin, und das »Pesthaus« wurde zur Unterbringung verarmter Kranker, als Lazarett und militärmedizinische Ausbildungsstätte genutzt. 1727 erhielt diese einmalige Lehrstätte vom Soldatenkönig Friedrich Wilhelm den Namen »Charité« (frz. »Barmherzigkeit«), und Berlin entwickelte sich zu einem Zentrum der medizinischen Wissenschaften.

1810 wurde die Berliner Universität gegründet. Erster Dekan wurde Christoph Wilhelm Hufeland, der u. a. die Einführung des Pockenschutzes förderte. Viele bekannte Ärzte wirkten an der Charité. Gelehrte wie Rudolf Virchow, Robert Koch, der die Milzbrand-, Tuberkel- und Choleraerreger entdeckte, oder Emil Behring, der Seren gegen Diphtherie und Tetanus entwickelte, begründeten ihren Weltruf. Acht Nobelpreisträger begannen hier ihren wissenschaftlichen Weg. Noch heute sind sie mit Denkmälern und Straßennamen im Berliner Stadtbild lebendig.

Das Nazi-Regime und die DDR-Regierung kontrollierten die Arbeit der Ärzte und missbrauchten die Klinik für ihre Zwecke. Nach der Wiedervereinigung wurde die Charité umstrukturiert, ist seit 1995 Universitätsklinikum der Humboldt-Universität und versucht, den einstigen Weltruf wiederzuerlangen.

Die Charité im 19. Jahrhundert. Stahlstich von Finden nach Stock, um 1850.

The Charité hospital in the nineteenth century. Steel engraving by Finden nach Stock, around 1850.

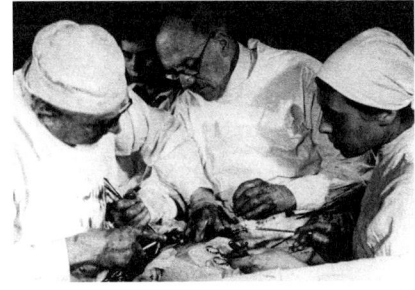

Virchow in seinem Arbeitszimmer in der Charité. 1896.
Rechts: Herzoperation in der Charité in den 1970er Jahren.

Left: Virchow in his study at the Charité, 1896
Right: Heart operation at the Charité during the 1970s.

CHARITÉ

In 1710, the Prussian king Friedrich I had a quarantine house built to accommodate potential victims of plague, thus laying the foundations for today's University Clinic in Friedrich-Wilhelm-Stadt. Berlin was spared the threatened epidemic and the 'plague house' was used for impoverished patients, as a military hospital, and as a military medical training centre. In 1727, the soldier king, Friedrich Wilhelm, called this unique place of learning the 'Charité' (French for 'mercy' or 'compassion'), and Berlin became a centre of medical science.

Berlin University was founded in 1810. The first dean was Christoph Wilhelm Hufeland, who, amongst other things, encouraged the introduction of smallpox immunization. Many famous doctors worked at the Charité, where scholars such as Rudolf Virchow, Robert Koch, who discovered the causes of anthrax, tuberculosis, and cholera, and Emil Behring, who developed serums against diphtheria and tetanus, established their international reputations. Eight Nobel Prize winners began their scientific careers here. Berlin remembers them to this day through monuments and street names.

The Nazi regime and East German government controlled the work of the doctors and abused the clinic for their own ends. After reunification, the Charité was reorganized, becoming the University Clinic of Humboldt University in 1995 and endeavouring to regain its former international reputation.

Friedrich II. von Preußen, genannt der Große, war ein Schöngeist. Während seiner Regierungszeit blühen Kultur und Wissenschaft. So baut er etwa die Preußische Staatsoper und den Berliner Dom und lässt am Tiergarten Vergnügungszelte aufbauen.

Friedrich II (the Great) of Prussia was an aesthete. Culture and science flourished during his rule. He built the Prussian State Opera, for example, and the Berliner Dom (Berlin Cathedral) and had pleasure tents erected in the Tiergarten.

Während des siegreich geführten Siebenjährigen Krieges, aus dem Friedrich II. im März 1763 zurückkehrt, hat sich der König ganz auf den Kampf konzentriert. Preußen steigt zur Weltmacht auf, sein König genießt nach der Schlacht in der Schlosskapelle von Charlottenburg das »Te Deum« von Graun. Selten ist er noch in Berlin.
Meist hält er sich im Schloss Sanssouci in Potsdam auf, das 1747 fertig gestellt wurde.

Throughout the successful Seven Years' War, from which he returned in March 1763, king Friedrich II concentrated all his energy on the battle. Prussia was fast becoming a world power. After the fighting, the King enjoys Graun's 'Te Deum' in the chapel of the Charlottenburg Palace. He is rarely to be found in Berlin any more, but spends most of his time in Schloss Sansoucci (Sanssouci Palace) in Potsdam, which was completed in 1747.

SCHLOSS BELLEVUE

Wer wissen will, ob der Bundespräsident in der Stadt ist, braucht nur einen Blick zu Schloss Bellevue im Spreeweg 1 hinüberzuwerfen. Ist er daheim, weht die Bundesfahne auf seinem Amtssitz. Die elegante weiße, dreiflügelige Schlossanlage, die barocke und frühklassizistische Baustile vereint, liegt inmitten eines herrlichen Parks mit einem Teich, Terrassen und Skulpturen, der, wenn der Hausherr nicht da ist, Spaziergängern offen steht.

Das Schloss wurde 1785 von dem Architekten Philip Daniel Boumann als Stadtresidenz für Prinz August Ferdinand von Preußen geschaffen und hat eine bewegte Geschichte hinter sich. Große Persönlichkeiten der Weltgeschichte – Napoleon, Wilhelm von Humboldt und Friedrich Schiller – waren hier zu Gast. Im 19. Jahrhundert diente es als Gästehaus und Museum. Nach seiner Zerstörung im Zweiten Weltkrieg wurde es in den 50er Jahren restauriert und ist seit 1959 der Amtssitz des Bundespräsidenten.

Die Schlossanlage heute. The palace buildings today.

SCHLOSS BELLEVUE

If you want to know whether the Federal president is in town, all you need to do is look across to Schloss Bellevue on the Spreeweg. If he is at home, the national flag will be flying above his official residence. This elegant, white, three-sided building, which combines both baroque and neo-classical architecture, is surrounded by a splendid park, complete with a small lake, terraces, and sculptures. When the President is not in residence, the park is open to the public.

The palace was built in 1785 by the architect Philip Daniel Boumann as a residence for Prince August Ferdinand of Prussia and has witnessed many historical events. Leading figures of world history have stayed here; for example, Napoleon, Wilhelm von Humboldt, and Friedrich Schiller. During the nineteenth century, it was used as a guesthouse and museum. It was destroyed in the Second World War but was restored in the 50s and, since 1959, has been the official seat of the Federal President.

Innenansicht, 1938.   View of the interior, 1938.

ZEIT DER REVOLUTIONEN
A TIME OF REVOLUTIONS

Nach der Niederlage Preußens gegen Frankreich wurde die Hauptstadt Berlin von Napoleon besetzt. Am 27. Oktober 1806 zog der Eroberer durch das Brandenburger Tor in die Stadt ein. Zum Zeichen des Sieges ließ er die Quadriga vom Brandenburger Tor entfernen; erst 1814 kehrte die Skulptur auf ihren Platz zurück.

Berlin entwickelte sich zum Zentrum einer patriotischen Bewegung gegen die napoleonische Fremdherrschaft. Gleichzeitig gewannen so auch Bestrebungen nach gesellschaftlichen Reformen im preußischen Staat mehr Einfluss. König Friedrich Wilhelm III. erklärte: »Der Staat soll durch geistige Kräfte ersetzen, was er an materiellen verloren hat.«

Vom 18. bis 22. April 1809 fand die erste Berliner Kommunalwahl statt. 102 Stadtverordnete erhielten ein Mandat und wählten den einzigen Adligen, Leopold von Gerlach, zu ihrem Vorsitzenden. Wenig später wurde er der erste Oberbürgermeister Berlins. Am 6. Juli 1809 wurden die neuen Mandatsträger in der Nikolaikirche feierlich in ihr Amt eingeführt. Zur gleichen Zeit wandte sich der Philosoph Johann Gottlieb Fichte in seinen »Reden an die deutsche Nation« gegen die napoleonische Herrschaft. Er war der erste frei gewählte Rektor der 1810 gegründeten Berliner Universität.

When France defeated Prussia, the capital, Berlin, was occupied by Napoleon. The conqueror marched into the city through the Brandenburg Gate on 27 October 1806. To mark his victory, he had the Quadriga removed from the Brandenburg Gate, and the sculpture was not returned to its place until 1814.

Berlin became the centre of a patriotic movement against the foreign rule of Napoleon. At the same time, attempts to bring about social reform in Prussia gained more influence. King Friedrich Wilhelm III declared: 'The state must replace its material losses with spiritual powers'. The first local election in Berlin took place from 18-22 April 1809. One-hundred-and-two city councillors won seats and elected Leopold von Gerlach, the only nobleman among them, as their leader. Shortly afterwards, he became the first Mayor of Berlin. On 6 July 1809, the new members formally took office at a ceremony in the Nikolaikirche. The philosopher Johann Gottlieb Fichte also spoke out against the Napoleonic masters in his 'Reden an die deutsche Nation' ('Speeches to the German Nation'). He was the first freely elected Rector of Berlin University, which was founded in 1810.

The year 1819 saw the end of the era of reform. The king gave the Chief of Police, Karl Albrecht von Kamptz, exceptional

Seite 46/47: »Blick vom Dach der Friedrich-Werderschen Kirche auf das Friedrichsforum«. Außerdem im Bild die Hedwigskirche, die Königliche Bibliothek und die Oper. 1835, Gemälde von Eduard Gaertner (1801-1877).

Pages 46/47: 'View from the roof of the Friedrich Werdersche Church onto the Friedrichsforum'. Also visible are the Hedwigskirche (Church of St Hedwig), the Königliche Bibliothek (Royal Library), and the Opera House. Painting by Eduard Gaertner (1801-1877), dated 1835.

1819 endete die Reformära: Der König gab dem Polizeidirektor Karl Albrecht von Kamptz außerordentliche Vollmachten, eine Verhaftungswelle folgte. Zur gleichen Zeit gab Karl Friedrich Schinkel der Stadt mit klassizistischen Bauten wie der Neuen Wache oder dem Neuen Schauspielhaus ein neues Gesicht.

Im März 1848 gingen die Bürger in Berlin – wie in fast ganz Deutschland – auf die Barrikaden und forderten mehr demokratische Mitbestimmung. Doch die Revolutionäre hatten keinen Erfolg. Die Unruhen forderten 250 Tote, der König behielt die Oberhand.

Berlin war zu dieser Zeit alles andere als fortschrittlich. Lebensbedingungen und hygienische Verhältnisse blieben für das Gros der sprunghaft steigenden Bevölkerung unerträglich: fehlende Wasserversorgung und Kanalisation, schlechte Straßen, Platzmangel und Epidemien prägten das Bild. Erst der Ausbau der Kanalisation ab 1873 verbesserte die Lage.

Nach Gründung des Deutschen Reiches 1871 wurde der preußische König Wilhelm I. zum Kaiser und Berlin zur Hauptstadt Deutschlands. Die Stadt boomte. 1877 hatte sie die Millionengrenze überschritten, Vorstädte wurden eingemeindet. Der technische Fortschritt beschleunigte sich rasant: 1865 wurde die erste Rohrpostlinie in Betrieb genommen, Werner von Siemens entdeckte die Prinzipien der elektrischen Stromversorgung. Auch das Schienennetz der Metropole wurde immer dichter. 1880 besaß Berlin neun Fernbahnhöfe.

Gleichzeitig verelendeten seit 1890 viele Arbeiterfamilien: Hunger, Wohnungsnot und Arbeitslosigkeit wurden zur Schattenseite des Wachstums.

powers and a wave of arrests followed. At the same time, Karl Friedrich Schinkel changed the face of the city with such classical buildings as the Neue Wache (New Guardhouse) and the Neues Schauspielhaus (New Theatre).

In March 1848, the citizens of Berlin – as in almost the whole of Germany – manned the barricades and demanded more participation in democracy. The revolutionaries, however, were unsuccessful. The unrest claimed 250 lives, and the king remained in power.

Berlin at this time was anything but progressive. Living conditions were still unbearable for the majority of the population, which was increasing by leaps and bounds. The characteristic picture is of inadequate water supplies and sewerage systems, bad roads, lack of space, and epidemics. The situation did not improve until extensions to the sewerage system commenced in 1873.

When the German Empire was founded in 1871, King Wilhelm I of Prussia became Emperor and Berlin became the capital of Germany. The city boomed. By 1877, its population was over one million. Technological progress was rapid. In 1865, the first pneumatic dispatch system was put into service, and Werner von Siemens discovered the principles of providing electric current. The capital's railway network was also growing. By 1880, Berlin had nine mainline stations.

After 1890, many working-class families became impoverished. Hunger, homelessness, and unemployment were the dark side of the city's growth.

Unter Reichsfreiherr Karl vom und zum Stein erlangt die Städteordnung Gesetzeskraft. Das Reformwerk beendet die Bevormundung der Bürger durch den absolutistischen Staat. Durch ihre Mitwirkung soll das Interesse für den Staat und seine politischen Aufgaben geweckt werden. Am 6. Juli 1809 erfolgt die Amtseinführung der ersten Stadtverordneten in der Nikolaikirche.

Under Reichsfreiherr Karl vom und zum Stein, the municipal statutes became law. The reforms put an end to control of the people by an absolutist state. Involving them was intended to awaken their interest in the state and its political tasks. The first of Berlin's representatives were inaugurated into office on 6 July 1809 in the Nikolaikirche (Church of St Nicholas).

Die Bilder ähneln sich:
Die preußischsächsischen Truppen werden in den Schlachten bei Jena und Auerstedt von den Franzosen vernichtend geschlagen. Am 27. Oktober 1806 zieht Napoleon I. durch das Brandenburger Tor in Berlin ein. Auf seinem Weg zurück nach Frankreich nimmt er die Quadriga mit. Nach dem Sieg in den Befreiungskriegen von 1814/1815 lässt sich Friedrich Wilhelm III. am 7. August 1814 an gleicher Stelle als Befreier des deutschen Vaterlandes feiern.

The pictures resemble one another: Prussian troops from Saxony suffer a terrible defeat at the hands of the French in the battles of Jena and Auerstedt. On 27 October 1806, Napoleon I marches into Berlin through the Brandenburg Gate. On his way back to France, he captures the Quadriga. Following his victory in the Wars of Liberation of 1814/1815, Friedrich Wilhelm III is celebrated in the very same spot on the 7 August 1814 as the liberator of the German fatherland.

KARL FRIEDRICH SCHINKEL

Karl Friedrich Schinkel (1781–1841) war der größte der preußischen Baumeister und der wichtigste Vertreter des deutschen Klassizismus. Er überführte die antike Formensprache in eine ihm eigene visionäre und von vielen schon als frühmodern empfundene Architektur. Sicherlich schien den Zeitgenossen der dorische Stil auch als geeignet, »den spartanischen Geist des preußischen Militärs zu betonen« (Ernst Gombrich).

Dabei begann Schinkels Karriere wenig vielversprechend. Nach seinem Studium reiste er in Ermangelung größerer Bauaufträge zunächst einige Jahre durch Europa und entwarf Panoramen und Bühnendekorationen. 1815 wurde er dann Geheimer Oberbaurat im neu eingerichteten Staatsbauamt und ab 1830 Leiter dieses Amtes. Aus der Zeit nach 1815 datieren die meisten seiner berühmten Bauten, Die Neue Wache (1816), die NikolaiKirche in Potsdam (1830-49), die Bauakademie (1831-36), das Schauspielhaus (1818) und das Haus seines Freundes Wilhelm von Humboldt.

Schinkel prägte das Gesicht des alten Berlins mit etwa 30 Bauten. Die meisten wurden von den jeweiligen Machthabern oder im Krieg zerstört, einige wie die Neue Wache Unter den Linden, die Schlossbrücke oder die Friedrich-Werdersche Kirche, die heute das Schinkel-Museum beheimatet, sind erhalten oder wiederaufgebaut und zählen zu den wichtigsten touristischen Attraktionen der Hauptstadt.

Altes Museum (erbaut 1823-29).   **Old Museum (built 1823-29).**

KARL FRIEDRICH SCHINKEL

Karl Friedrich Schinkel (1781-1841) was Prussia's greatest architect and the most eminent exponent of German classicism. He adapted the classical style and transformed it into his own unique and visionary style of architecture, considered by many to be a forerunner of early modernism. Be that as it may, his contemporaries certainly felt that the Doric style of his designs was eminently suited to emphasizing the 'Spartan spirit of the Prussian military' (Ernst Gombrich).

Schinkel's career, however, got off to a less than auspicious start. His studies completed and no major building commissions forthcoming, he spent the next few years travelling around Europe, designing panoramas and stage sets. In 1815, he was appointed Geheimer Oberbaurat (senior surveyor) of the newly established Prussian Building Commission, eventually becoming its director from 1830 onwards. His most famous architectural achievements date from the post-1815 period. These include the Neue Wache (Royal Guardhouse) (1816), the Nicolai Church in Potsdam (1830-49), the Bauakademie (School of Architecture) (1831-36), the Schauspielhaus (Concert Hall) (1818), and the house of his friend, Wilhelm von Humboldt.

Approximately thirty buildings in old Berlin once bore witness to Schinkel's architectural influence in the city. Most of these were destroyed by respective ruling powers or during the war. Some of them, however, such as the Neue Wache on Unter den Linden, the Schlossbrücke (Palace Bridge) and the Friedrichswerdersche Church, which today houses the Schinkel Museum, have been preserved or reconstructed and are regarded as some of the city's main tourist attractions.

Links: »Das Innere der Friedrich-Werderschen Kirche«, Aquarell, 1832, von Friedrich Wilhelm Klose. Rechts: Ansicht der Vorderfront des Schauspielhauses (erbaut 1818-21). Nach der Zerstörung im Zweiten Weltkrieg wurde das Gebäude bis 1984 wiederaufgebaut.

Left: 'The interior of the Friedrich Werdersche Church', a watercolour by Friedrich Wihelm Klose, 1832. right: Façade of the Schauspielhaus (built 1818-21). The building was reopened in 1984 following its destruction in World War II.

Peter Joseph Lenné hatte den Tiergarten 1833-39 zu einer englischen Parkanlage umgestaltet. 1840 legt er König Friedrich IV. mit seinen Vorschlägen zur Gestaltung Berlins erstmals einen planerischen Gesamtentwurf der Stadt vor. Oben links: Der Schafgraben. Oben rechts: Eisläufer auf der zugefrorenen Spree hinter den Zelten im Tiergarten.

Ice-skaters on the frozen Spree behind the tents in the Tiergarten. Peter Joseph Lenné converted the Tiergarten in 1833-39 into an English-style park (the photo shows the Schafgraben). In 1840, he presents King Friedrich IV with an overall design concept with proposals for remodelling the city of Berlin.

MUSEUMSINSEL

»Eine Freistätte für Kunst und Wissenschaft« wollte der preußische König Friedrich Wilhelm IV. 1835 auf der Spree-Insel schaffen. Bereits in dem ersten der insgesamt fünf Gebäude, dem Alten Museum von Karl Friedrich Schinkel, das 1830 fertiggestellt wurde, hatte er seinen Museumsgedanken manifestiert. Es ist das älteste Berliner Museumsgebäude überhaupt und machte Kunstschätze erstmals der Öffentlichkeit zugänglich. Erst hundert Jahre später, 1930, wurde seine Vision mit der Fertigstellung des Pergamon-Museums vollendet.

Die Nationalsozialisten bauten die Insel nicht weiter aus – im Gegenteil: sie verkauften bzw. vernichteten zahlreiche Gemälde. Der Zweite Weltkrieg tat sein Übriges. Die Gebäude wurden bis zu 70 Prozent zerstört. Sie werden derzeit wieder aufgebaut und die während der Teilung in Ost- und Westdeutschland verteilten Sammlungen zum größten Teil zusammengeführt.

Umgeben von Spree und Kupfergraben sind Altes Museum, Neues Museum, Alte Nationalgalerie, Bode-Museum und Pergamon-Museum, die die archäologischen Sammlungen und die Kunst des 19. Jahrhunderts beherbergen, ein Zeugnis für die Entwicklung des öffentlichen Kunstraums in Berlin. Im Jahr 1999 ernannte die UNESCO das Gebäudeensemble der Museumsinsel zum Weltkulturerbe.

Links: Die Alte Nationalgalerie (1862-76 erbaut), Bildpostkarte, um 1900.
Rechts: Die Museumsinsel heute.

left: The Old National Gallery (built 1862-76). Picture postcard, around 1900.
Right: Museum island today.

MUSEUM ISLAND

In 1835, the Prussian King Friedrich Wilhelm IV decided to create 'a haven of art and science' on this island in the Spree. His interest in museums was already evident from the first of the eventual five buildings to be built, the Old Museum, designed by Karl Friedrich Schinkel and completed in 1830. This is Berlin's oldest museum and was the first to make art treasures accessible to the public. It was not until a hundred years later in 1930, however, that the king's vision finally came to fruition with the completion of the Pergamon Museum.

The Nazis did not continue with the island's development. On the contrary, they sold or destroyed many of the paintings. The Second World War took care of the rest. Nearly 70 per cent of the buildings were destroyed. Reconstruction work is currently underway, however, and the collections, which were divided during the split between East and West Germany, are by and large being reunited.

Encircled by the Spree and Kupfergraben are the Old Museum, New Museum, Old National Gallery, Bode Museum, and Pergamon Museum, containing archaeological collections and 18th-century art treasures, a testimonial to the development of public museums and art galleries in Berlin. In January 1999, UNESCO awarded this cluster of buildings on Museum Island world cultural heritage status.

August Borsig gründet nach dem ersten gelungenen Eisenguss am 22. Juli 1837 seine Maschinenbauanstalt und Eisengießerei in der Chausseestraße 1. Hier widmet er sich vor allem dem Bau der ersten Dampflokomotiven und wird zum Lokomotiven-König Berlins. Die Firma Siemens & Halske wird zehn Jahre später gegründet. Sie baut 1879 die erste elektrische Eisenbahn (oben links), am 3. Juli 1897 geht das Unternehmen an die Börse (rechts). Der Maler Adolph von Menzel hält die Faszination und die Anstrengung der Arbeit in einem Walzwerk in seinem berühmten Gemälde »Eisenwalzwerk« fest (nächste Seite).

Industrialization

Following the first successful iron casting on 22 July 1837, August Borsig inaugurated his engineering works and iron foundry in the Chausseestraße. His overriding interest was in building the first steam locomotives and he became Berlin's locomotive king. The firm of Siemens & Halske was founded ten years later and in 1879 produced the first electric railway (above left). On 3 July 1897, the firm went public on the stock exchange (right). In 'Iron-rolling Mill' (overleaf), the painter Adolph von Menzel has captured the atmosphere of the fascinating and back-breaking nature of work in a rolling mill.

Adolph von Menzel:
Eisenwalzwerk, 1875.

**Adolph von Menzel:
Iron Rolling Mill, 1875.**

In den Salons werden Reformdebatten geführt. Zu den führenden Intellektuellen gehören Freiherr vom und zum Stein, Jakob und Wilhelm Grimm, Bettina von Arnim, Wilhelm Freiherr von Humboldt, Georg Friedrich Wilhelm Hegel.

Great Thinkers in Athens on the Spree
The salons became centres for debate on reform. Some of the leading intellectuals of the day included Freiherr vom und zum Stein, Jakob and Wilhelm Grimm, Bettina von Arnim, Wilhelm Freiherr von Humboldt, and Georg Friedrich Wilhelm Hegel.

Seit Anfang März fordern Menschen aus allen Schichten der Bevölkerung in täglichen Volksversammlungen u. a. das Recht auf Presse- und Redefreiheit, die Amnestie politisch Inhaftierter, politische Gleichberechtigung usw. Nach heftigen Auseinandersetzungen auf den Straßen gesteht der König schließlich Reformen zu. Doch der Freudentaumel endet im Barrikadenkampf, hier in der Breite Straße am 18./19. März 1848.

March Revolution
From early March, meetings were held on an almost daily basis by people from all walks of life, whose demands included freedom of speech and of the press, an amnesty for political prisoners, and political equality. Violent clashes on the streets finally forced the king to accede to reforms, but the jubilations end in fighting on the barricades, as pictured here in the Breite Straße on 18-19 March 1848.

Am 26. Februar 1871 beendet der Vorfriede von Versailles die Kampfhandlungen im Deutsch-Französischen Krieg, die deutschen Truppen kehren zurück. Auf dem Potsdamer Bahnhof wird am 22. März 1871 die Gardelandwehr empfangen. Am 18. Januar 1871 wird König Wilhelm I. von Preußen im Spiegelsaal des Schlosses von Versailles zum Deutschen Kaiser ausgerufen. Hier in seinem Arbeitszimmer im Palais Unter den Linden. Am 11. Mai 1878 verübt der 20jährige Gelegenheitsarbeiter Max Hödel in Berlin ein Revolver-Attentat auf Wilhelm I. Der Kaiser, der sich durch das »Sozialistengesetz« in der Arbeiterschaft unbeliebt gemacht hatte, bleibt unverletzt.

The King of Prussia becomes Emperor
On 26 February 1871, the armistice Treaty of Versailles marked the end of hostilities in the Franco-German War, and German troops returned home. The Gardelandwehr (Guards Militia) is welcomed at Potsdam Station on 22 March 1871. On 18 January 1871, King Wilhelm I of Prussia was proclaimed German emperor in the Hall of Mirrors at the Palace of Versailles. He is shown here in his study in the Palais Unter den Linden. On 11 May 1878, he was the victim of an assassination attempt, when a 20-year-old casual labourer, Max Hödel, fired a revolver at him in Berlin. The Kaiser, who was unharmed, had made himself unpopular among the working classes as a result of his Sozialistengesetz (Socialist Bill).

Die Stadt ruft: Vor den Toren Berlins herrscht Armut, dahinter Wohnungsnot. Dennoch versprechen sich viele Arbeit von der boomenden Spreemetropole, in der das Leben zunehmend vom Verkehr geprägt ist (hier: Rosenthaler Tor).

The city beckons: Beyond the gates of Berlin, poverty was rife, but within the city accommodation was in short supply. Despite this, many people still hoped to find work in the booming Spree metropolis, a city increasingly dominated by traffic (Here: the Rosenthaler Gate)

Straßenbilder
Der Potsdamer Platz erhält 1884 die erste elektrische Straßenbeleuchtung in Berlin. Die Meierei Bolle liefert Milch mit Wagen aus dem Umland in die Stadt. Mit dem Plakatieren von Informationen und Werbung verdienen Zettelkleber ihr Geld. Die erste Litfaßsäule hatte der Berliner Buchdrucker Ernst Litfaß 1855 in Berlin aufgestellt.

Impressions
In 1884 the first electric street lighting was installed at Potsdam Square.
The dairy Bolle delivers milk from the surrounding countryside to the city.
In 1855 the Berlin book printer Ernst Litfaß put up the first advertizing column.

Die Berliner Luft dürfte angesichts von Industrie, Verkehrsaufkommen, unzureichender Sanitäranlagen und Kohleheizungen in manchen Teilen der Stadt nicht gerade Wohlgeruch verströmt haben. Der Komponist Paul Lincke (1866-1946) hatte sie in seinem Marsch berühmt gemacht (Bild rechts). Die Menschen zog es ins Grüne. Kinder vergnügten sich im Zoo, Herren im Grunewald. Vielleicht hat der Genuss einer Berliner Weißen diese Herren übermütig werden lassen.

The air in Berlin apparently had a reputation for being somewhat less than fresh in some parts of the city, as a result of the industry, heavy traffic, inadequate sanitary facilities, and coal-fired heating systems. It even provided the inspiration for a piece of music, a march by composer Paul Lincke (1866-1946) (illustration right). People sought the countryside. Children loved to visit the zoo, while the menfolk headed for the Grunewald, perhaps to enjoy a glass or two of Berliner Weiße beer.

Der 1811 von Friedrich Ludwig »Turnvater« Jahn gegründete Turnplatz beherbergt gegen Ende des Jahrhunderts auch eine Gartenwirtschaft. Gepflegter geht es im Innenhof des Café Linden mit maurischem Brunnen zu, doch auch Amüsierlokale finden regen Zuspruch.

The gymnastics club founded by Friedrich Jahn, 'the father of physical education', in 1811 also incorporated a beer garden by the end of the century. The courtyard of the Café Linden with its Moorish fountains provides a more elegant setting, but the cheaper haunts are also very popular.

Werkunterricht für Knaben in einer Berliner Schule. Die Zahl der Arbeitslosen wächst – Menschen hoffen auf Arbeit in den Fabriken wie im Elektromobilbau bei den AEG – Automobilwerken in Berlin.

Instruction for young boys in a Berlin school. The number of unemployed is growing – people hope for work in the factories, for example at the AEG car works in Berlin.

OTTO VON BISMARCK

Keinem anderen Deutschen sind mehr Denkmäler errichtet worden als ihm. Der ebenso verehrte wie geschmähte »Eiserne Kanzler« gilt als der Begründer des deutschen Nationalstaates und als glänzender Stratege, der erkannte, dass ein Nationalstaat nur in ausgewogenen europäischen Verhältnissen bestehen kann.

Bismarck stammte aus einem bedeutenden altmärkischen Adelsgeschlecht und war ab 1848 konservativer Abgeordneter in der Zweiten Kammer im Erfurter Landtag sowie Gesandter am Frankfurter Bundestag. Die Erfahrung der Revolution von 1848 prägte ihn tief und verstärkte seine Überzeugung von der Notwendigkeit eines starken Staates. Unruhen und Revolutionen waren ihm ein Gräuel. Er glaubte nicht an Ideen, sondern an die Kraft des Interessenausgleichs. Er wollte am monarchisch geprägten Staat festhalten, sozialistische Tendenzen bekämpfen und trotzdem die Arbeiter auf seiner Seite haben. Ein epochemachendes Ergebnis seiner Politik war das von ihm entwickelte deutsche Sozialsystem mit der Einführung der Sozialversicherung. Bismarck war davon überzeugt, mit der autoritären Interessen- und Machtpolitik, die er ab 1862 als Preußischer Ministerpräsident und ab 1871 als Reichskanzler vertrat, dem deutschen Volk nur Gutes zu tun. Trotzdem musste er an den Widersprüchen, die er lange im Gleichgewicht zu halten verstand, scheitern. Am 20. März 1890 wurde er von Kaiser Wilhelm I. entlassen.

Letzter Besuch Bismarcks in Berlin auf Einladung Kaiser Wilhelms II.

Bismarck's last visit to Berlin at the invitation of Kaiser Wilhelm II.

OTTO VON BISMARCK

Otto von Bismarck has had more monuments erected in his honour than any other German. The 'Iron Chancellor', who was, by turns, both revered and reviled, is regarded as the founder of the German nation-state and an outstanding strategist, who recognized that a nation-state could only exist if a balance existed between the European powers.

Bismarck was born in Altmark, Prussia, the son of a high-ranking aristocratic family. From 1848, he was an elected Conservative member of the Second Chamber, the Erfurt Diet, as well as representative at the Frankfurt National Assembly. He was deeply influenced by his experience of the Revolution of 1848, which served to reinforce his belief in the need for a strong state. He had a horror of unrest and revolution. He believed not so much in ideas but in trying to reconcile conflicting interests. He clung to the concept of a state based on monarchy and opposed socialist tendencies, yet, at the same time, wanted the working classes on his side. One of his most epoch-making political achievements was to devise a social system incorporating a social insurance scheme for German workers.

Bismarck was firmly convinced that the German people could derive nothing but benefit from his authoritarian brand of representational and power politics, with which he governed from 1862, first as Prussian Prime Minister and later, from 1871, as Imperial Chancellor. Ultimately, however, it was these conflicting interests that he had managed to hold in check for so long which brought about his downfall. On 20 March 1890, he was relieved of office by Kaiser Wilhelm I.

Der »Eiserne Kanzler« im Reichstag 1888.   The 'Iron Chancellor' in the Reichstag 1888.

»Es ist nicht leicht, unter Bismarck Kaiser zu sein« soll Kaiser Wilhelm I. angeblich gesagt haben. Als er am 9. März 1888 stirbt, nehmen Tausende an den Beisetzungsfeierlichkeiten teil. Drei Monate später wird der Kronprinz als Wilhelm II. Deutscher Kaiser und König von Preußen. Hier bei einem Besuch des österreichischen Kaisers Franz Joseph in Berlin.

'It is not easy being Emperor under Bismarck', as Kaiser Wilhelm I is reputed to have said. After his death on 9 March 1888, thousands of people attended his funeral. Three months later, the Crown Prince is proclaimed Wilhelm II, German emperor and King of Prussia, pictured here during a visit to Berlin by the Austrian emperor Franz Joseph.

GLANZ UND ELEND DER GRÜNDERZEIT

SPLENDOUR AND POVERTY OF THE EARLY YEARS

Der wichtigste Umbruch im 19. Jahrhundert war neben der Bürgerlichen Revolution von 1848 und der Reichsgründung 1871 die Industrielle Revolution mit ihren epochalen Folgen für das Leben der Menschen in den Industriestädten. In der »Gründerzeit« von 1871 bis um die Jahrhundertwende, als die Industrialisierung an Dynamik zulegte, wuchs die Einwohnerzahl Berlins von 900.000 auf über 2,7 Millionen. Die Stadt explodierte, es entstanden neue Bauaufgaben wie Bahnhöfe, Kaufhäuser, Fabriken, und die Massen der Arbeiter, die in die Stadt strömten, brauchten Wohnungen. Ab Mitte des Jahrhunderts wurden auf Veranlassung des Oberbaurats James Hobrecht rational geplante Häuserblocks gebaut, die nach einem einheitlichen Muster strukturiert waren. Die typische Berliner Mietskaserne bestand aus Vorderhäusern, Seitenflügeln und Hinterhäusern. Bis zu sechs dieser umbauten Höfe waren hintereinander gestaffelt. Querstraßen zur Erschließung der großen Blocks wollte man vermeiden, da sie zusätzliche Kosten für die Bauherren verursachten.

Die Vorderhäuser der Wohnblöcke waren hell und komfortabel, für die besser gestellten sozialen Schichten gedacht und zur Straße hin mit repräsentativen historistischen Fassaden verkleidet. In den Hinterhäusern und Kellerwohnungen wohnten Arbeiter, Dienstboten und kleine Handwer-

Alongside the Civil Revolution of 1848 and the founding of the German Reich in 1871, the most important radical change in 19th-century Germany was the Industrial Revolution, with its incredible consequences for people living in the towns. During the German industrial revolution, from 1871 to 1900, the number of people living in Berlin rose from nine hundred thousand to over 2.7 million. The city underwent a population explosion; there were commissions for new buildings such as railway stations, department stores, and factories, and the masses of workers that streamed into the city needed somewhere to live. From the middle of the century, at the instigation of the municipal buildings surveyor, James Hobrecht, rationally planned apartment blocks were built to a standard plan. The typical Berlin 'tenement' comprised buildings to the front, side wings, and rear, creating a yard in the centre. Often up to six of these yards surrounded by buildings were backed up one behind the other. Wherever possible, connecting streets that would have opened up the large blocks were avoided, as their construction would cause the clients additional expense.

The buildings at the front of the residential blocks were light and comfortable, intended for the better-off social strata and finished with imposing historic façades on the street side. In the houses to the rear and the basement apartments,

Seite 78/79: Meyers Hof, Ackerstraße 132 in Berlin-Wedding. Erbaut 1874.

Pages 78/79: Meyers Hof, Ackerstraße 132 in Berlin-Wedding. Built 1874.

ker in dunklen und beengten, oft viel zu feuchten Wohnungen, in der Regel ohne eigene Toilette oder eigenes Bad. Nicht ohne Grund entstanden zu dieser Zeit die öffentlichen Bäder in den Städten. In den Hinterhöfen waren zudem Gewerbebetriebe angesiedelt, und in den Quergebäuden der Blockbebauung waren ganze Fabriketagen angelegt. Diese Mischung der Funktionen war charakteristisch für die Quartiere der Arbeiterschaft.

Wurden früher Häuser in individuellem Auftrag gebaut, so war der Bau jetzt die massenhafte industrialisierte Herstellung von Wohnungen für einen Markt, der bedient werden musste, und auf dem Spekulanten mit der steigenden Nachfrage ihr Geschäft machten.

Mit wachsender Einwohnerzahl wurde Berlin bis 1900 zur größten Mietskasernenstadt der Welt. Besonders in den Arbeiterbezirken von Neukölln, Prenzlauer Berg, Kreuzberg, Wedding und Friedrichshain, aber auch in Charlottenburg, wurden die Mietskasernen immer gleich straßenweise hochgezogen und oft noch feucht bezogen. Ärmere Erstmieter konnten gegen Mietnachlass die neuen Häuser »trockenwohnen«. Die schnell wachsenden Elendsquartiere hat Heinrich Zille in seinen oft bitter ironischen Zeichnungen festgehalten.

Bis heute ist die Struktur der Berliner Innenstadtbezirke geprägt durch die Mietskasernenarchitektur. Nach den Flächensanierungskonzepten der 60er und 70er Jahre sind die alten Fabriketagen und Gartenhäuser der Hinterhöfe in den 80er Jahren zu beliebten Wohnquartieren geworden.

workers, servants, and artisans lived in narrow, dark, and damp apartments, generally with no toilet or bath of their own. It was with good reason that public baths first appeared in the towns around this time. Small businesses were also accommodated in the backyards and, in the buildings constructed across a block, whole floors of factories were installed. This combination of functions was typical of the working class areas of Berlin.

Whereas houses had previously been built to individual commission, now dwellings were mass-produced on a scale for a market that had to be served. With the increasing demand, it was also a market in which speculators did good business.

As a result of this population increase, by 1900 Berlin had become the largest tenement town in the world. Especially in the working class areas of Neukölln, Prenzlauer Berg, Kreuzberg, Wedding, and Friedrichshain, but also in Charlottenburg, the tenements rose up whole streets at a time and people moved in while they were still damp. Poorer tenants renting a brand-new property could pay a reduced rent and 'live the apartment dry'. Heinrich Zille captured these expanding slum quarters in his frequently ironic drawings.

Even now, tenement architecture is still a dominant feature of the structure of Berlin's inner city areas. Following the redevelopment plans of the 1960s and 70s, in the 1980s the old factory floors and rear buildings in the backyards became popular residential areas.

Die Gründerzeit war in Berlin, wie auch in den anderen Industriestädten Deutschlands, geprägt durch zahlreiche neue Gebäude, die den neuen Wohlstand repräsentierten. Das Warenhaus Hermann Tietz (oben) in der Leipziger Straße (1898–1900 erbaut) war der Inbegriff für den gründerzeitlichen Prunk der Jahrhundertwende.

Like in other industrial cities, the period of promoterism, or Wilhelminian style, in Berlin was stamped by numerous new buildings, which represented the new wealth. The department store Hermann Tietz (above) at Leipziger Straße (built 1898-1900) epitomized the Wilhelminian pomp at the turn of the century.

Auch der internationale Jugendstil prägte viele Wohn- und Geschäftsräume. Hier das Lokal der Continental-Havanna-Compagnie in der Mohrenstraße 11/12, 1899.

The international art nouveau stamped several living and business offices as well. Here, the saloon of the Continental-Havanna-Compagnie on Mohrenstraße 11/12, 1899.

Während sich die Massen der nach Berlin geströmten Arbeiter in engen und feuchten Hinterhofwohnungen drängten, imitierten die zu Geld gekommenen Industriellen in großbürgerlichen Salons die Einrichtungsstile des Adels. Wohnzimmer einer Berliner Wohnung im Louis-Quinze-Stil.

While the masses of the employees flocking to Berlin crowded in crammed-in backyard flats, the industrialist who gained wealth imitated the furnishing style of the aristocracy in their upper class parlours. Louis-Quinze-Style living room of a Berlin apartment.

HOTEL ADLON

Am Pariser Platz, der »guten Stube« Berlins, erfüllte sich der Hotelier und Weinhändler Lorenz Adlon 1907 einen Traum: ein Hotel der Luxusklasse, das den großen Häusern in Paris und London ebenbürtig sein sollte. Mit Unterstützung von Kaiser Wilhelm II. schenkte er Berlin das modernste, schönste und luxuriöseste Hotel der damaligen Zeit, in dem sich bald die Welt traf und gekrönte Häupter ein und aus gingen. Kaiser Wilhelm floh aus den zugigen Räumen seines Schlosses ins Adlon, und das Auswärtige Amt nutzte das Hotel als »inoffizielles« Gästehaus.

Das Haus entwickelte sich zu einem Tummelplatz der kulturellen und politischen Welt. Könige, Zaren, Maharadschas standen hier ebenso im Gästebuch wie die Namen Einstein, Sauerbruch, Rockefeller, Stresemann, Furtwängler, Karajan oder Charlie Chaplin. Marlene Dietrich wurde hier entdeckt.

Im Verlauf der Geschichte wurde das Adlon auch zum Schauplatz politischer und diplomatischer Entscheidungen. Während der NS-Zeit galt es als »die kleine Schweiz in Berlin«. Die internationale Prominenz aus Politik und Gesellschaft gab sich auch während der Olympischen Spiele 1936 hier die Klinke in die Hand. Die SS und auch Adolf Hitler mieden das

Grandhotel mit Tradition: das Adlon auf einer Bildpostkarte 1928 und Außenansicht von 1935.

HOTEL ADLON

It was on Pariser Platz, Berlin's 'parlour', that the hotel owner and wine merchant Lorenz Adlon fulfilled a dream in 1907: a luxury hotel intended to rival the leading hotels in Paris and London. With the support of Kaiser Wilhelm II, he gave Berlin the most modern, most beautiful, and most luxurious hotel of the time, where soon the whole world would meet and crowned heads would come and go. Kaiser Wilhelm fled the draughty rooms of his palace to the Adlon, and the Department of State used the hotel as an 'unofficial' guesthouse.

The hotel became a playground for the world of culture and politics. Kings, tsars, and maharajas were listed in the guest book alongside names such as Einstein, Sauerbruch, Rockefeller, Stresemann, Furtwängler, Karajan, and Charlie Chaplin. Marlene Dietrich was discovered at the Adlon.

During the course of history, the Adlon also became the scene of political and diplomatic decisions. During the Nazi period, it was viewed as 'Berlin's Little Switzerland'. The SS and Adolf Hitler avoided it. The 1936 Olympic Games brought the hotel to further international prominence through politics and society. Astonishingly, the Adlon even

Grand Hotel with tradition: The Adlon on a 1928 postcard and a view of the exterior in 1935.

Adlon. Das Haus überdauerte erstaunlicherweise selbst den Zweiten Weltkrieg, dann wurde es aber durch einen verheerenden Brand im Jahre 1945 zerstört, dessen Ursache bis heute nicht geklärt ist.

Die ehemalige DDR richtete in einem erhaltenen Seitenflügel wieder ein Hotel ein, später ein Lehrlingswohnheim. 1964 wurde der Bau zwar noch einmal renoviert, wurde aber 1984 ganz abgerissen, um einem Wohnkomplex Platz zu machen. Als 1989 die Mauer fiel, erwarb die Hotelbetriebsgesellschaft Kempinski die Genehmigung für den Wiederaufbau des Hotels Adlon. Am 23. August 1997 eröffnete der Bundespräsident Roman Herzog an der gleichen Stelle, wo es in den 20er Jahren seine große Zeit hatte, das neue Hotel Adlon.

Auf 6.000 Quadratmetern haben die Berliner Architekten Rüdiger Patzschke und Rainer-Michael Klotz einen Luxuspalast mit Ballsaal, Banketträumen, Salons, Restaurants, kugelsicheren Präsidentensuiten, Fitnessbereich und allem, was ein hochmodernes Spitzenhotel heute auszeichnet, gebaut, und die Gästeliste liest sich auch heute wieder wie ein »Who is who« des internationalen Jet-set.

Hotelierehepaar Louis und Hedda Adlon.
1921 übernahm Louis Adlon das Hotel von seinem Vater Lorenz Adlon.

Hotelier couple, Louis and Hedda Adlon. Louis Adlon took over the hotel from his father, Lorenz Adlon, in 1921.

survived the Second World War, only to be destroyed in 1945 by a devastating fire, the cause of which is still not clear.

The former German Democratic Republic re-established a hotel in a surviving wing, which later became a lodging house for apprentices. In 1964, the building was once again renovated, but totally demolished in 1984 to make way for a housing development. When the Berlin Wall fell in 1989, the Kempinski hotel management company obtained permission to rebuild the Hotel Adlon. On 23 August 1997, the German President, Roman Herzog, opened the new hotel in exactly the same location of its heyday in the 1920s.

The Berlin architects Rüdiger Patzschke and Rainer-Michael Klotz built a luxury palace covering six thousand square metres, complete with ballroom, banquet rooms, drawing rooms, restaurants, bullet-proof presidential suites, a fitness suite, and everything else that now goes toward making an ultra-modern luxury hotel. And once again the Adlon guest list reads like a 'Who's who' of the international jet set.

Das neue Adlon (oben) wurde von 1995-97 am Pariser Platz erbaut.

The new Adlon (above) was built in the Pariser Platz between 1995-97.

Bürgerstolz und Handelsfleiß: Im Fotoalbum einer Berliner Unternehmerfamilie präsentieren sich die Eltern stolz mit ihren Töchtern vor einer Rikscha im Garten des Hauses (oben u. links).
Im Kontor eines Kaufmanns die leitenden Angestellten (unten links), auf einer Parkbank ein Ehepaar im Sonntagsstaat (rechts).

Bourgeois pride and trading diligence: In a picture book of a Berlin entrepreneur family the parents proudly present themselves together with their daughters in front of a rickshaw in the garden of their house (above left). In a branch office of a merchant the directive staffers (left); on a bench a married couple in their Sunday outfits (right).

Die Vorderfronten der Mietshäuser waren in der Regel repräsentativ gestaltet und mit reichhaltigem Ornamentschmuck in den unterschiedlichsten historischen Stilen versehen. Berliner Mietshaus mit Geschäften, um 1910.

The fascias of the tenement blocks were generally very imposing and ornately decorated in a variety of historic architectural styles. Berlin tenement block with three shops (1910).

Blick in einen Berliner Hinterhof, um 1900. In den Hinterhöfen der Mietskasernen lagen Trostlosigkeit und Hinterhofromantik oft nah beieinander. Hier waren meist noch Gewerbebetriebe, Kutschereien oder Werkstätten untergebracht.

View of a Berlin backyard around 1900: Wretched living conditions and backyard romance often existed side by side within these tenement blocks. They were mostly home to shops, coachhouses, and workshops.

HEINRICH ZILLE

An dem Haus Sophie-Charlottenstraße 88 im Berliner Stadtteil Charlottenburg ist eine Gedenktafel angebracht, die an Heinrich Zille erinnert. Der »Pinselheinrich« (geb. 1858) wohnte hier von 1892 bis zu seinem Tode 1929 und stellte seine »Milljöh-Studien« an, die er mit bitterer Ironie auf den Skizzenblock brachte. Die verheerenden Wohnverhältnisse und die gesellschaftlichen Missstände wurden zum Thema seiner sozialkritischen Arbeiten, in denen er den Alltag der Berliner Hinterhöfe und Kellerwohnungen jener Zeit festhielt. Seine Motive waren die Menschen auf der Straße und in den Kneipen, die Arbeiter, die derben Bierkutscher, die leichten Mädchen.

Zille, dessen kritische Zeichnungen und Fotos die Gesellschaft schockieren sollten, wurde oft als simpler »Witzblattzeichner« abgetan. Dennoch, er war ein wichtiger Künstler in der Tradition des Realismus von Hogarth oder Daumier. Schon früh hatte er für die bekannten Zeitschriften »Jugend« und »Simplizissimus« gearbeitet. Seine Zeichnungen wurden darüber hinaus in verschiedenen grafischen Mappen und Büchern publiziert wie z.B. »Hurengespräche« (1913) oder »Das große Zille-Album« (1927). 1924 wurde er als Professor an die Berliner Akademie der Künste berufen. Zilles Bedeutung für die Kunst zu Beginn des 20. Jahrhunderts weit über Berlin hinaus ist unumstritten.

Heinrich Zille, der »Pinselheinrich«, hat das Leben in den Berliner Hinterhöfen und Destillen in oft sehr bitter-ironischen Zeichnungen und Skizzen festgehalten. Ein Selbstbildnis von 1919 zeigt ihn hier im Regen stehend bei der Arbeit.

Heinrich Zille, nicknamed 'Paintbrush Henry', was known for his often bitterly ironic drawings and sketches portraying life in Berlin's backyards and bars. This self-portrait from around 1919 shows him at work in the rain.

HEINRICH ZILLE

On the wall of the house at No. 88, Sophie-Charlottenstraße in Berlin's Charlottenburg district, is a plaque commemorating the painter Heinrich Zille. 'Henry the Paintbrush' (born 1858) lived here from 1892 until his death in 1929. It was here that he produced his 'Milljöh-Studien' ('Milieu Studies'), a series of sketches rooted in a sense of caustic irony. His work, which focussed on contemporary everyday life in Berlin's backyards and tenement buildings, formed a critical social commentary on the wretched living conditions and social injustices that he deplored. His subjects were people on the street or in bars, labourers, rough brewery wagon drivers, and prostitutes.

Zille, whose critical sketches and photographs were intended to shock society, was frequently dismissed as simply a 'comic artist'. In truth, however, he was an important artist, pursuing the tradition of realism and in the same league as Hogarth and Daumier. He began his career early on, working for established magazines such as 'Jugend' and 'Simplizissimus'. His sketches were also published in various graphic collections and books; for example, 'Hurengespräche' ('Conversations with Whores') (1913) and 'Das große Zille-Album' (1927). In 1924, he was appointed Professor of the Berlin Academy of Arts. There is no doubt that Zille's influence on early 20th-century art extended far beyond the confines of Berlin itself.

Neben zahlreichen anderen Büchern und Mappen mit Zeichnungen und Grafiken hat Zille 1908 das Buch »Kinder der Straße. 100 Berliner Bilder« veröffentlicht. (links: Titelbild der Erstausgabe, rechts: typische Berliner Hinterhofszene aus dem Buch).

Zille's many books and collections of drawings and sketches include 'Children of the Street. 100 Pictures of Berlin', published in 1908. (left: title page of the first edition; right: typical Berlin backyard scene as illustrated in the book).

Hinterhof eines Wohnhauses in der Dorotheenstraße, Berlin Mitte, um 1885. Die Wohnblöcke der Dorotheenstraße sind der späteren Stadtentwicklung gewichen. Heute befindet sich hier, mitten im neuen Regierungsviertel das Jakob-Kaiser-Haus, ein Verwaltungsblock mit Tausenden von Büros und Konferenzräumen.

Backyard of a housing block in the Dorotheenstraße, Central Berlin, around 1885: The Dorotheenstraße tenement blocks were demolished to make way for more recent development in the city, including the Jakob-Kaiser-Haus, an administrative building housing thousands of offices and conference rooms, situated right in the heart of what is now the new government district.

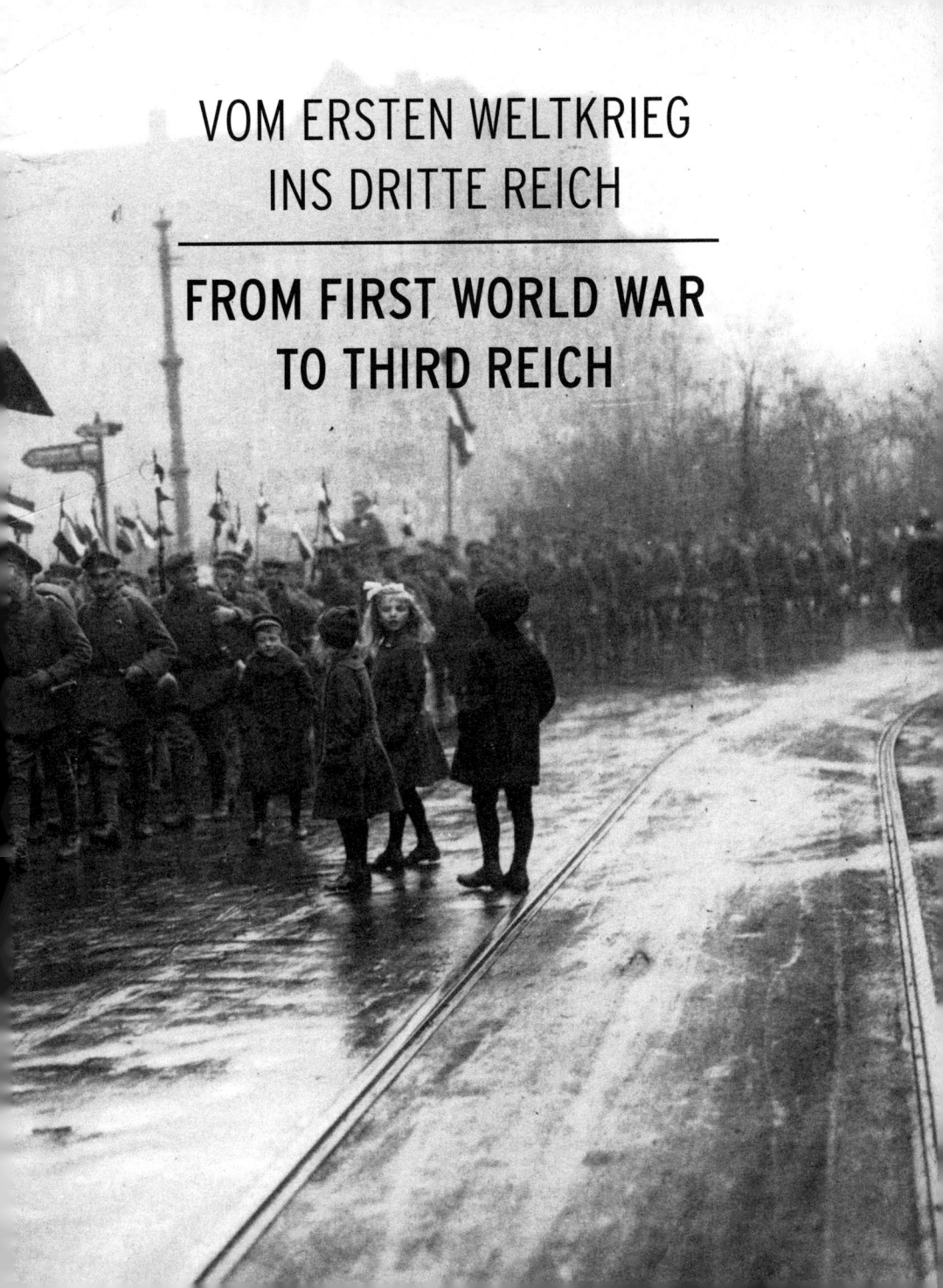

VOM ERSTEN WELTKRIEG INS DRITTE REICH

FROM FIRST WORLD WAR TO THIRD REICH

Der Ausbruch des Ersten Weltkriegs im Jahr 1914 löste in Berlin eine Welle patriotischer Kriegsbegeisterung aus.

Doch schon bald wurde die Bevölkerung Berlins von der bitteren Realität eingeholt: Wie in allen Großstädten, so führte der Krieg auch hier zu gravierenden Versorgungsengpässen. Ab 1915 wurden in Berlin Brot, Fleisch, Kartoffeln und andere Grundnahrungsmittel rationiert. Der harte Winter des Jahres 1917 ging als »Kohlrübenwinter« in die Geschichte ein.

Die Unzufriedenheit der Bevölkerung wuchs. In den Rüstungsbetrieben kam es zu Streiks gegen Hungersnot und Krieg. Die SPD spaltete sich – zu unüberbrückbar waren die Gegensätze zwischen den gemäßigten Sozialdemokraten unter Friedrich Ebert und Philipp Scheidemann und dem linken Flügel: im April 1917 gründete sich die Unabhängige Sozialdemokratische Partei Deutschlands (USPD).

Im November 1918 erreichten die Unruhen ihren Höhepunkt: in Berlin brach am 9. November ein Generalstreik aus, Soldaten und Arbeiter bildeten Räte. Reichskanzler Prinz Max von Baden gab die Abdankung Kaiser Wilhelms II. bekannt; um 14 Uhr rief Philipp Scheidemann, Fraktionsvorsitzender der SPD, im Reichstag die Deutsche Republik aus. Wenig später proklamierte Karl Liebknecht, Mitglied der USPD, von einem

The outbreak of the First World War in 1914 set off a wave of patriotic enthusiasm for war in Berlin.

The population of Berlin was, however, soon overtaken by harsh reality; as in all big cities, the war led to serious food shortages. From 1915, bread, meat, potatoes, and other basic foodstuffs were rationed. The hard winter of 1917 has gone down in history as the 'swede winter'.

Dissatisfaction among the population increased. In the armaments factories there were strikes against famine and war. The SPD split; the differences between the moderate Social Democrats under Friedrich Ebert and Philipp Scheidemann and the left wing were irreconcilable. The Independent Social Democratic Party of Germany (USPD) was founded in April 1917.

Unrest peaked in November 1918. A general strike broke out in Berlin on 9 November; soldiers and workers formed councils. The Chancellor, Prinz Max von Baden, announced the abdication of Kaiser Wilhelm II. At 2.00 p.m. Philipp Scheidemann, the SPD leader, proclaimed the German Republic in the Reichstag. Shortly afterwards Karl Liebknecht, a member of the USPD, proclaimed the 'Free Socialist Republic' from one of the balconies of Berlin Castle. In January 1919, he and

Seite 96/97: Der Krieg endete in einer Katastrophe, und die, die zurück kamen, waren froh, dass sie überlebt hatten. Heimkehr der Gardetruppen am 10. Dezember 1918. Ein Infanterieregiment passiert den Bayrischen Platz in Berlin-Schöneberg.

Pages 96/97: The war ended in disaster and those who returned home were just relieved to have survived at all. Homecoming of the Guards Regiment on 10 December 1918. An Infantry regiment passing the Bayrischer Platz in Berlin-Schöneberg.

Balkon des Berliner Schlosses aus die »Freie Sozialistische Republik«.

Im Januar 1919 wurden er und Rosa Luxemburg als Anführer der neu gegründeten Kommunistischen Partei (KPD) ermordert. Im März endete der Generalstreik der Berliner Arbeiterschaft auf Befehl des SPD-Reichswehrministers Gustav Noske blutig: 1.200 Menschen starben.

1920 wurde die Stadt Berlin mit ihren umliegenden Dörfern und Städten zu »Groß-Berlin« mit knapp vier Millionen Einwohnern vereinigt.

Ein Jahr später entstand mit der AVUS die erste Autobahn im Deutschen Reich. 1924 öffnete die erste deutsche Funkausstellung ihre Tore, 1926 die erste Grüne Woche. Im selben Jahr gründete der Ullstein-Verlag das größte und modernste Druckhaus Europas.

Auch Film und Theater feierten Goldene Zwanziger: Filme wie »Berlin – Sinfonie einer Großstadt« von Walter Ruttmann oder Fritz Langs »Metropolis« sind heute Klassiker. 1928 wurde Bertolt Brechts Welterfolg »Die Dreigroschenoper« uraufgeführt. Die Bohéme versank in Amusement und Jazzfieber.

Das politisch-wirtschaftliche Klima verschärfte sich dagegen extrem. 1922 wurde der Außenminister Walther Rathenau von Rechtsextremisten ermordet. Inflation und Arbeitslosigkeit ebneten den Nationalsozialisten den Weg. Ende 1929 waren 450.000 Berliner arbeitslos. Die Nazis kamen erstmals ins Rathaus. Am 30. Januar 1933 ernannte Reichspräsident Paul von Hindenburg Hitler zum Reichskanzler: Der »Trommler« war am Ziel.

Rosa Luxemburg were assassinated as the leaders of the newly founded Communist Party (KPD). In March, the general strike by the Berlin workforce came to a bloody end, on the orders of the SPD Defence Minister Gustav Noske; 1,200 died.

In 1920, the city was joined with the surrounding towns and villages to form 'Greater Berlin' with almost four million inhabitants. One year later, the AVUS, which started life as a privately built test track, became the first autobahn in Germany. In 1924, the first German Radio Exhibition opened its gates, and 1926 saw the first 'Grüne Woche' agricultural exhibition. In the same year, the Ullstein-Verlag founded the biggest and most modern print works in Europe. The cinema and theatre also celebrated the 'golden twenties'. Films like 'Berlin – Symphony of a City' by Walter Ruttmann, and Fritz Lang's 'Metropolis' have since become classics. Bertolt Brecht's world wide success 'The Threepenny Opera' was first performed in 1928. The bohemian world was plunged into entertainment and jazz fever.

By contrast, the political and economic climate was becoming extremely tense. In 1922, the Foreign Minister, Walther Rathenau, was assassinated by right-wing extremists. Inflation and unemployment paved the way for the National Socialists. At the end of 1929, there were 450,000 unemployed in Berlin. The Nazis were elected to the town hall for the first time. On 30 January 1933, President Paul von Hindenburg appointed Hitler Chancellor. 'Der Trommler' ('the Drummer') had achieved his goal.

August 1914: Die Kriegsbegeisterung in Europa erreichte ihren Höhepunkt. In patriotischen Kundgebungen wie im Berliner Lustgarten bekundeten die Menschen ihre »Vaterlandstreue« und Kriegsbereitschaft.

August 1914: War fever in Europe was reaching a climax. Patriotic rallies were held, such as this one in Berlin's Lustgarten park, proclaiming the people's 'loyalty to the fatherland' and their willingness to go to war.

28. August 1914: Abfahrt eines Truppentransports von einem Berliner Bahnhof. Noch ahnten die Kriegsfreiwilligen nicht, was ihnen bevorstand, und zogen begeistert gegen den französischen »Erbfeind«.

28 August 1914: A troop transport leaving Berlin railway station. At this stage, these volunteer soldiers still had no idea of what was to come and set off, full of enthusiasm, to fight the French 'arch enemy'.

Die Kaiserin überreicht den Offizieren des I. Garde-Regiments zum Abschied Rosen.

Kriegsbegeisterung von höchster Stelle: Kaiserin Auguste Viktoria überreicht den Offizieren des 1. Garde-Regiments zum Abschied Rosen. Solche Szenen wurden als Fotopostkarten zu beliebten Geschenken und Andenken. Der Kitsch um Reich und Krieg fand seinen Niederschlag auch auf unzähligen Sammeltassen, Wandtellern und Biergläsern. So sollte der »Hurra-Patriotismus« in alle Bevölkerungsschichten getragen werden.

War fever at the highest level: Empress Auguste Viktoria presents each officer of the 1st Guards Regiment with a farewell rose. Such scenes were captured on postcards and became popular gifts and keepsakes. The commercial kitsch spawned in the name of Empire and war also extended to innumerable commemorative cups, wall plates, and beer glasses. This flag-waving patriotism embraced all sectors of society.

Anfangs verlief noch alles nach Plan, und in der Heimat konnten Siege vermeldet werden: Am 2. September 1914 wurden auf einer Truppenparade in Berlin die ersten Kriegstrophäen und Beutestücke stolz präsentiert. Ein Zug mit erbeuteten Geschützen passiert Zeughaus und Schlossbrücke.

To begin with, everything went according to plan, and the initial reports home boasted of victories. On 2 September 1914, the first trophies and spoils of war were proudly displayed during a military parade in Berlin. A train carrying captured guns passes the Zeughaus and Schlossbrücke.

Der Krieg hatte die sozialen Probleme, die durch die Industrialisierung entstanden waren, noch verschärft. Viele Arbeiterfamilien lebten in schlechten Wohnungen und schlimmsten hygienischen Bedingungen. Eine Berliner Arbeiterwohnung im Dachgeschoss um 1918.

The war served to exacerbate the social problems that had arisen in the wake of industrialization. Many working families lived in poor apartments, in conditions of the worst possible hygiene. A Berlin working family's attic apartment around 1918.

Die nationale Begeisterung von 1914 war bis 1918 Ernüchterung, Kriegsmüdigkeit und innenpolitischen Spannungen gewichen. Nach dem Aufstand der Matrosen in Kiel, die gegen eine Weiterführung des Krieges protestierten, griffen am 9. November 1918 auch in Berlin schnell revolutionäre Aufstände um sich. Truppenteile schlossen sich mit aufständischen Arbeitern zusammen, um die alten Machthaber abzulösen. Auch die Garde-Ulanen-Kaserne in Berlin wurde an die Mitglieder des Arbeiter- und Soldatenrates übergeben.

The national enthusiasm of 1914 had, by 1918, been replaced by disillusionment, war weariness, and political tension within the country. Following an uprising by sailors in Kiel, in protest against a continuation of the war, there were also spontaneous outbreaks of revolutionary unrest on 9 November 1918 in Berlin itself. Troop units joined forces with protesting workers in an effort to depose the old rulers. The Garde-Ulanen barracks in Berlin was handed over to the Workers' and Soldiers' Council.

Die Berliner Bahnhöfe wurden zu Sammelstellen und Durchfahrtslagern für die heimkehrenden Kriegsgefangenen aus Sibirien. Das Rote Kreuz versuchte trotz des katastrophalen Mangels im Land die Heimkehrer zu verpflegen.

Berlin's railway stations became collection points and transit camps for prisoners-of-war returning from Siberia. Despite dreadful shortages throughout the country, the Red Cross did its best to provide care for the men returning home.

Demonstration im Lustgarten für die Freilassung der letzten 115 Kriegsgefangenen aus Frankreich.

Demonstrations in the Lustgarten park calling for the release of the last 115 prisoners-of-war held in France.

Die zurückgekehrten Soldaten fanden in der Heimat Hunger, wirtschaftliches Chaos und revolutionäre Unruhen vor. Sie sahen ihr bisheriges Weltbild in Frage gestellt, fanden keine Arbeit und mussten sich mit Gelegenheitsjobs über Wasser halten. Dass sich Soldaten 1918/19 als fliegende Händler oder Zigarettenverkäufer betätigen mussten, war keine Seltenheit und förderte Unzufriedenheit und radikale Ansichten.

What the soldiers were faced with on their return home was hunger, economic chaos, and revolutionary unrest. The world as they had known it no longer existed. There was no work for them and they had to make ends meet doing casual jobs. It was not unusual in 1918/19 for former soldiers to find themselves relegated to working as pedlars, cigarette sellers, or selling Christmas confectionery and this, in turn, led to dissatisfaction and radical views.

TROTZ ALLEDEM!

Mit diesen Worten reagierte Karl Liebknecht (1871–1919) am 15. Januar 1919 in der »Roten Fahne« auf die Niederlage der Revolution. Die Schrift ist eine flammende Anklage gegen die Herrschenden und gleichzeitig Vermächtnis. Er und seine Weggefährtin Rosa Luxemburg (1871–1919) werden noch am selben Tag von Soldaten der Garde-Kavallerie-Schützen-Division verhaftet, in das Freikorps-Hauptquartier im Hotel Eden verschleppt, misshandelt, verhört und anschließend ermordet. Die Presse vermeldete am nächsten Tag, Karl Liebknecht sei auf der Flucht erschossen, Rosa Luxemburg vom tobenden Mob gelyncht worden. Die Meldung löste auch in weiten Teilen der bürgerlichen Öffentlichkeit Empörung aus.

Im von schweren Unruhen geprägten Berliner Winter 1918/1919 kämpften Karl Liebknecht und Rosa Luxemburg, beide Gründungsmitglieder des Spartakusbundes, als führende Köpfe auf der Seite der Aufständischen. Nach der Abdankung des Kaisers proklamiert Philipp Scheidemann vom Reichstagsgebäude die »Deutsche Republik«, zwei Stunden später ruft Liebknecht vom Balkon des Berliner Schlosses die »Freie Sozialistische Republik« aus. Die Novemberrevolution nimmt ihren Anfang, und erst mit der Niederschlagung des Januaraufstandes durch die Regierung am 12. Januar 1919 nehmen die blutigen Auseinandersetzungen ihr Ende. Der Kampf um die Errichtung einer Räterepublik ist gescheitert.

Karl Liebknecht und Rosa Luxemburg bei der Vorbereitung des Gründungsparteitages der KPD (Zeichnung, 1950).
Rosa Luxemburg 1914 in Berlin.

Karl Liebknecht and Rosa Luxemburg preparing for the founding Congress of the KPD (Drawing, 1950).
Rosa Luxemburg, Berlin 1914.

DESPITE EVERYTHING!

These words were Karl Liebknecht's (1871-1919) reaction to the collapse of the revolution, published on 15 January 1919 in the 'Red Flag'. The article, which turned out to be his final legacy, was a fierce indictment of the ruling powers. He and his partner Rosa Luxemburg (1871-1919) were arrested the same day by soldiers of the Garde-Kavallerie-Schützen-Division and taken to the Hotel Eden, the corps headquarters, where they were assaulted, interrogated, and subsequently murdered. Press reports the next day claimed that Karl Liebknecht had been shot whilst attempting to escape and that Rosa Luxemburg had been lynched by the rampaging mob. These reports unleashed a wave of public indignation, even among the middle classes.

During the winter of 1918-19, Berlin had been plagued by serious unrest. Karl Liebknecht and Rosa Luxemburg, both founding members of the Spartakusbund, were prominent figures on the side of the insurgents. Following the abdication of the Kaiser, Philipp Scheidemann proclaimed the 'German Republic' from the Reichstag building. Just two hours later, Liebknecht proclaimed a 'Free Socialist Republic' from the balcony of the Palace. This signalled the start of the November Revolution and it was not until the government's defeat of the January uprising on 12 January 1919 that the bloody violence came to an end. The struggle to establish a soviet republic had failed.

Durch Granattreffer während der Revolutionstage zerstörtes Wohnhaus im Dezember 1918.

A housing block demolished by a grenade during the days of the Revolution in December 1918.

Die Revolution hinterlässt ihre Spuren: Begräbnisfeierlichkeiten für die Revolutionsopfer am 20. November 1918. Der Trauerzug am Brandenburger Tor.

The Revolution leaves its mark: Funeral ceremonies for the victims of the revolution on 20 November 1918. The funeral cortège at the Brandenburg Gate.

Schon im Dezember 1918 war an Berliner Plakatsäulen offen zum Mord an Karl Liebknecht und Rosa Luxemburg aufgerufen worden. Am 4. Januar 1919 hält Liebknecht vor dem Ministerium des Innern (Unter den Linden) seine letzte öffentliche Ansprache, in der er vor den Demonstranten die sofortige Entlassung der Soldaten fordert. Am 15. Januar wird er ermordet.

Posters had been appearing all over Berlin since December 1918, openly calling for the murder of Karl Liebknecht and Rosa Luxemburg. On 4 January 1919, Liebknecht delivered his last public address before a crowd of demonstrators outside the Ministry of the Interior on Unter den Linden, demanding the soldiers' immediate release. He was murdered on 15 January.

Reichskanzler Friedrich Ebert hatte gegen die Aufstände Regierungstruppen eingesetzt. Das verstärkte die Spaltung der Linken und führt, mit anderen Ursachen, zum Austritt der USPD aus dem Rat der Volksbeauftragten und zur Gründung der KPD. Im Januar 1919 kommt es in Berlin zum Spartakusaufstand mit blutigen Kämpfen zwischen regierungstreuen Truppen und Freikorps auf der einen Seite und Revolutionären auf der anderen Seite. An allen wichtigen Punkten der Stadt werden Straßen und Plätze besetzt (unten). Auch in Berlin-Friedrichshain, in der Andreas-/ Ecke Lange Straße, werden Barrikaden errichtet (oben).

Reichskanzler Friedrich Ebert called in government troops to deal with the demonstrators. This widened the split with the left wing and was one of the factors which led to the USPD quitting the Rat der Volksbeauftragten (National Delegates' Council), founding the KPD, and, in January 1919, inciting the Spartacus uprising during which bloody clashes occurred between pro-government troops and the Freikorps on the one side and revolutionaries on the other. Streets and squares were occupied at all strategic points throughout the city (below). Barricades were erected in Berlin-Friedrichshain and the Andreas-/Ecke Lange Straße, to name but a few (above).

Januar 1919: Im Berliner Zeitungsviertel, wie hier in der Großen Frankfurter Straße, feuern Regierungstruppen hinter einer Barrikade aus Zeitungspapierrollen auf Spartakisten. Noch bis Mai tobt in Deutschland ein Bürgerkrieg mit Tausenden von Todesopfern.

January 1919: In Berlin's newspaper district, here in the Große Frankfurter Straße, government troops behind a barricade of rolled-up newspapers fire on Spartakists. The civil war in Germany continues until May, claiming thousands of victims.

Trauerzug durch Berlin: Am 25. Januar 1919 werden Karl Liebknecht und Rosa Luxemburg auf dem Friedhof Berlin-Friedrichsfelde beigesetzt.

Funeral procession in Berlin: Karl Liebknecht and Rosa Luxemburg are laid to rest at Berlin-Friedrichsfelde Cemetery on 25 January 1919.

Berlin im Ausnahmezustand. Die Arbeiterschaft befindet sich im Generalstreik.
Reichswehrminister Noske verhängt den Belagerungszustand und lässt regierungstreue Truppen gegen die Streikenden vorgehen.

Berlin in a state of emergency: The workers have called a general strike. Reichswehrminister Noske proclaims a state of siege and calls in government troops to intervene against the strikers.

Berlin, Juli 1919: Auch die Angestellten der Berliner Verkehrsbetriebe streiken. Überall, wie hier auf dem Potsdamer Platz, kommt es zum Chaos.

Berlin, July 1919: Berlin's public transport workers also go on strike. Chaos reigns everywhere, as seen here in Potsdam Square.

WAS DARF SATIRE?

Der Schriftsteller und Journalist Kurt Tucholsky wurde am 9. Januar 1890 als Sohn eines jüdischen Kaufmanns in Berlin geboren. Schon als Jugendlicher veröffentlichte er erste Texte.

Ab 1913 schrieb er u. a. für die sozialdemokratische Zeitung »Vorwärts« und Siegfried Jacobsohns Zeitschrift »Schaubühne«, die später »Weltbühne« hieß. Tucholskys Artikel, Gedichte und Chansons kritisierten mit satirischer Schärfe die gesellschaftlichen Missstände der Weimarer Republik. Nach seinen Erfahrungen als Soldat im Ersten Weltkrieg trat Tucholsky als überzeugter Pazifist auf. Wie viele linke Intellektuelle jener Zeit kämpfte er gegen Nationalismus, Militarismus, eine korrupte Justiz und obrigkeitshörige Beamte.

Zu Markenzeichen des brillanten Kritikers wurden Pseudonyme wie Kaspar Hauser, Peter Panter, Ignaz Wrobel und Theobald Tiger. Sein Selbstverständnis: »Der Satiriker ist ein gekränkter Idealist: er will die Welt gut haben, sie ist schlecht, und nun rennt er gegen das Schlechte an.«

Ab 1924 lebte Tucholsky als Korrespondent für »Weltbühne« und »Vossische Zeitung« größtenteils im Ausland, 1929 emigrierte er, resigniert über die politische Entwicklung in Deutschland nach Hindas in Schweden. Schon vor der Machtübernahme der Nationalsozialisten beschrieb er in Gedichten wie »Das Dritte Reich« oder »Joebbels« das heraufziehende Unheil. 1933 wurden die Bücher Kurt Tucholskys im Deutschen Reich verboten und verbrannt, er selbst ausgebürgert. Nach schwerer Krankheit beging er 1935 im schwedischen Exil Selbstmord.

Gesellschaftskritiker mit Berliner Witz: Kurt Tucholsky.

Critics' society with native Berlin wit: Kurt Tucholsky.

WHAT CAN SATIRE DO?

The author and journalist Kurt Tucholsky, son of a Jewish businessman, was born in Berlin on 9 January 1890. His first writings were published while still an adolescent. In 1913, he started writing for such publications as the Social Democratic newspaper 'Vorwärts' and Siegfried Jacobsohn's journal 'Schaubühne', later renamed 'Weltbühne'.

Tucholsky's articles, poems and satirical political songs sharply criticized the social outrages of the Weimar Republic. As a result of his experiences as a soldier in the First World War, Tucholsky became a convinced pacifist. Like many left-wing intellectuals at the time, he fought against nationalism, militarism, a corrupt judicial system, and authoritarian officials.

His trademarks included pseudonyms like Kaspar Hauser, Peter Panter, Ignaz Wrobel, and Theobald Tiger. His view of the satirist's role is that 'the satirist is a wounded idealist. He wants to the world to be good; it is bad, and so he attacks what is bad'.

After 1924, Tucholsky mostly lived abroad as a correspondent for 'Weltbühne' and 'Vossische Zeitung'. In 1929, he emigrated to Hindas in Sweden, having become disillusioned by the political developments in Germany. Even before the Nazis seized power, he described the impending disaster in poems such as 'Das Dritte Reich' ('The Third Reich') and 'Joebbels'. In 1933, Kurt Tucholsky's books were banned and burned in the German Reich, and he was deprived of his citizenship. In 1935, after a serious illness, he committed suicide while in exile in Sweden.

1932 steht Tucholskys Freund, der »Weltbühne«-Herausgeber Carl von Ossietzky (Mitte), wegen »Landesverrats« vor Gericht.

In 1932, Tucholsky's friend and editor of the 'Weltbühne' ('World Stage') magazine, Carl von Ossietzky, is on trial for 'treason'.

Die Folgen von Revolution und Bürgerkrieg verschärfen die sozialen Gegensätze im Berlin der 20er Jahre. Viele Menschen, vor allem Kinder, sind unterernährt und erhalten ihre Mahlzeiten in öffentlichen Suppenküchen (oben). Familien des Großbürgertums, darunter auch nicht wenige Kriegsgewinnler, haben weiterhin ihre Hausangestellten. Berliner Waschfrauen um 1920 (unten).

The Revolution and civil war merely serve to highlight the social inequalities in Berlin in the 1920s. Many people, children in particular, are undernourished and rely on public soup kitchens for their meals (above). Upper middle-class families, some of whom have actually profited from the war, have managed to retain their servants. Berlin washerwomen around 1920 (below).

Wie von der Außenwelt unberührt: Großbürgerliches Herrenzimmer in einer Berliner Wohnung um 1920.

Untouched by the outside world: An upper middle-class gentleman's smoking-room in a Berlin apartment around 1920.

WALTER GROPIUS

Walter Gropius gilt als der führende Wegbereiter der klassisch modernen Architektur. Der Schüler von Peter Behrens gründete 1919 in Weimar das später weltberühmte Bauhaus und war bis 1928 sein Direktor. Anschließend arbeitete er als Architekt in Berlin, wo er bereits ab 1926 zusammen mit Hans Scharoun, Hugo Häring und Otto Bartning im Bezirk Spandau die Siemensstadt, eine Werkssiedlung mit etwa 1300 Wohnungen für die Arbeiter der Siemenswerke, plante und baute. Als 1933 das Bauhaus unter Druck der Nationalsozialisten geschlossen wurde, emigrierte Gropius zunächst nach London und anschließend, wie andere berühmte Vertreter des Bauhauses, in die USA. Nach dem Krieg wurde Gropius erneut in Berlin tätig. 1957 wurde im Rahmen der Internationalen Bauausstellung nach seinen Entwürfen im Hansaviertel ein neungeschossiges Wohnhaus gebaut. Den Namen des Architekten ehrt darüber hinaus eine gigantische Siedlung. Gropiusstadt, ursprünglich als BBR-Siedlung (Britz-Buckow-Rudow) bezeichnet, war das größte Bauprojekt der Nachkriegszeit in Westberlin. 50.000 Menschen sollten in den 17.000 Wohnungen dieser geplanten Trabantenstadt unterkommen. Beauftragt mit dem Vorhaben wurde die »Gemeinnützige Heimstätten AG Walter Gropius«. Unter der Regie von Gropius' Büro TAC (The Architects Collaborative) in den USA arbeiteten 50 Architekten an dem Mammutprojekt. Gleichwohl scheiterte das ambitionierte Vorhaben zumindest im Hinblick auf Gropius' Intention, eine Modellstadt zu schaffen, die ein menschliches Wohnen ermöglichen sollte. Laufend geänderte Pläne und Etatkürzungen durch den Senat sorgten dafür, dass letztlich nur ein unmotiviertes Dickicht von Hochhäusern entstand, von dem sich Gropius ausdrücklich distanzierte. Trotzdem erhielt die Trabantenstadt drei Jahre nach seinem Tod seinen Namen.

Links: Das Wohnhaus im Hansa-Viertel ließ Walter Gropius (Mitte) für die Internationale Bauausstellung 1957 erbauen.

Rechts: Bauhaus-Archiv in Berlin-Tiergarten, 1976-79 von Walter Gropius erbaut.

Left: The appartment building in the Hansa-Viertel Walter Gropius built for the International Construction Exhibition 1957.
Right: Bauhaus-Archive in Berlin Tiergarten, built by Walter Gropius 1976-79.

WALTER GROPIUS

Walter Gropius is considered as one of the leading pioneers of classical modern architecture. A pupil of Peter Behrens, in 1919 he founded the Bauhaus in Weimar, which would go on to become world-famous, and of which he was director until 1928. He then worked as an architect in Berlin where, from 1926 onwards, and together with Hans Scharoun, Hugo Häring, and Otto Bartning, he designed the Siemensstadt in the Spandau district, a company housing development with around thirteen hundred apartments for people working at the Siemens factory. When in 1933 the Bauhaus was closed due to pressure from the National Socialists, Gropius emigrated, first to London and then, like other famous representatives of the Bauhaus, to America.

After the war, Gropius returned to work in Berlin. In 1957, as part of the International Building Exhibition, a nine-storey apartment block was built in the Hansa quarter using his designs. A huge housing development also honours the architect's name. Gropiusstadt, originally called the BBR-housing development (Britz-Buckow-Rudow), was the largest building project of the postwar period in West Berlin. The intention was to house fifty thousand people in the seventeen thousand apartments of this planned satellite town. The 'Gemeinnützige Heimstätten AG Walter Gropius' was commissioned to carry out the project. Under the management of Gropius' TAC (The Architects' Collaborative) in America, fifty architects worked on this mammoth enterprise. Constantly amended plans and budget cuts by the Senate however ensured that ultimately only an aimless jungle of high-rise apartments was created, from which Gropius expressly distanced himself. The satellite town was nevertheless named after him, three years after his death.

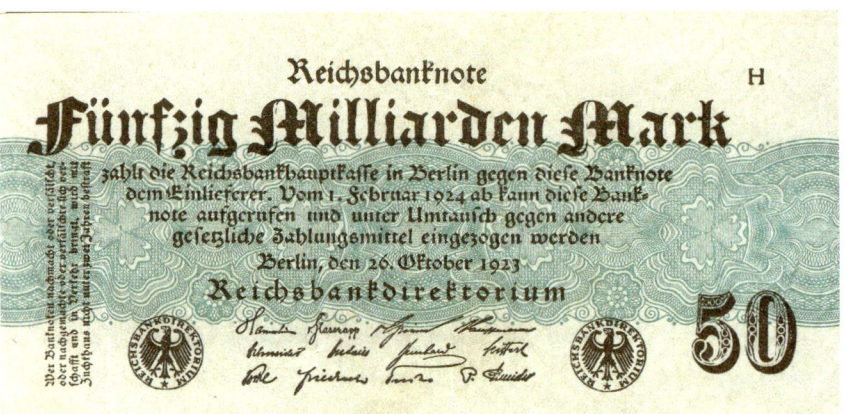

Milliarden ohne Wert: Auf dem Höhepunkt der Inflation von 1923 ist das deutsche Geld nichts mehr wert.

Worthless billions: When inflation reached its peak in 1923, Germany currency was completely worthless.

In Berlin waren die 20er Jahre zunächst nicht, und schon gar nicht für alle, die »Goldenen Zwanziger Jahre«: Bettelnde Frau an einer Straßenecke, 1923.

The 1920s were by no means the 'Golden Twenties' for everyone: Women begging on a street corner, 1923.

Berlin 1925: Nach Krieg, Revolution und Inflation stabilisiert sich die wirtschaftliche Situation in Deutschland. In Berlin wird der Potsdamer Platz wieder zum Zentrum einer pulsierenden Großstadt. Nach dem Eingemeindungsgesetz von 1920 ist Berlin jetzt mit fast 4 Millionen Einwohnern die zweitgrößte Stadt Europas und mit einer Fläche von 878 Quadratkilometern flächenmäßig eine der größten Städte der Welt.

Berlin 1925: War, revolution, and inflation finally give way to a greater degree of economic stability in Germany. Potsdam Square once again becomes the heart of a pulsating city. Territorial reform in 1920 makes Berlin the second largest city in Europe and, with nearly 4,000,000 inhabitants over an area of 878 square kilometres, one of the biggest cities in the world.

Die »Goldenen Zwanziger Jahre« waren in Berlin von Avantgardekunst und Varieté, vor allem aber durch die großen Sportereignisse geprägt: die großen Boxkämpfe und die Radrennen im Berliner Sportpalast wurden zu Legenden.

The 'Golden Twenties' era in Berlin was characterized not only by avantgarde art and entertainment, but also by major sports events: Championship boxing tournaments and cycle races in Berlin's Sportpalast became legendary.

Die 20er Jahre waren die Zeit der großen Boxer: hier Max Schmeling und Jack Stanley (Großbritannien) im Berliner Sportpalast am 7. Januar 1927. Stanley ging in der 8. Runde zu Boden.

The 1920s was the era of great boxers: Pictured here are Max Schmeling and Jack Stanley (Great Britain) in Berlin's Sportpalast on 7 Januray 1927. Stanley was knocked out in the 8th round.

Deutschland erlebte von 1924 bis 1929 einen wirtschaftlichen und technologischen Aufschwung. Die Autorennen auf der AVUS standen in dieser Zeit gleichermaßen für technologischen Fortschritt, sportliche Leistung und waren gesellschaftliche Ereignisse. Hier der Start zum 3. Rennen über 180 km auf der AVUS in Berlin.

From 1924 to 1929, Germany experienced an economic and technological upturn. The AVUS motor races at that time symbolized not only technological progress and sporting achievement but were also a social event. Pictured here is the start of the 3rd 180-km AVUS race in Berlin.

Auf der AVUS präsentierte Fritz Opel 1928 auch sein Aufsehen erregendes Raketenauto.

Fritz Opel introducing his rocket-propelled car at the AVUS in 1928.

Internationalität und Exotik prägten das Berliner Leben: die amerikanische Sängerin und Revuetänzerin Josephine Baker trat in Berlin auf. Bei einem Gastspiel im Februar 1926 fuhr sie in einem Straußengespann durch die Straßen der Stadt.
Berliner Nachtleben 1925: Vor dem Eingang des Varieté-Theaters Scala in der Lutherstraße 22 posieren die »Scala-Girls«.

International and exotic influences have always left their mark on the city: American singer and dancer Josephine Baker performed in Berlin. During a guest visit in February 1926, she drove through the streets of Berlin in an ostrich-drawn carriage.
Berlin night life 1925: The 'Scala-Girls' pose in front of the variety theatre Scala in the Lutherstraße 22.

Auch die deutsche Unterhaltungsindustrie boomt: Der Frühling von Berlin, 1924.

The booming German entertainment industry: Spring in Berlin, 1924.

BERTOLT BRECHT

Bertolt Brecht (1898–1956) war ohne Zweifel einer der bedeutendsten Theatermacher des 20. Jahrhunderts.

Nach ersten Erfolgen als Dramatiker zog Brecht 1924 nach Berlin und wurde Dramaturg an Max Reinhardts Deutschem Theater. Zu dieser Zeit begann sein Studium marxistischer Schriften. Mit der »Dreigroschenoper« gelang Brecht 1928 ein erster großer Erfolg am Theater am Schiffbauerdamm. Es war das erste Stück des von Brecht erfundenen epischen Theaters, bei dem die Zuschauer sich nicht mit dem Bühnengeschehen identifizieren, sondern es mit kritischer Distanz beobachten sollen.

1933 musste der Kommunist Brecht das nationalsozialistische Deutschland verlassen, 1935 wurde er ausgebürgert. Im amerikanischen Exil entstanden politisch motivierte Stücke wie »Der aufhaltsame Aufstieg des Arturo Ui« oder »Galileo Galilei«.

Nach dem Zweiten Weltkrieg lebte Brecht mit seiner Frau Helene Weigel kurz in der Schweiz, bevor er 1949 nach Ost-Berlin übersiedelte. Dort gründeten sie das »Berliner Ensemble«, das ab 1954 im Theater am Schiffbauerdamm zu einer weltberühmten experimentellen Bühne wurde.

Bertolt Brecht unterstützte wie viele Intellektuelle der jungen DDR zunächst uneingeschränkt die SED. Er sprach sich gegen den Aufstand staatskritischer Demonstranten am 17. Juni 1953 aus und wurde mit mehreren Staatspreisen ausgezeichnet. In seinen letzten Lebensjahren geriet er jedoch zunehmend in ideologische und ästhetische Konflikte mit dem DDR-Staat. Bertolt Brecht starb 1956 in Berlin und wurde auf dem Dorotheenstädtischen Friedhof beigesetzt.

Welterfolge des Herrn B.: 1928 wird Brechts »Dreigroschenoper« uraufgeführt, 1941 »Mutter Courage und ihre Kinder« (mit Helene Weigel in der Titelrolle). Nach dem Krieg gründen Bertolt Brecht und seine Lebensgefährtin das Berliner Ensemble in Ostberlin.

Mr. B's international successes: 1928 sees the premier of Brecht's 'Threepenny Opera', followed by 'Mother Courage and her Children' in 1941 (with Helene Weigel in the title role). After the war, Bertolt Brecht and his partner founded the Berliner Ensemble in East Berlin.

BERTOLT BRECHT

Bertolt Brecht (1898-1956) was one of the most significant playwrights of the twentieth century.

After his early successes as a dramatist, he moved to Berlin in 1924 and took up the post of dramaturg at Max Reinhardt's Deutsches Theater. It was at this time that he began to study Marxist writings. The 1928 'Dreigroschenoper' ('Threepenny Opera') was Brecht's first great success at the Theater am Schiffbauerdamm. It was the first play of the 'epic theatre' genre invented by Brecht, in which the audience must not identify with events on stage but observe them from a critical distance.

As a communist, Brecht had to leave Nazi Germany in 1933 and was deprived of his citizenship in 1935. While in exile in America, he wrote politically motivated plays such as 'Der aufhaltsame Aufstieg des Arturo Ui' ('The Resistible Rise of Arturo Ui') and 'Galileo Galilei'.

After the Second World War, Brecht and his wife Helene Weigel lived in Switzerland for a short time, before moving to East Berlin in 1949. There, they founded the Berliner Ensemble which from 1954 onwards made the Theater am Schiffbauerdamm world famous as an experimental theatre.

Like many intellectuals in the new German Democratic Republic, Bertolt Brecht at first supported the SED (Socialist Unity Party of Germany) without reservation. He came out against the rebellious anti-state demonstrators on 17 June 1953 and was distinguished by the award of a number of state prizes. In the last years of his life, however, he increasingly came into ideological and aesthetic conflict with the East German State. Bertolt Brecht died in 1956 in Berlin and is buried in the Dorotheenstadt cemetery.

Der Künstler Otto Dix hat in seinen Bildern Glanz und Elend des Großstadtlebens der 20er Jahre so treffend festgehalten wie kein anderer. Mittelteil des Tryptichons »Großstadt« (1927/28).
(Stuttgart, Staatsgalerie)

In his pictures, painter Otto Dix captured the extremes of glitter and misery in 1920s Berlin better than anyone else: Central section of the 'Großstadt' triptych (1927/28) (Stuttgart, municipal gallery).

Auch die Künstler zeigten sich vom Boxsport begeistert. George Grosz (1893-1959), Wieland Herzfelde und John Heartfield beim Boxtraining; im Hintergrund Erwin Piscator. Berlin, um 1924.

Artists also developed an interest in boxing: George Grosz (1893-1959), Wieland Herzfelde and John Heartfield at boxing training; in the background, Erwin Piscator, Berlin, around 1924.

Die 20er Jahre waren auch in Berlin die Zeit des sozialen Wohnungsbaus. Der Architekt Bruno Taut baute 1925 bis 1931 in Berlin-Neukölln die sogenannte Hufeisensiedlung Britz.

During the 1920s, Berlin, like other cities, experienced a boom in social housing development: Architect Bruno Taut built the so-called Britz Horseshoe settlement in the Berlin-Neukölln district between 1925 and 1931.

GOTT SEI DANK, BERLINERIN

Der Weltstar Marlene Dietrich (1901–1992) war durch und durch Berlinerin. Als Lola in Josef von Sternbergs »Der Blaue Engel« verkörperte sie perfekt die kesse Göre im Berlin der 20er Jahre. Nach diesem internationalen Erfolg ging sie zusammen mit ihrem Regisseur und Liebhaber nach Hollywood. Mit Filmen wie »Marokko«, »Shanghai Express« oder »The devil is a woman« begründete sie ihren Ruhm als androgyne Diva, drehte mit den Top-Regisseuren des amerikanischen Kinos: Billy Wilder, Alfred Hitchcock und Orson Welles. Filmangebote aus dem nationalsozialistischen Deutschland lehnte Marlene Dietrich, die 1937 die amerikanische Staatsbürgerschaft annahm, konsequent ab.

Nach dem Zweiten Weltkrieg nahmen viele Berliner der Schauspielerin, die mittlerweile als Entertainerin die Konzertsäle in aller Welt füllte, ihr Engagement gegen Nazi-Deutschland übel. Bei einem Berlin-Besuch 1960 beschimpfen sie sie als »Landesverräterin« und fordern »Marlene, go home!«.

Obwohl sie in ihrer Heimatstadt nicht immer auf Gegenliebe stieß, publizierte die Dietrich ihre Memoiren 1987 unter dem Titel »Ich bin, Gott sei Dank, Berlinerin«. Nach ihrem Tod 1992 wurde sie ihrem Wunsch entsprechend auf dem Friedhof in der Stubenrauchstraße in Berlin-Friedenau beigesetzt. Heute heißt ein Teil des Potsdamer Platzes »Marlene-Dietrich-Platz«.

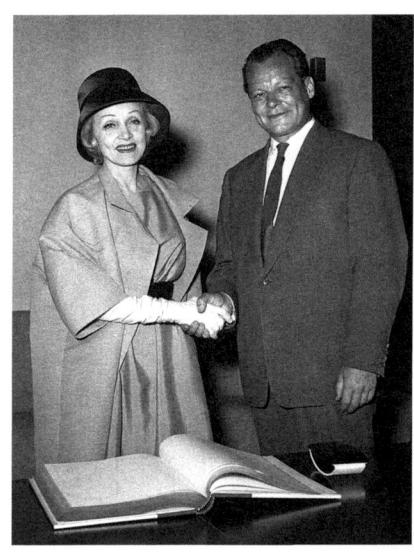

A star is born: Die junge Marlene Dietrich, bekannt geworden durch den »Blauen Engel«, posiert vor einer Opel-Limousine.

Der Regierende Bürgermeister Willy Brandt begrüßt Marlene Dietrich, die im Mai 1960 erstmals wieder Deutschland besucht.

A star is born: The young Marlene Dietrich, made famous by the film 'The Blue Angel', poses in front of an Opel limousine.

The Mayor of West Berlin, Willy Brandt, welcomes Marlene Dietrich, who in May 1960 is making her first visit back to Germany.

THANK GOODNESS, A BERLINER

The world famous film star Marlene Dietrich (1901-1992) was a Berliner through and through. As Lola in Josef von Sternberg's 'The Blue Angel', she was the perfect embodiment of the saucy young girl of 1920s Berlin. After this international success, she and Sternberg, her director and lover, went to Hollywood. With films like 'Marocco', 'Shanghai Express' and 'The Devil is a Woman', she became famous as the androgynous goddess of the silver screen and worked with the top American film directors Billy Wilder, Alfred Hitchcock, and Orson Welles. Dietrich, who became an American citizen in 1937, consistently turned down offers of films from Nazi Germany.

After the Second World War, many Berliners bore a grudge against the actress – who had meantime turned entertainer and was filling concert halls all over the world – for the stand she had taken against Nazi Germany. When she visited Berlin in 1960, they called her a traitor to her country and shouted 'Marlene, go home!'.

Although she was not always well received in the city of her birth, Dietrich published her memoirs in 1987 under the title 'Ich bin, Gott sei Dank, Berlinerin' ('Thank Goodness I'm a Berliner' – published in English as 'My Life'). When she died in 1992, she was buried according to her wishes in the cemetery in Stubenrauchstraße in Berlin-Friedenau. Part of the Potsdamer Platz has now been named 'Marlene-Dietrich-Platz'.

Berlin 1929, das Ende der goldenen Jahre: Die von den USA ausgehende Wirtschaftskrise wird zur Weltwirtschaftskrise und erreicht auch Deutschland. Während in den Theatern und Varietés noch immer das kulturelle Leben blüht, wachsen vor den Berliner Arbeitsämtern und Zahlstellen die Schlangen von Erwerbslosen.

Berlin 1929, the end of a golden era: The economic crisis in the USA spreads worldwide. While cultural life continues to thrive in theatres and variety halls, the queues of unemployed outside Berlin's labour exchanges and job centres grow longer.

13. Juni 1931: Nach dem Zusammenbruch des zweitgrößten deutschen Geldinstitutes, der Darmstädter und Nationalbank (Danat-Bank) bleiben die Berliner Banken geschlossen. Tausende von Anlegern und Kunden drängen sich vor den Banken Berlins.

13 June 1931: Following the collapse of Germany's second biggest financial institution, the Darmstädter und Nationalbank (Danat Bank), Berlin's banks remain closed. Thousands of customers and investors throng outside Berlin's banks.

Die Stunde der Demagogen: Adolf Hitler 1930 auf einer Veranstaltung im Berliner Sportpalast. Die soziale Krise radikalisiert die Massen. Die Reichstagswahlen von 1930 bringen sowohl den Kommunisten als auch der NSDAP, die plötzlich zur zweitstärksten Fraktion wird, erhebliche Zuwächse.

The hour of the dictator: Adolf Hitler, 1930 at a rally in Berlin's Sportpalast. The social crisis pushes the masses into radical action. The Reichstag elections of 1930 result in considerable gains for the KPD as well as the NSDAP, which suddenly finds itself the second biggest parliamentary party.

Wahlkampf 1930: Joseph Goebbels spricht auf einer Kundgebung der NSDAP im Lustgarten.

Election campaign 1930: Joseph Goebbels speaking at an NSDAP rally in the Lustgarten Park.

Die Reichstagswahl von 1932 führt zum Rücktritt der Regierung Brüning. Sein Nachfolger als Reichskanzler wird Franz von Papen, hier beim Verlassen seines Berliner Wahllokals am 31. Juli 1932. (links: Wahlpropaganda an einer Litfaßsäule)

The 1932 Reichstag elections result in the resignation of Brüning's government. His successor as Imperial Chancellor is named as Franz von Papen, seen here leaving his Berlin polling station on 31 July 1932. (left: Election slogans on an advertising pillar)

November 1932: Die Wahlen ändern nichts. Die soziale Misere bleibt bestehen, die Radikalität wächst. Oben: Streikposten der Angestellten der städtischen Verkehrsgesellschaft protestieren gegen weitere Lohnsenkungen. Rechts: Kommunistische Demonstration vor dem Berliner Dom.

November 1932: The elections change nothing. Social problems remain unsolved and the demand for radical solutions grows. Above: Pickets of employees of the public transport system protesting against further wage reductions. On the right: Communist demonstration in front of Berlin Cathedral.

DIE ZENTRALE DER NS-MACHT

NERVE CENTRE OF NAZI POWER

Nachdem die Nationalsozialisten bereits in der zweiten Hälfte der 20er Jahre in Deutschland immer mehr an Einfluss gewonnen hatten, überstürzten sich im Jahr 1933 die Ereignisse. Berlin wurde zum Schauplatz der nationalsozialistischen »Machtergreifung«: Am 30. Januar wurde Adolf Hitler zum Reichskanzler ernannt. Das war der Auftakt eines brutalen Terrorfeldzugs der NSDAP gegen ihre politischen Gegner, die Kommunisten und Sozialdemokraten, die immer noch in vielen Vierteln Berlins eine starke Anhängerschaft hatten.

In der Nacht vom 27. zum 28. Februar wurde das Reichstagsgebäude durch Brandstiftung zu einem großen Teil zerstört. Als Tatverdächtiger wurde der holländische Kommunist Marinus van der Lubbe festgenommen. Dieses Ereignis nutzten die Nationalsozialisten sofort für ihre Propaganda- und Verfolgungsaktion gegen KPD und SPD.

Raffinierte Propagandamaßnahmen kennzeichneten auch den weiteren Machtausbau der NSDAP. So wurden die Olympischen Spiele, die 1936 in Berlin stattfanden, vom Nazi-Regime geschickt zur Selbstdarstellung genutzt. Indessen nahmen die Ausschreitungen gegen die Juden in allen Teilen Deutschlands immer brutalere Formen an und gipfelten in der Nacht vom 9. zum 10. November 1938 in der Pogromnacht: Schlägertrupps der SA und Mitglieder der NSDAP zündeten in ganz Deutschland Syn-

After the National Socialists had become increasingly influential in the second half of the twenties in Germany, events in 1933 came thick and fast. Berlin became the scene of the Nazi seizure of power. On 30 January, Adolf Hitler was appointed Chancellor. That was the start of a brutal campaign of terror by the Nazi Party (NSDAP) against their political opponents, the Communists (KPD) and the Social Democrats (SPD), who still had a strong following in many quarters of Berlin. During the night of 27-28 February, the Reichstag building was largely destroyed by fire. The Dutch Communist Marinus van der Lubbe was arrested on suspicion. The Nazis immediately used this event for their own propaganda purposes and reprisals against the KPD and SPD.

Refined propaganda measures were also characteristic of the way the Nazi Party further extended its powers. For instance, the Nazi regime cleverly made use of the Olympic Games, which were held in Berlin in 1936, in order to promote itself. Meanwhile, the excesses against the Jews in all parts of Germany took ever more brutal forms, culminating in the pogrom of the night of 9-10 November 1938. A strike force of storm troopers and members of the Nazi Party set fire to synagogues and Jewish shops all over Germany. Twenty-

Seite 154/155:
18. Juli 1940: Berliner und Brandenburger Truppen ziehen nach dem Sieg über Frankreich im Parademarsch durch die Stadt.

Pages 154/155:
18 July 1940: Berlin and Brandenburg troops parade through the city in celebration of France's defeat.

agogen und jüdische Geschäfte an. In dieser Nacht wurden 29 jüdische Warenhäuser vernichtet, 191 Synagogen niedergebrannt, 7.500 Läden und 171 Wohnhäuser zerstört; 91 Juden wurden getötet. In den darauf folgenden Tagen wurden weitere 35.000 Juden verhaftet und in Konzentrationslager deportiert.

Am 1. September 1939 gab Hitler vor dem in der Krolloper versammelten Reichstag die Eröffnung des Krieges gegen Polen bekannt. Nach anfänglichen Siegen zeichnete sich die unausweichliche Niederlage Deutschlands ab. Zogen am 18. Juli 1940 noch die heimkehrenden Soldaten in einem Triumphzug durch die Stadt, so mussten die Berliner schon ab dem 25. August die ersten Luftangriffe auf ihre Stadt erleben. Am Ende des Jahres 1943 waren 400.000 Berliner obdachlos. Je näher die Niederlage rückte, um so aggressiver wurde die Propaganda des Nazi-Regimes. Am 18. Februar 1943 fragte Reichspropagandaminister Joseph Goebbels in seiner berühmten Rede im Berliner Sportpalast noch: »Wollt Ihr den totalen Krieg?« – am 1. August desselben Jahres leitete er die ersten Evakuierungsmaßnahmen für Berlin ein. Über 700.000 Berliner verließen in der zweiten Jahreshälfte ihre Stadt. Am 25. April 1945 schlossen sowjetische Truppen Berlin ein. Am 2. Mai kapitulierte der Stadtkommandant. Hitler hatte am 30. April – im Bunker der Berliner Neuen Reichskanzlei Selbstmord begangen. Ab dem 5. Juni stand Berlin unter der Kontrolle der Alliierten.

nine Jewish stores were destroyed that night, 191 synagogues were burned down, 7500 shops and 171 dwelling houses were destroyed, and 91 Jews were killed. In the following days, a further thirty-five thousand Jews were arrested and deported to concentration camps.

On 1 September 1939, Hitler announced the start of the war against Poland to the Reichstag, which had assembled in the Krolloper. After some early victories, the inevitability of German defeat became apparent. Though the returning troops marched through the city in triumphal procession on 18 July 1940, the Berliners had to experience the first air attacks on their city as early as 25 August. At the end of 1943, four hundred thousand Berliners were without a roof over their heads.

The closer they came to defeat, the more aggressive the Nazi regime's propaganda became. On 18 February 1943, propaganda minister Joseph Goebbels asked in his famous speech in the Berlin Palace of Sport: 'Do you want total war?'. On 1 August of the same year, he introduced the first evacuation measures for Berlin; over seven hundred thousand Berliners left the city in the second half of the year. On 25 May 1945, Soviet troops surrounded Berlin. On 2 May, the commandant of the city capitulated. Hitler had already committed suicide a week earlier – on 30 April – in the bunker of the New Berlin Reichskanzlei. From 5 June, Berlin was under Allied control.

30. Januar 1933, der Tag der »Machtergreifung«:
SA und SS ziehen zur Feier der »Machtübernahme«
im Fackelzug durch das Brandenburger Tor
(für einen Propagandafilm wurde diese Szene im
Sommer 1933 nachgestellt).

30 January 1933, the day that marked the 'seizure of power': A torchlight procession of SA and SS members winds its way through the Brandenburg Gate to celebrate the Nazi takeover of power (the entire performance was repeated in the summer of 1933 for the sake of a propaganda film).

25. Februar 1934: Rudolf Hess spricht von München aus über Rundfunk den Treue-Eid auf Adolf Hitler vor.

25 February 1934: Rudolf Hess swears an oath of allegiance to Adolf Hitler in a radio broadcast from Munich.

In der Nacht vom 27. Auf den 28. Februar wird das Reichstagsgebäude durch Brandstiftung größtenteils zerstört. Blick vom Brandenburger Tor auf das brennende Gebäude am Morgen des 28. Februar.

During the night of 27–28 February, the Reichstag building is badly damaged in an arson attack. (View of the burning building the next morning from the Brandenburg Gate).

DER REICHSTAG

Der Reichstag symbolisiert wie kein anderes Gebäude die wechselvolle Geschichte des Deutschen Parlamentarismus. Im März 1871 trat der erste durch allgemeine, gleiche, direkte und geheime Wahlen gewählte gesamtdeutsche Reichstag zusammen. Schnell wurde der Ruf nach einem Gebäude laut, das die neue Macht der im Parlament repräsentierten Bürger zum Ausdruck bringen sollte. Doch bis die frei stehende Vierflügelanlage nach Entwürfen von Paul Wallot vollendet war, vergingen über zwanzig Jahre.

In der Weimarer Republik spielte der Reichstag eine zentrale Rolle. Hier rief der Sozialdemokrat Philipp Scheidemann am 9. November 1918 die Republik aus, die am 23. März 1933 – eingeleitet vom Reichstagsbrand – mit der Selbstentmachtung des Parlaments und dem »Ermächtigungsgesetz« endete. Bis zum Ende des Zweiten Weltkrieges wurde das Gebäude nicht mehr für parlamentarische Zwecke genutzt.

Zu Beginn der 50er Jahre wurde die beschädigte Kuppel gesprengt, 1955 der Wiederaufbau beschlossen. Paul Baumgarten vollendete erst 1973 die Ausbauarbeiten. Das Zentrum bildete ein vollständig hergerichteter Plenarsaal für die Abgeordneten eines wiedervereinigten Deutschland. Erst am 4. Oktober 1990 trat hier das erste gesamtdeutsche Parlament zusammen. Kaum ein Jahr später wurde beschlossen, Parlament und Regierung nach Berlin zu verlegen und das Reichstagsgebäude zum Sitz des Bundestages zu erheben, im September 1999 erfolgte der Umzug des Deutschen Bundestages nach Berlin.

Um seine demokratische Nutzung sichtbar zu machen, ließ der britische Architekt Sir Norman Foster den Reichstag mit einer begehbaren Glaskuppel ausstatten, die nachts von innen beleuchtet wird.

»Wrapped Reichstag«. Vor dem Umbau macht der Verhüllungskünstler Christo das Reichstagsgebäude 1995 zum Kunstwerk und lenkt die Aufmerksamkeit der Weltöffentlichkeit auf das Gebäude.
Christo und Jeanne-Claude: Verhüllter Reichstag, Berlin 1971-1995. Foto: Wolfgang Volz, © Christo

THE REICHSTAG

No other building symbolizes the chequered history of German parliamentarianism as significantly as the Reichstag. The first session of the unified German Reichstag was held in March 1871, the result of a universal, equal, direct, and secret ballot. It was not long before people were calling for a building that would suitably reflect the newfound power of their newly enfranchised representatives. More than twenty years were to pass, however, before the new four-winged building, designed by Paul Wallot, was completed.

The Reichstag was to play a key role during the years of the Weimar Republic. It was from this building that Philipp Scheidemann, the Social-Democrat politician, proclaimed the Republic on 9 November 1918, which lasted until 23 March 1933. Events – beginning with the Reichstag fire – eventually culminated in the passing of the 'Ermächtigungsgesetz' ('Enabling Act'), which robbed parliament of its powers. The building was not used for parliamentary purposes again until after the Second World War.

In the early fifties, the severely damaged cupola was blown up and, in 1955, the decision was taken to reconstruct the building. Paul Baumgarten was commissioned with the work but it was not until 1973 that reconstruction was completed. The building was designed around a fully equipped plenary chamber in anticipation of a reunified Germany. It was not until 4 October 1990, however, that the reunified German parliament held its first session here. Less than a year later, it was decided to transfer the German parliament and government to Berlin and to make the Reichstag building the seat of the Bundestag (German parliament). In September 1999, the Bundestag moved to Berlin.

In order to highlight the Reichstag's democratic function, its architect, Sir Norman Foster, incorporated a glass cupola into its design which is illuminated at night from within.

'Wrapped Reichstag': In 1995, before its renovation, Christo, an artist renowned for similar works of this kind, attracted international attention by 'wrapping' the Reichstag building and turning it into an art exhibit. Christo and Jeanne-Claude: Wrapped Reichstag, Berlin 1971-1995. Photo: Wolfgang Volz, © Christo.

Die gläserne Kuppel war eine architektonische Meiserleistung. Ihr wurde symbolträchtig eine steinerne Kaiserkrone aufgesetzt. Die Giebel-Inschrift »Dem Deutschen Volke« wurde erst im Jahre 1916 nach dem Entwurf des Jugendstilkünstlers Peter Behrens angebracht.

The glass cupola represents a masterpiece of architectural achievement and is topped with a symbolic imperial crown of stone. The inscription on the pediment, 'Dem Deutschen Volke' ('To the German People'), was a feature added in 1916 after a design by Peter Behrens of the Jugendstil School of Art.

Die Kuppel und der Plenarsaal d
Nacht vom 27. auf den 28. Febru
zerstört. Das Ereignis leitet das
Machtübernahme durch die Nat

The Reichstag's dome and pler
an arson attack during the nig
the end of the Weimar Republi
power.

gsgebäudes werden in der
ch Brandstiftung größtenteils
eimarer Republik und die
sten ein.

er were severely damaged in
February. This event heralded
led the Nazis' takeover of

Seit September 1999 tagt der Deutsche Bundestag in dem von Sir Norman Foster umgebauten Reichstagsgebäude. Die gläserne Kuppel ist begehbar.

Since September 1999, the restored Reichstagbuilding with its accessible glass cupola, designed by Sir Norman Foster, has been the seat of the German Bundestag

1. Mai 1934: Abfahrt Hitlers nach seiner Rede an die Jugend am Feiertag der nationalen Arbeit im Lustgarten.

1 May 1934: Hitler taking his leave after addressing an audience of young people at a National Labour Day rally in the Lustgarten.

19. August 1934: Propagandawagen der Hitlerjugend in der Wilhelmstraße am Wahltag.

19 August 1934: Hitler Youth canvassing from a campaign car in the Wilhelmstraße on polling day.

Olympia 1936: Die Nationalsozialisten nutzen die Olympischen Spiele in Berlin, um sich noch einmal weltoffen zu geben. Die ganze Stadt wird zur Propagandabühne. Festliche Illumination Unter den Linden / Ecke Friedrichstraße.

Olympia 1936: The Olympic Games in Berlin form a perfect showpiece with which the Nazis hope to Oimpress the rest of the world. The entire city becomes a propaganda showcase. Festive lights illuminating Unter den Linden and the corner of Friedrichstraße.

Das Olympiastadion und das Reichssportfeld wurden 1934-36 für die Olympischen Spiele 1936 erbaut.

The Olympic Stadium and Reichs sports arena were built between 1934–36 in readiness for the 1936 Olympic Games.

Die Olympiade als Propagandaspektakel: Die bis heute umstrittene Regisseurin Leni Riefenstahl inszeniert die Spiele in dem Dokumentarfilm »Fest der Völker« (Deutschland 1936).

The Olympics as a propaganda exercise: Leni Riefenstahl, whose reputation as a controversial director persists to this day, produces a documentary film of the Games entitled 'Festival of Nations' (Germany 1936).

Leni Riefenstahl während der Dreharbeiten zum Olympia-Film »Fest der Völker« 1936.

Leni Riefenstahl during the filming of the Olympics film 'Festival of Nations' 1936.

August 1936: Der Amerikaner Jesse Owens wird zum Liebling der Berliner, hier nach seinem Weltrekord im 100-m-Lauf, umringt von Autogrammjägern und Presseleuten.

August 1936: American athlete Jesse Owens wins the hearts of Berliners, seen here surrounded by autograph hunters and the press after his world record in the 100-m sprint.

Reichssportfeld, am letzten Tag der Olympiade: Bierzapfer hinter ihrem Verkaufsstand.

The Reichs sports arena on the last day of the Olympics: Beer sellers behind their stalls.

Adolf Hitler wollte Berlin zur »Welthauptstadt Germania« machen. Mit zahlreichen monumentalen Gebäuden soll die Stadt inszeniert werden.
1938 lässt Hitler von Albert Speer die Neue Reichskanzlei bauen. Nachtaufnahme der Großbaustelle, 7. Mai 1938.

Adolf Hitler's ambition was to turn Berlin into the 'world capital of Germania'. His plans to rebuild the city included many grandiose architectural projects. In 1938, Hitler commissions Albert Speer to build the new Reichskanzlei (Chancellery) building. A night-time photo of the vast building site, 7 May 1938.

Neue Reichskanzlei, Haupteingang mit Wache, Voßstraße. Das Gebäude sollte eine Art Neo-Klassizismus vermitteln, strahlt aber eher eine düstere Monumentalität aus.

The new Reichskanzlei building, main entrance with guard, Voßstraße. Though modelled on a neo-Classical style, the building inclines more towards an oppressive monumentality.

Die nationalsozialistische Kunstideologie vertrat eine diffuse Vorstellung von Gesamtkunstwerk. Die Neue Reichskanzlei war mit Skulpturen von Arno Breker ausgestattet.

Nazi ideology with regard to art was based on a somewhat diffuse concept of art as a whole. The new Reichskanzlei building was decorated with sculptures by Arno Breker.

Auch das Innere der Neuen Reichskanzlei war von dumpfer Monumentalität geprägt. Das Arbeitszimmer des Führers.

The interior of the new Reichskanzlei building likewise gave an impression of subdued monumentality. The Führer's study.

Hitlers Planung für die Reichshauptstadt basierte auf einem monumentalen Achsenkreuz. Blick nach Osten, auf die neu gestaltete Ost-West-Achse (ehem. Charlottenburger Chaussee, heute Straße des 17. Juni) und die Siegessäule.

Hitler's plans for the Reich's capital city were based on a monumental coordinate system. View to the East, onto the new East-West axis (formerly known as Charlottenburger Chaussee, now Straße des 17. Juni) and the Victory Column.

Eine gigantische Kongresshalle sollte zum Höhepunkt der stadtplanerischen Maßnahmen werden. Hier im Modell, daneben als Größenvergleich ein Modell des Brandenburger Tores und des Reichstags.

A huge Congress Hall was to be the crowning glory of the city's architectural design, a model of which is pictured here, next to models of the Brandenburg Gate and Reichstag building which demonstrate the scale if it.

Ufa-Gelände in Berlin-Tempelhof (Luftaufnahme). Die 1917 gegründete Universum Film Aktiengesellschaft (Ufa) hatte Berlin in den 1920er Jahren zu einer Metropole des internationalen Films gemacht.

The grounds of the Universal Film Company (Ufa) in Berlin-Tempelhof (aerial view).
Ufa, which was formed in 1917, helped turn Berlin into an international film capital.

Hollywoodstars kamen noch in den 1930er Jahren nach Berlin: Douglas Fairbanks mit Ehefrau Mary Pickford vor dem Brandenburger Tor.

Hollywood stars continued to visit Berlin in the 30s: Douglas Fairbanks with his wife, Mary Pickford, in front of the Brandenburg Gate.

Lichter der Großstadt: Ufa-Filmpalast an der Friedrichstraße bei Nacht, 1938.

Lights of the metropolis: a night-time view of the Ufa film palace on the Friedrichstraße, 1938.

Die Nationalsozialisten bemächtigten sich auch der Filmwirtschaft. Hitler als Ehrengast bei der Filmerstaufführung »Morgenrot« der Ufa. Links: Alfred Hugenberg mit Ehefrau, rechts neben Hitler Franz von Papen. 1937 wurde die Ufa auf Betreiben des Reichspropagandaministers Joseph Goebbels verstaatlicht.

The Nazis also took over the film industry. Hitler as the guest of honour at the première of the Ufa film 'Morgenrot'. On the left: Alfred Hugenberg with his wife; on the right, next to Hitler, is Franz von Papen. In 1937, the Ufa film studios were nationalized on the advice of Joseph Goebbels, Minister of Propaganda.

9./10. November 1938: Das wahre Gesicht des Nationalsozialismus tritt in Berlin in seiner ganzen Brutalität zu Tage. In der Pogromnacht werden Einrichtungen und Geschäfte jüdischer Bürger zerstört und geplündert.

9-10 November 1938: The true face of Nazi brutality begins to emerge in Berlin. Jewish shops and businesses were wrecked and plundered during the pogroms that night.

JÜDISCHES LEBEN IN BERLIN

In einem Handwerksbrief der Wollweber aus dem Jahr 1295 werden Juden in Berlin erstmals erwähnt. Heute ist Berlin laut AJC (American Jewish Committee) die am schnellsten wachsende jüdische Gemeinde der Welt. Dazwischen liegen 700 Jahre wechselvollen jüdischen Lebens in Berlin.

Die heutige jüdische Gemeinde gründet sich auf Familien, die – aus Wien vertrieben – 1671 nach Berlin kamen. Erst 200 Jahre später, mit der Gründung des Deutschen Reiches, wurden sie den übrigen Bürgern gleichgestellt. Damals wurde die Metropole Berlin zum Zentrum jüdischen Lebens in Deutschland. In den Zwanziger Jahren prägten Juden wie Walter Benjamin, Albert Einstein, Ernst Lubitsch, Max Reinhardt und Arnold Schönberg das kulturell-intellektuelle Klima des Landes.

Vor der Machtübernahme der Nationalsozialisten im Jahr 1933 zählte die jüdische Gemeinde Berlins ca. 200.000 Mitglieder (und damit ein Drittel der Juden des Deutschen Reiches). Bis 1945 zerstörten Verfolgung und Holocaust das jüdische Leben vollständig.

Als in der Reichspogromnacht 1938 die Berliner Synagogen brennen (rechts in der Prinzregentenstraße), beginnt für die Juden eine Zeit des Terrors und der Vertreibung. 1939 sammeln sich in der Meineckestraße auswanderungswillige Juden vor einem Reisebüro.

JEWISH LIFE IN BERLIN

The first mention of Jews in Berlin is in a letter from the wool weavers' guild dating from 1295. According to the AJC (American Jewish Committee), Berlin is now the fastest growing Jewish community in the world. In between lie seven hundred years of eventful Jewish life in Berlin.

The present day Jewish community is founded on families arriving in Berlin in 1671, after being driven out of Vienna. Not until two hundred years later, at the time of German unification, were they granted equal status with other citizens. Then the city of Berlin became the centre of Jewish life in Germany. In the twenties, Jews such as Walter Benjamin, Albert Einstein, Ernst Lubitsch, Max Reinhardt, and Arnold Schönberg had a formative influence on the cultural and intellectual climate of the country.

Before the Nazis seized power in 1933, the Jewish community in Berlin numbered about two hundred thousand (one-third of the Jews in the German Reich). By 1945 Jewish life had been utterly destroyed by persecution and the holocaust.

The burning of the Berlin synagogues during the 'Night of Broken Glass' ('Kristallnacht' or 'Reichspogromnacht') (right, in Prinzregentenstraße), marks the beginning of a period of terror and deportation for Jews. Jews willing to emigrate gather in front of a travel agency in Meineckestraße in 1939.

Vor allem Zuwanderern aus Osteuropa ist es zu verdanken, dass in Berlin heute wieder 12.000 Menschen zur jüdischen Gemeinde gehören. Wie kein anderes Gebäude symbolisiert das neu eröffnete Jüdische Museum ein lebendiges Zentrum deutsch-jüdischer Geschichte. Der international beachtete Bau von Daniel Libeskind wurde 2001 feierlich eingeweiht. Ein weiteres Denkmal weist von der Vergangenheit in die Zukunft: Nach den Entwürfen des New Yorker Architekten Peter Eisenman wird eine Gedenkstätte für die ermordeten Juden Europas errichtet, die 2004 fertiggestellt sein soll.

Erinnerung und Neuanfang: 1988 begann der Wiederaufbau der von Eduard Knoblauch 1859-66 erbauten Synagoge in der Oranienburger Straße. Ein Jahr früher wurde am ehemaligen Bahnhof Putlitzbrücke ein Mahnmal für die von dort deportierten Juden eingeweiht.

The fact that Berlin now has a Jewish community of twelve thousand members is mainly the result of immigration from Eastern Europe. More than any other building, the recently opened Jewish Museum symbolizes the living centre of German Jewish history. The internationally respected building by Daniel Libeskind was formally opened in 2001. One other monument points the way from the past to the future. A memorial to the murdered Jews of Europe, designed by New York Architect Peter Eisenman, is under construction and is scheduled for completion in 2004.

Remembrance and a new beginning: In 1987, at the former Putlitz Bridge train station, a memorial to the Jews deported from there was officially unveiled. One year later, work began on reconstructing the Oranienburger Straße synagogue built by Eduard Knoblauch between 1859 and 1866.

Am 1. September 1939 überfällt Deutschland Polen und eröffnet den Zweiten Weltkrieg. Zu Beginn des Krieges marschierten nach dem Sieg über Frankreich die Berliner und Brandenburger Truppen noch im Parademarsch durchs Brandenburger Tor und wurden als Sieger empfangen.

On 1 September 1939, Germany invades Poland, triggering World War 2. In the early days of the war, Berlin and Brandenburg troops marching through the Brandenburg Gate after the defeat of France are given a hero's welcome.

Erste britische Bombenangriffe auf Berlin gab es schon 1940. Nach der Niederlage in Stalingrad verstärkten sich aber die Angriffe (oben: Verbände der US-Luftwaffe über Berlin).

1940 saw the first British bombing raids on Berlin. After the defeat at Stalingrad, the number of air raids increased. (Above: US airforce squadrons over Berlin).

April 1942: Schwere Flak in Feuerbereitschaft auf dem Flak-Turm des Zoo-Bunkers.

April 1942: Heavy anti-aircraft guns ready for action on the anti-aircraft turret above the Zoo bunker.

Was Goebbels mit seiner Frage nach dem »totalen Krieg« meinte, erfuhren die Berliner ab 1943 in aller Deutlichkeit: ausgebombte Familien nach Angriffen der alliierten Luftstreitkräfte.

From 1943 on, Berliners began to discover all too clearly what Goebbels meant when he spoke of 'total war': Families bombed out of their homes as a result of Allied air raids.

Der brennende Französische Dom auf dem Gendarmenmarkt nach einem Angriff der Alliierten am 24. Mai 1944.

24 May 1944: Flames engulfing the French Cathedral in the Gendarmenmarkt following an Allied air attack.

Das Ende des braunen Wahnsinns: Am 30. April 1945 hissen Soldaten der Roten Armee die Sowjetflagge auf dem Reichstagsgebäude. Das Foto des russischen Fotografen Jewgeni Chaldej ging in die Fotogeschichte ein. Es war allerdings gestellt und mehrmals von verschiedenen Blickpunkten aufgenommen.

The brown madness is finally over: On 30 April 1945, Red Army soldiers raise the Soviet flag above the Reichstag building. This photo by Russian photographer Yevgeniy Chaldey has become a landmark of photographic history despite it being posed for and taken from several different angles.

Am Ende des Krieges war Berlin eine Ruinenlandschaft mit 75 Millionen Kubikmetern Schutt. Hier der Eingang zum U-Bahnhof Französische Straße.

By the end of the war, Berlin was a city in ruins, buried under 75 million cubic metres of rubble. Here, the entrance to the Französische Straße underground station.

Ku'damm 1945: Ansicht der zerstörten Kaiser-Wilhelm-Gedächtniskirche.

Ku'damm 1945: View of the badly damaged Kaiser Wilhelm Memorial Church.

Das ganze Ausmaß der Zerstörung: Blick auf Schöneberg mit Viktoria-Luise-Platz und Gasometer in der Bayreuther Straße (heute Welser Straße). Luftaufnahme, 1945.

The full extent of the destruction: View of Schöneberg with the Viktoria-Luise-Platz and the gasometer in the Bayreuther Straße (now known as Welser Straße). Aerial view, 1945.

Durch die Bombenangriffe der Alliierten kamen etwa 50.000 Berliner ums Leben, über die Hälfte aller Gebäude waren beschädigt, ein Drittel des Wohnraums zerstört. Zwei Männer sitzen erschöpft und verzweifelt vor ausgebombten Häusern in der Französischen Straße.

The Allied air attacks killed around 50,000 Berliners, damaged over half the buildings, and destroyed one-third of all homes. Two men sitting exhausted and in despair outside bombed-out houses in the Französische Straße.

Rückkehr der Berliner in ihre zerstörte Stadt.

Berliners returning home to the ruins of their city.

NEUBEGINN IN OST UND WEST

NEW BEGINNINGS IN EAST AND WEST

8. Mai 1945, die Stunde Null. Berlin lag in Trümmern. Über 600.000 Wohnungen völlig zerstört, nur noch knapp 3 Millionen Menschen lebten hier. Die alliierten Besatzungsmächte USA, Sowjetunion, Großbritannien und Frankreich teilten die Stadt in vier Sektoren auf. Die Bevölkerung litt unter der schlechten Ernährungslage. Daraufhin organisierte die private amerikanische Hilfsaktion CARE die Verteilung von Lebensmittelpaketen.

1946 startete der Wiederaufbau der Ruinenstadt. Neben technischem Gerät fehlten männliche Arbeitskräfte, so dass vor allem dienstverpflichtete »Trümmerfrauen« die Aufräumungsarbeiten vorantrieben. Zusätzlich setzte den Berlinern im Dezember 1946 eine schwere Kältewelle zu: Lungenentzündung, Grippe und Ruhr grassierten.

Im März 1948 verließ die Sowjetunion den Alliierten Kontrollrat aus Protest gegen Pläne, in den westlichen Besatzungszonen verfassungsgebende Versammlungen einzuberufen. Der Kalte Krieg verschärfte sich, die Teilung Deutschlands – und damit auch Berlins – rückte näher. Dies zeigte sich auch bei der Währungsreform. Am 23. Juni 1948 ordnete die sowjetische Militäradministration an, die Mark der SBZ in allen vier Sektoren einzuführen. Einen Tag später verfügten die westlichen Stadtkommandanten für ihre Sektoren die Umstellung auf Westmark. Die Sowjets reagierten mit der Berliner Blo-

8. May 1945, zero hour. Berlin lay in ruins. With over six hundred thousand dwellings completely destroyed, the population of Berlin had fallen to barely three million. The Allied occupying forces of the USA, Soviet Union, Britain, and France divided the city into four sectors. The situation regarding food for the population was dire and, in response, the private American aid agency CARE organized the distribution of food parcels.

In 1946, work began on reconstructing the ruined city. The demands of the task were far too great for the available technical equipment and workforce, so that the clearing work was speeded up primarily by drafting in 'Trümmerfrauen' ('rubble women'). The Berliners were also hard hit by a severe cold snap in December 1946; pulmonary disease, flu, and dysentery were rife.

In March 1948, the Soviet Union left the Allied Control Council, in protest at plans to convene constituent meetings in the western occupied zones. The Cold War intensified, the partition of Germany – and thus also of Berlin – came ever closer, and was further exemplified by the currency reform. On 23 June 1948, the Soviet military administration ordered that the mark used in the Soviet occupied zone be introduced in all four sectors. The very next day, the western city governors ordered the currency for their sectors to

Seite 204/205: Eine Stadt in Ausnahmesituation: Während der sowjetischen Blockade 1948 wird Berlin von den Westmächten aus der Luft versorgt. Kinder jubeln den amerikanischen »Rosinenbombern« zu.

Pages 204/205: The city in a state of emergency: During the Soviet blockade in 1948, supplies are airlifted into Berlin by the Western powers. Children cheering the US 'currant bombers'.

ckade: Land- und Wasserwege zwischen Berlin und den westlichen Besatzungszonen wurden für den Passagier- und Güterverkehr gesperrt. Oberbürgermeister Ernst Reuter forderte: »Ihr Völker der Welt (...) Schaut auf diese Stadt und erkennt, daß Ihr diese Stadt und dieses Volk nicht preisgeben dürft und preisgeben könnt!« Fast ein Jahr lang versorgten die Westalliierten den Westteil der Stadt über eine Luftbrücke. Westdeutschland half der finanziell angeschlagenen Stadt ab April 1949 mit einer Sondersteuer, dem »Notopfer Berlin«. Nach dem Ende der Blockade am 12. Mai 1949 waren die politische und ökonomische Teilung Berlins besiegelt, im selben Jahr zwei deutsche Staaten gegründet.

Trotz aller Schwierigkeiten blühte das kulturelle Leben wieder auf: Die Berliner Universität wurde 1946 wieder eröffnet, die Technische und die Freie Universität neu gegründet. Die Theaterszene boomte mit Welterfolgen wie Bertolt Brechts »Mutter Courage«, die Presselandschaft zählte schon 1947 wieder 20 Zeitungen.

Ab 1950 verbesserte sich die wirtschaftliche Lage Berlins, obwohl viele Flüchtlinge aus der DDR und Ostberlin in den Westen kamen. Am 17. Juni 1953 protestierten Zehntausende DDR-Arbeiter in Berlin gegen das Regime. Der Aufstand wurde von sowjetischen Truppen niedergeschlagen. Drei Jahre später kam es als Reaktion auf den Volksaufstand in Ungarn wieder zu Demonstrationen. 1958 forderte Chruschtschow, Westberlin zu einer »entmilitarisierten, freien Stadt« zu machen. Die Krise in Berlin eskalierte mit dem Bau der Mauer am 13. August 1961.

be converted to the West German mark. The Soviets responded with the 'Berlin blockade'. Mayor Ernst Reuter demanded: 'People of the world (...) Look at this city and recognize that you should not and cannot abandon this city and its people!'.

For almost a year, the western allies brought provisions to the western part of the city via an airlift. From 1949, West Germany helped the financially ruined city by means of a special tax, 'Berlin emergency aid'. When the blockade was lifted on 12 May 1949, the political and economic division of Berlin was achieved, the two German states being established in the same year.

Despite all the difficulties, cultural life flourished again; Berlin University reopened in 1946, and the Technical and Free Universities were founded. The theatre scene blossomed with international successes such as Bertolt Brecht's 'Mother Courage' and, as early as 1947, the press were once again producing 20 newspapers.

From 1950, the economic situation in Berlin improved, despite the arrival of many refugees fleeing to the west from the German Democratic Republic and East Berlin. On 17 June 1953, ten thousand GDR workers protested in Berlin against the regime. The uprising was put down by Soviet troops. Three years later, there were once again demonstrations in response to the people's uprising in Hungary. In 1958, Khrushchev demanded that West Berlin be made into a 'demilitarized free city'. The Berlin crisis escalated with the construction of the Wall on 13 August 1961.

Aus Trümmern auferstehen: Gemäß dem Gesetz des Alliierten Kontrollrats vom 14. Januar 1946 sollten so genannte »Trümmerfrauen« für die Beseitigung von Trümmern dienstverpflichtet werden. Sie wurden zum Sinnbild für Überlebenswillen und Wiederaufbau nach dem Krieg.

A city rising from the ashes: Following an order issued by the Allied Control Council on 14 January 1946, so-called 'Trümmerfrauen' ('rubble women') were co-opted into service to clear away the rubble. They came to symbolize the post-war determination to survive and rebuild.

Momente der Nachdenklichkeit: Hobbymaler vor der Ruine der Hl.-Kreuz-Kirche, Blücher- / Ecke Urbanstraße in Berlin-Kreuzberg.

Contemplative moments: Amateur painters outside the Hl.-Kreuz Church, Blücher-/corner of Urbanstraße in Berlin's Kreuzberg district.

Normalität im Ausnahmezustand: Fahrradfahrer auf dem Trümmerschutt an der Oranienstraße in Berlin-Kreuzberg.

Moments of normality during the state of emergency: Cyclists on the rubble in the Oranienstraße, Kreuzberg.

Notstand als Normalzustand: In der unmittelbaren Nachkriegszeit herrschte wie überall auch in Berlin eine große Lebensmittelknappheit. Kartoffellieferung zur Versorgung der Bevölkerung.

The state of emergency becomes a normal way of life: In the immediate aftermath of the war, Berlin, like everywhere else, suffered major food shortages. Potatoes being delivered to feed the population.

Die Zeit der materiellen Not war gleichzeitig auch eine Zeit des Neubeginns. In Berlin beharrten Kommunisten und Sozialdemokraten zunächst erfolgreich auf ihrer Eigenständigkeit. Der Zusammenschluss zu einer sozialistischen Einheitspartei konnte nur in der Sowjetischen Besatzungszone stattfinden, während in Berlin SPD und SED nebeneinander bestanden. Im Mai 1948 demonstrierte die SED in Ostberlin für ein Volksbegehren »Für ein ungeteiltes demokratisches Berlin«.

Trotz seines Sonderstatus entwickelte sich auch Berlin in den Ost- und West-Sektoren sehr schnell ganz unterschiedlich. Die Straßennamen im Ostsektor waren in lateinischer und kyrillischer Schrift geschrieben, so wie an der Kreuzung Invaliden- / Chausseestraße.

This period of material hardship was also a time for fresh beginnings. Communists and Social Democrats in Berlin successfully asserted themselves. Only in the Soviet occupation zone, however, did they amalgamate into a single Socialist Unity Party (SED). In the rest of Berlin, the SPD (German Socialist Party) and SED existed alongside one another. In May 1948, the SED held a demonstration in East Berlin calling for a referendum in support of 'an undivided democratic Berlin'.

Despite its special status, Berlin's development soon began to take very different directions in the Eastern and Westers sectors. The street names in the former were written in Latin and Cyrillic, as at the junction of the Invaliden- and Chausseestraße.

Die am 18. Juni 1948 von den Westmächten durchgeführte Währungsreform sollte sich mit Rücksicht auf den Viermächtestatus zunächst nicht auf Berlin erstrecken. Als aber die sowjetische Besatzungsmacht ihrerseits am 23. Juni die Ost-Mark in Berlin einführt, dehnen die Westmächte am 24. Juni den Geltungsbereich der West-Mark auch auf die Westsektoren Berlins aus. Ergebnis ist ein ungebremster Ansturm auf Banken und Wechselstuben (links).

Die sowjetische Militärverwaltung nimmt dies zum Anlass, die Westsektoren der Stadt »wegen technischer Störungen« auf sämtlichen Land- und Wasserwegen vollständig abzusperren. Nur noch drei Luftkorridore bleiben geöffnet. Die Westmächte reagieren sofort und versorgen Berlin aus der Luft.
Die Berliner Luftbrücke wird zum Symbol für den Lebens- und Freiheitswillen der Berliner. Die so genannten »Rosinenbomber« der amerikanischen Streitkräfte werden bei ihrer Landung auf dem Flughafen Tempelhof von den Berlinern begrüßt (oben).

The currency reform introduced on 18 June note: add 1948 by the Western powers was not originally intended to encompass Berlin because of its special Four-Power status. When the Soviet occupying power went ahead and introduced the East Mark in Berlin on 23 June, however, the Western powers responded on 24 June by extending the West Mark to include the Western sectors of Berlin. This led to a frenzied rush on banks and foreign currency exchange outlets (left).

The Soviet military authorities used this as an excuse to close off all road and rail links and waterways to the West, citing 'technical problems' as the reason. Only three air corridors remained open. The Western powers reacted with the utmost speed and began supplying the city by air. The Berlin air bridge became a symbol of Berliners' determination to survive and preserve their freedom. US transport planes, or 'currant bombers', as they were known, being welcomed by Berlin residents after landing at Tempelhof airport (above).

Die Versorgung Berlins wird, unter schwierigsten Bedingungen, zu einer grandiosen logistischen Meisterleistung. Care-Pakete werden über Zwischenlager in den Westsektoren Deutschlands nach Berlin eingeflogen.

Keeping Berlin supplied under such difficult conditions was a masterpiece of logistical achievement. Care packages are flown into Berlin via transit camps in the Western sectors of Germany.

Verteilung von Care-Paketen an Senioren, Berlin 1948.

Handing out care packages to senior citizens, Berlin 1948.

Westberlin wird von den Westmächten über die Luftbrücke versorgt: Arbeiter laden Tausende von Kohlensäcken vom LKW in ein wartendes Flugzeug auf dem Flugplatz Celle, von wo alliierte Militärmaschinen nach Berlin starten.

The Western powers air lift supplies into West Berlin: Workers load thousands of coal sacks brought in by lorry onto a waiting plane at Celle airport, the departure point for Allied military planes leaving for Berlin.

Dezember 1948: Die »Rosinenbomber« fliegen alle 90 Sekunden nach Berlin und warten auf dem Flughafen Tempelhof auf das Löschen ihrer Ladung. Höhepunkt war der 16. April 1949, als im Abstand von 62 Sekunden 1344 Flüge in Berlin landeten und 12.940 Tonnen in die Stadt brachten.

December 1948: The 'currant bombers' take off for Berlin every 90 seconds, then wait at Tempelhof airport for their cargo to be offloaded. The record day for airlifts was 16 April 1949, when 1,344 planes landed in Berlin at 62-second intervals, bringing 12,940 tonnes of supplies to the city.

»Heart gifts for Berliners« Geschenke zum Valentinstag, Februar 1949. Der amerikanische Fotograf Tony Vaccaro hat die Luftbrücke in seinen Fotos dokumentiert und zu einem Stück Fotogeschichte gemacht.

'Heart gifts for Berliners' arriving for Valentine's Day in February 1949. US photographer Tony Vaccaro documented the airlift in a series of photos, turning it into a chapter of photographic history.

Auch Strom und Gas wurden von den Sowjets gesperrt. Eine Berliner Mutter bereitet ihren Kindern eine Mahlzeit aus Kartoffelmehl auf einem Spirituskocher.

Electricity and gas supplies were also cut by the Soviets. A Berlin woman preparing a meal from potato flour for her children over a spirit stove.

Ernst Reuter, der regierende Bürgermeister von Westberlin, fordert in seiner Rede am 9. September 1948 Beistand für die blockierte Stadt. Sein Appell »Völker der Welt – schaut auf diese Stadt« geht um die Welt.

In a speech on 9 September 1948, Ernst Reuter, the governing mayor of West Berlin, calls for assistance for his beleaguered city. His appeal, 'Nations of the world – look to this city', was broadcast worldwide.

12. Mai 1949: Die Blockade ist beendet. Berlin ist wieder auf dem Landweg erreichbar, die Luftbrücke wird aber noch bis zum Oktober aufrecht gehalten. Von Juli 1948 bis Mai 1949 haben amerikanische und britische Flugzeuge in über 200.000 Flügen etwa 1,8 Millionen Tonnen Güter in die Stadt geflogen. Jetzt drängen sich Berlinerinnen vor den Schaufensterauslagen der Metzgereien, wo es wieder Wurst und Frischfleisch gibt.

12 May 1949: The blockade is over. Berlin is accessible by road again, although the airlift continues until October. Between July 1948 and May 1949, US and British planes made over 200,000 flights, bringing around 1.8 million tonnes of supplies into the city. The women of Berlin crowd outside the shop windows of the city's butchers, where sausage and fresh meat are finally on display again.

»Hurra wir leben noch«: Am 12. Mai starten um 7 Uhr morgens am Pariser Platz die ersten Interzonenbusse mit den bekannt gewordenen Plakaten, die die unzerstörbare Lebenslust der Berliner nach der überstandenen Blockade ausriefen.

'Hurra wir leben noch' ('Hurray, we've survived'): On 12 May, at 7 o'clock in the morning, the first of the inter-zone buses leaves Pariser Platz bedecked with the posters which would become such a common sight, illustrating the Berliner people's inextinguishable zest for life in the wake of the blockade.

Mitarbeiter des Funkhauses RIAS (»Rundfunk im amerikanischen Sektor«) in Berlin-Schöneberg feiern das Ende der Blockade.

Staff of RIAS broadcasting station (Radio in the American Sector) in Berlin-Schöneberg celebrate the ending of the blockade.

PACK DIE BADEHOSE EIN...

sang 1951 die siebenjährige Berliner Göre Cornelia Froboess. Mit ihrem Lied von den kleinen Alltagsfreuden der Nachkriegszeit sang sie den Wannsee in die Köpfe der Deutschen und setzte einem der größten Binnenseebäder Europas ein musikalisches Denkmal.

Seit 1907 ersetzte die 260 Hektar große Ausbuchtung der Havel vor allem Arbeitern die Vergnügungen eines Badeurlaubs. Im Laufe der Zeit sorgten Strandkörbe, Liegestühle, Umkleidekabinen, Buden und das 1929 terrassenförmig angelegte Strandbad, das heute dem Verfall überlassen ist, auf dem 1275 Meter langen Sandstrand für Ostsee-Flair.

Auch wohlhabende Berliner wussten die Vorzüge des Großen und des Kleinen Wannsees zu schätzen. Die Villenkolonie Alsen wurde 1863 als Sommerfrische für das Großbürgertum gegründet, die Villenkolonie Schwanenwerder zählt auch heute zu den nobelsten Adressen Berlins.

1942 erlangte das Gewässer traurige Berühmtheit. Am 20. Januar wurde auf der Wannsee-Konferenz die Deportation der europäischen Juden beschlossen und organisiert. Seit 1992 ist das Haus in Berlin-Zehlendorf eine nationale Gedenk- und Bildungsstätte.

Zu Blockade- und Mauerzeiten die wichtigste Wasserfreizeitanlage der Berliner, ist der Wannsee heute eines der vielen natürlichen Gewässer in und um Berlin, die die Stadt im Sommer zu einem Paradies für Badefans und Wassersportler machen.

Badefreuden in der Großstadt: im Wasser und beim Paartanz.

A bathing resort on the city's doorstep. Having fun in the water or enjoying a dance

GET YOUR SWIMMING THINGS TOGETHER...

sang Berlin's 7-year-old child star, Cornelia Froboess, in 1951. Her song about life's little pleasures in post-war Germany turned the Wannsee into a household name throughout the country and, in so doing, created a musical monument to one of Europe's largest inland bathing resorts.

The Wannsee extends over an area of 260 hectares at a point where the Havel river widens out into a lake and, since 1907, has provided the working population, in particular, with all the pleasures of a bathing resort. Over the years, deckchairs, sun-beds, changing cabins, kiosks, and a terraced bathing beach, created in 1929 but now sadly neglected, have recreated the atmosphere of a Baltic coast resort along its 1,275 metres of sandy beach.

Well-to-do Berliners likewise came to appreciate the advantages of the Großer and Kleiner Wannsee suburbs. A colony of villas was established at Alsen in 1863 as a summer retreat for the upper classes, while the Schwanenwerder villa district is still one of Berlin's most exclusive addresses.

In 1942, the lake gained tragic notoriety, for it was here that the Wannsee Conference was held on 20 January for the purpose of planning the deportation of European Jews. In 1992, the building in Berlin-Zehlendorf was made a national memorial and educational centre.

During the years of blockade and the Wall, the Wannsee was Berlin's most important recreational lake resort. Nowadays, it is just one of the many natural lakes in and around Berlin which make the city a summer paradise for swimmers and water sports enthusiasts alike.

Berlin erwacht langsam wieder zum Leben: Wahl der »Miss Berlin« 1950.

Berlin gradually returns to life: The 'Miss Berlin' competition in 1950.

Auch die Westberliner Theaterszene lebt auf: Hier das 1949 gegründete Kabarett »Die Stachelschweine« unter der Leitung von Wolfgang Gruner im Burgkeller am Kurfürstendamm.

The West Berlin theatre scene also comes to life again: Pictured here, 'Die Stachelschweine' cabaret club, which opened in 1949 and was run by Wolfgang Gruner in the Burgkeller on the Kurfürstendamm.

Frühlingserwachen 1950:
mit dem Motorrad unterwegs zum Paddeln.

Spring awakening:
Off to the lakeside by motorbike.

Ferienlager im Grunewald. Holiday camp in Grunewald.

3. Juli 1950: Das KaDeWe wird in der Tauentzienstraße in Schöneberg wieder eröffnet. 600 Verkäuferinnen wurden eingestellt und Tausende von Kunden und Schaulustigen strömen in den Konsumtempel. Wegen des starken Andrangs muss die Polizei schon kurz nach der Eröfnung die Eingänge wieder schließen und kann die Kunden nur schubweise einlassen.

3 July 1950: The KaDeWe department store reopens in Schöneberg's Tauentzienstraße. Six hundred sales personnel were hired, and customers and curious window shoppers flocked in their thousands to this cathedral of consumerism. The crowds were so dense that no sooner had the store opened than police were forced to close the entrance doors, allowing in only a few people at a time.

KEIN FRÄULEINWUNDER

Sie war eine Provokation für die junge Bundesrepublik. Schon in ihren frühen Filmen entsprach Hildegard Knef (1925-2002) nicht dem blonden Fräuleinwunder. Eine kurze Nacktszene in »Die Sünderin« wurde im prüden Klima der Adenauer-Ära zum großen Skandal. Hildegard Knef floh Richtung Hollywood. Nach einigen Filmproduktionen spielte sie ab 1954 zwei Jahre lang mit großem Erfolg im Broadway-Musical »Silk Stockings« von Cole Porter. Die Knef avancierte zum internationalen Star.

Trotzdem blieb sie Deutschland – und besonders Berlin – immer verbunden. Als Schriftstellerin und Chansonsängerin schuf das Multitalent moderne Klassiker wie »Für mich soll´s rote Rosen regnen«. Ihr markant-rauchiges Timbre machte sie zur »größten Sängerin ohne Stimme« (Ella Fitzgerald). 1970 veröffentlichte sie mit ihrer Autobiografie »Der geschenkte Gaul« einen Weltbestseller. Hildegard Knef war eine öffentliche Frau, die persönliche Erfahrungen – Krebs, Scheidung, Schönheitsoperationen – enttabuisierte.

Zuletzt lebte Hildegard Knef wieder in Berlin, wo sie 2002 starb. Sie wurde auf dem Friedhof Berlin-Zehlendorf begraben.

Allroundtalent mit Koffer in Berlin: Die Schauspielerin, Sängerin und Schriftstellerin Hildegard Knef.

NO MISS PERFECT

She provoked the wrath of the new Federal Republic. Even in her early films, Hildegard Knef (1925-2002) failed to match the ideal of blond feminine perfection. A brief nude scene in 'Die Sünderin' (The Sinner) caused a furore in the prudish climate of the Adenauer era. Hildegard Knef fled to Hollywood. In 1954, after making a number of films, she opened in the Broadway Musical 'Silk Stockings' by Cole Porter, and appeared in it for two years with great success. Knef was on the way to international stardom.

Nevertheless, she always maintained her links with Germany, especially Berlin. A multitalented writer and singer of satirical songs, she created such modern classics as 'Für mich soll´s rote Rosen regnen' (It should rain red roses for me). The striking smoky timbre of her voice made her 'the greatest singer without a voice', as Ella Fitzgerald put it. In 1970 she published her autobiography 'Der geschenkte Gaul' (The Gift Horse), which became a world best seller. Hildegard Knef was a woman in the public eye, who lifted the taboo on personal experiences – cancer, divorce, and cosmetic surgery.

Hildegard Knef finally returned to Berlin, where she died in 2002. She is buried in the cemetery of Berlin-Zehlendorf.

All-round talent with luggage in Berlin: The actress, singer, and author, Hildegard Knef.

Eine Reihe von Westberliner Polizisten markiert die Grenze des britischen Sektors am Potsdamer Platz, um Zwischenfällen nach der Kundgebung am 1. Mai 1950 auf dem Platz der Republik vorzubeugen.

West Berlin police line the border with the British sector in Potsdam Square to deter incidents following the May Day rally in 1950 in the Platz der Republik.

27.-30. Mai 1950: in Ost-Berlin findet das von der Freien Deutschen Jugend (FDJ) organisierte »1. Deutschlandtreffen« statt. 700. 000 Jugendliche, darunter auch 30.000 aus der Bundesrepublik Deutschland, nehmen an dem Treffen teil. Die Veranstaltung steht im Zeichen scharfer Angriffe gegen die Bundesregierung in Bonn. Höhepunkt ist ein achtstündiger Vorbeimarsch von mehr als einer halben Million Menschen an einer Ehrentribüne nahe dem Lustgarten. Etwa 30.000 FDJ-Angehörige nutzen trotz Verbots die Gelegenheit zu einem Abstecher in den Westteil der Stadt.

27–30 May 1950: The Free German Youth (FDJ) organizes its '1st Germany Rally' in East Berlin, attended by 700,000 young people including 30,000 from the Federal Republic. The event becomes a platform for fierce attacks on the Federal Government in Bonn. The climax of the rally is an 8-hour procession of over 500,000 people marching past a VIP stand near the Lustgarten. Despite the ban, around 30,000 FDJ members take advantage of the opportunity to visit the Western sector of the city.

Traditionen Ost: am 6. November 1950 wird in Ost-Berlin die Ruine des Stadtschlosses gesprengt, obwohl es wieder aufgebaut hätte werden können. Viele Menschen in Ost und West hatten sich dafür eingesetzt, aber die DDR-Führung wollte mit dem Abriss ganz bewusst den Bruch mit der preußischen Tradition Berlins dokumentieren.

Traditional Eastern style: On 6 November 1950, the badly damaged city palace in East Berlin was demolished, even though it could have been restored. Many people in both East and West Berlin were in favour of its restoration, but the GDR leaders wanted its demolition to signal a total break with Berlin's Prussian traditions.

Traditionen West: 17 Millionen Amerikaner stiften 1950 die »Freiheitsglocke«, gegossen nach dem Vorbild der »Liberty Bell«. Die Glocke wird vor dem Rathaus Schöneberg aufgestellt.

Traditional Western style: In 1950, 17 million Americans present Berlin with a 'liberty bell', modelled on the US original. The bell is mounted outside Schöneberg Town Hall.

Zweite Parteikonferenz der SED in Ost-Berlin vom 9. bis zum 12. Juli 1952. Aufmarsch von Mitgliedern der FDJ, Volkspolizei und SED-Aktivisten auf dem Marx-Engels-Platz. Beschlossen wird der vorrangige Aufbau der Schwerindustrie, die Kollektivierung der Landwirtschaft, der Aufbau von Streitkräften und die Verschärfung des Klassenkampfes. Das alles vor dem Hintergrund einer immer katastrophaleren Versorgungslage der Bevölkerung.

The SED holds its 2nd Party Congress in East Berlin from 9–12 July 1952. Members of the FDJ, People's Police, and SED activists converge in Marx-Engels Square. The Congress resolves to give priority to developing heavy industry, collectivizing agriculture, building up the armed forces, and intensifying the class struggle. Meanwhile, the supply situation in the country goes from bad to worse.

1952 verschlechtert sich die Situation zusehends. Immer mehr Menschen fliehen vom Ostteil der Stadt in den Westen. Links: Flüchtlinge aus der DDR vor einem Auffanglager in Charlottenburg.
Oben: Übergriff auf einen DDR-Grenzpolizisten, 1952.

In 1952, the situation worsens dramatically. Ever-increasing numbers of people are fleeing to the West from the Eastern part of the city. On the left: Refugees from the GDR at a reception camp in Charlottenburg. Above: A member of the GDR frontier police is assaulted in 1952.

Flüchtlinge aus Ostberlin vor dem Aufnahmelager in der Kuno-Fischer-Straße in Westberlin (links u. rechts außen).
Blick in einen Schlafsaal im Flüchtlingslager am Salzufer 10 in Westberlin (Mitte).

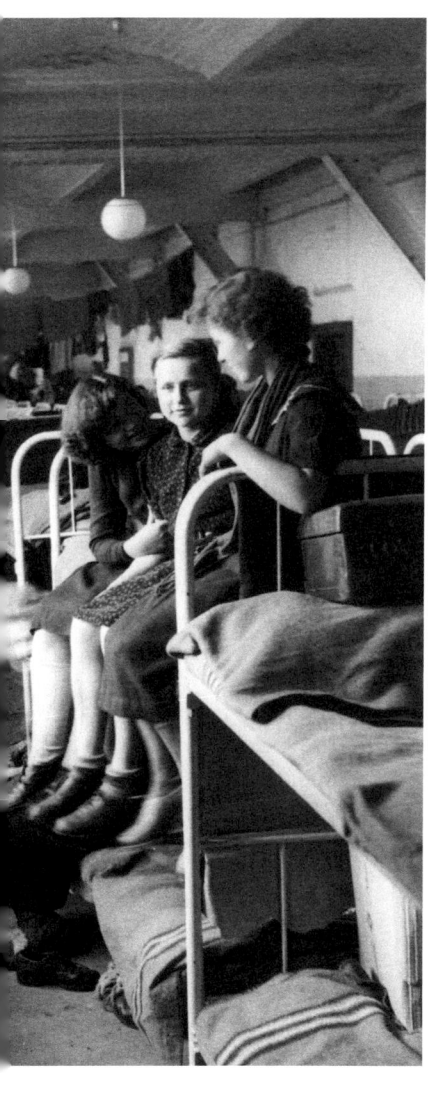

Refugees from East Berlin outside the reception camp in the Kuno-Fischer-Straße in West Berlin (left and far right).
View of a dormitory at the Salzufer No. 10 refugee camp in West Berlin.

An der Grenze zwischen amerikanischem und sowjetischem Sektor in der Friedrichstraße werden im Februar 1953 Sektorenschilder versetzt.

Sector signs being put up in February 1953 along the border between the American and Soviet sectors in the Friedrichstraße.

Zu Pfingsten, am 24. Mai 1953 findet der erste Gottesdienst nach dem Krieg in der Ruine der Kaiser-Wilhelm-Gedächtniskirche statt.

During the Whitsun celebrations, the first post-war church service is held on 24 May 1953 in the badly damaged Kaiser Wilhelm Memorial Church.

Die Umsetzung der Beschlüsse der 2. Parteikonferenz der SED vom Juli 1952 stürzte die DDR-Regierung innerhalb weniger Monate in ihre bis dahin schwerste Krise. Die Kollektivierung der Landwirtschaft und die Bevorzugung der Schwerindustrie führten zu dramatischen Engpässen in der Versorgung. Dazu kam im Mai die Erhöhung der Arbeitsnorm um 10%. Schon vorher hatten die Arbeiter in einzelnen Streiks ihrem Unmut Luft gemacht, aber jetzt kam es zu einem wütenden Volksaufstand. Am 17. Juni 1953 wird der Generalstreik ausgerufen und der Rücktritt der Regierung gefordert. Die Aufstände eskalieren rund um den Potsdamer Platz.

Within a few months, attempts to implement the resolutions of the 2nd SED Congress of July 1952 had thrown the GDR Government into its worst ever crisis. Collectivizing agriculture and prioritizing heavy industry meant severe shortages for the population. Matters came to a head in May when the government decreed that the average work rate should be increased by 10 per cent. Even prior to this, workers had been expressing their dissatisfaction in localized strike action, but now their anger escalated into a popular revolt. A general strike was called on 17 June 1953, calling for the government's resignation. Workers took to the streets all around Potsdam Square.

Auf dem Höhepunkt des Aufstandes vom 17. Juni rollen sowjetische Panzer gegen Demonstranten, die sich mit Pflastersteinen bewaffnet gegen die Übermacht stellen. Der Aufstand wird blutig niedergeschlagen.

As the rebellion reached its climax on 17 June, Soviet tanks moved in against the demonstrators who, armed with cobblestones, were no match for such a superior force. Soviet intervention brought the revolt to a bloody end.

In der zweiten Hälfte der 50er Jahre entwickelt sich in Westberlin nicht zu übersehender Wohlstand.
Links: Sommer am Strandbad Wannsee.
Oben: Die moderne Architektur der 50er Jahre prägt das Bild, wie im Restaurant im Palais am Funkturm.

During the latter half of the 50s, the lifestyle of West Berliners became conspicuously affluent. Pictured left: Summer at the Wannsee lakeside resort. Above: modern architecture of the 50s predominates, as reflected here in the Palais am Funkturm restaurant.

KUDAMM UND KADEWE

Der Kurfürstendamm (kurz: Kudamm) wurde im 16. Jahrhundert unter Kurfürst Joachim II. als Verbindungsstraße zwischen dem Stadtschloss und dem Jagdschloss Grunewald angelegt. Ab 1880 baute Bismarck den Kurfürstendamm zu einer 53 Meter breiten Prachtstraße nach dem Vorbild der Pariser Champs Elysée aus. Das gesellschaftliche Leben verlagerte sich vom historischen Kern »Unter den Linden« hierher. Der Boulevard spiegelt die Geschichte Berlins: Anfangs großbürgerliche Wohnstraße und Flaniermeile der Vorkriegsmetropole, entwickelte er sich zum Zentrum Westberlins, auf dem die Berliner Kennedy zujubelten und sich Ende der 60er Jahre die Studentenbewegung formierte. Heute ist der Kurfürstendamm nach denkmalpflegerischen Bemühungen wieder ein attraktiver Treffpunkt für Berliner und Touristen.

In der Tauentzienstraße am Kurfürstendamm präsentiert sich das Kaufhaus des Westens (KaDeWe). Der Konsumtempel nach Plänen des Architekten Emil Schaudt umfasste schon bei seiner Gründung im Jahr 1907 eine Verkaufsfläche von 24.000 qm auf fünf Etagen. Nach dem Zweiten Weltkrieg feierten 1950 180.000 Besucher die Wiedereröffnung des KaDeWe als symbolischen Neuanfang. Besonders beliebt: die legendäre sechste Etage mit ihrem exotischen Feinkostangebot. Daran hat sich nichts geändert: im zweitgrößten Kaufhaus Europas tummeln sich täglich 80.000 Besucher.

Glamour der Großstadt: Der Kurfürstendamm mit seinen zahlreichen Einkaufs- und Vergnügungsmöglichkeiten (rechts) und der Konsumtempel KaDeWe in der Tauentzienstraße.

KUDAMM AND KADEWE

The Kurfürstendamm (Kudamm for short) was built in the sixteenth century during the reign of Elector Joachim II to connect his castle in the city with the hunting lodge of Grunewald. In 1880, Bismarck began extending the Kurfürstendamm into a magnificent 53-metre-wide boulevard, modelled on the Champs-Elysées in Paris, and the high life moved here from the historic centre of Unter den Linden. The Kurfürstendamm reflects the history of Berlin. Originally a residential street for the haute bourgeoisie and the smart place for the citizens of the prewar capital to take a stroll, it became the centre of West Berlin, where the Berliners cheered Kennedy and where the student movement was formed at the end of the 1960s. Now preserved as an historical monument, it is once again an attractive meeting place for Berliners and tourists alike.

Situated in Tauentzienstrasse on the Kurfürstendamm is the department store Kaufhaus des Westens, otherwise known as the KaDeWe (or KDW). This temple of consumption, designed by the architect Emil Schaudt, had a sales area of twenty-four thousand square metres on five floors when it was founded back in 1907. After the Second World War, one hundred and eighty thousand customers celebrated its reopening in 1956 as the symbol of a new beginning. Especially popular is the legendary sixth floor with its exotic delicatessen. In this respect, nothing has changed: eighty thousand customers a day flock to this, the second largest department store in Europe.

The bright lights of the big city: The Kurfürstendamm with its numerous shopping and leisure opportunities (right) and the KaDeWe shrine to consumerism in Tauentzienstraße.

Am 11. Februar 1955 wählt das Berliner Abgeordnetenhaus Willy Brandt zu seinem neuen Präsidenten. Willy und Ruth Brandt beim Abflug in die USA auf dem Flughafen Tempelhof.

On 11 February 1955, Willy Brandt is elected the new President of Berlin's Chamber of Deputies. Willy and Ruth Brandt at Tempelhof airport, prior to their departure for the USA.

Am 4. September 1955 wird die Deutsche Staatsoper Unter den Linden mit einem großen Festakt wiedereröffnet. Ankunft der Gäste vor der Oper.

On 4 September 1955, the German State Opera is reopened with great ceremony on Unter den Linden. Invited guests arriving outside the Opera House.

Vom 22. Juni bis zum 3. Juli 1956 finden in Westberlin die 6. internationalen Filmfestspiele statt. Vor dem Gloria Palast am Kurfürstendamm drängen sich die Menschenmassen, um einen der prominenten Gäste zu sehen.

West Berlin hosts the 6th International Film Festival from 22 June to 3 July 1956. Crowds throng outside the Gloria Palace on Kurfürstendamm, desperate to catch a glimpse of one of the celebrities.

Berlin 1959:»Freie Stadt zwischen Stacheldraht« - Der Titel einer Broschüre des Bundesministeriums für Gesamtdeutsche Fragen beschreibt die paradoxe Situation Berlins Ende der 50er Jahre sehr treffend.

Berlin 1959: 'Free City Behind the Barbed Wire' - This title of a pamphlet, published by the Federal Ministry of All-German Affairs, perfectly encapsulates Berlin's paradoxical situation towards the end of the 1950s.

Nach dem Zweiten Weltkrieg wurde Berlin zur geteilten Stadt. In Westberlin entwickelte sich ein modernes städtisches Leben mit demokratischer Verfassung und aufkeimender Marktwirtschaft. Im sowjetischen Sektor kam es immer wieder zu Versorgungsengpässen, und die Menschen lebten in ständiger Angst vor Partei und Staatssicherheitsdienst. Aufgrund der wirtschaftlichen Misere und des rigiden Drucks des kommunistischen Systems flohen immer mehr Menschen nach Westdeutschland, und nachdem 1952 die Grenze zur Bundesrepublik geschlossen wurde, blieb aufgrund seines Viermächtestatus nur noch Berlin als Weg in den Westen. Um dieser Entwicklung zu begegnen, kündigte die sowjetische Regierung 1958 einseitig den Viermächtestatus und stellte den Westmächten ein Ultimatum zum Verlassen der Stadt. Nachdem diese, allen voran die USA, sich geweigert hatten, den freien Zugang zur Stadt und ihre Präsenz dort aufzugeben, spitzte sich die Lage 1961 zu. Die Zahl der Flüchtlinge stieg noch einmal rapide an. Um der Situation zu begegnen – seit 1949 hatten jedes Jahr Hunderttausende die DDR verlassen – entschloss sich die Regierung unter Walter Ulbricht zum Bau der Mauer. Am 13. August 1961 begannen Einheiten der Volkspolizei und der Nationalen Volksarmee mit der Abriegelung der Sektorengrenze. Von den 81 Übergangsstellen wurden die meisten geschlossen, wenig später die ersten Stacheldrahtverhaue und Betonpfähle gesetzt. Kurz

Seite 264/265: In letzter Minute: Am 15. August 1961 flüchtet ein Volksarmist nach der Abriegelung des sowjetischen Sektors in den Westen Berlins.

After the Second World War, Berlin became a divided city. West Berlin developed a modern urban way of life with a democratic constitution and a high standard of living. In the Soviet sector, there were once again shortages of supplies, and the people lived in constant fear of the party and state security police. As a result of the desperate economic situation and the inflexibility of the communist system, ever more people fled to West Germany. When, in 1952, the border to the Federal Republic was closed, Berlin, with its four-power status, was the only remaining route to the West.

To counter this development, the Soviet government unilaterally denounced the four-power status in 1958 and gave the Western powers an ultimatum to leave the city. The Western powers, and the USA in particular, refused to give up free access to the city and their presence there, and the situation came to a head in 1961. The number of refugees once again rose steeply. To counter this situation – since 1949 hundreds of thousands of people had left the GDR each year – the East German government, under Walter Ulbricht, decided to build the Wall. On 13 August 1961, units of the GDR national police force and army began to seal off the border with the other sectors. Of the 81 crossing points, 69 were blocked and, a little later, the first barbed wire entanglements and concrete posts were installed. Soon after, gangs of con-

Pages 264/265: Last-minute escape: On 15 August 1961, a soldier in the East German People's Army flees to West Berlin after the Soviet sector is sealed off.

darauf begannen Bautrupps unter Militärschutz die bis zu vier Meter hohe Mauer hochzuziehen. In dramatischen Aktionen retteten sich noch viele Menschen in letzter Minute in den Westen. Dann wurde die Mauer zur unüberwindlichen Todesfalle mit Wachtürmen, Bunkern und einem 100 Meter breiten Todesstreifen, bewacht von Grenztruppen, die den Befehl hatten, Flüchtige notfalls mit Waffengebrauch aufzuhalten.

In den 60er und 70er Jahren spielten sich in der geteilten Stadt die wichtigen Ereignisse auf der Straße ab: Im Westen demonstrierte die Außerparlamentarische Opposition (APO) gegen den Staat der restaurativen Väter, Im Osten marschierten Militär und FDJ auf den Paradestraßen, während Dissidenten wie der Liedermacher Wolf Biermann oder der Chemiker Robert Havemann überwacht wurden und Berufsverbot erhielten.

In den 70er Jahre brachte die Ostpolitik Willy Brandts und die Verhandlungen der Alliierten kleine Fortschritte für den innerdeutschen Austausch: 1971 vereinbarten die Bundesrepublik und die DDR das Transitabkommen, das den Besuchs- und Reiseverkehr zwischen Westberlin und der DDR erleichterte, und 1972 zusammen mit dem Viermächteabkommen in Kraft trat.

Trotzdem blieb die Mauer ein tiefer Riss durch das Herz der Stadt, Familien waren auseinander gerissen, Freundschaften zerstört und Westberlin zur Insel in einem diktatorischen System gemacht worden. Das änderte sich erst mit dem Fall der Mauer am 9. November 1989.

struction workers under military protection began to erect the Wall, which rose up to four metres high in places. Many more people managed to make dramatic, last minute escapes to the West. Then, the Wall became an insurmountable deathtrap complete with watchtowers, bunkers, and a 100m-wide strip of no man's land, patrolled by border troops who had been ordered to arrest refugees, using their weapons if necessary.

The important events of the 1960s and 70s spilled out onto the streets of Berlin, despite it being a divided city; In the West, protest demonstrations were held by the Extra-Parliamentary Opposition (APO) against the old order. In the East, members of the military and FDJ (Free German Youth) marched down the parade boulevards, while dissidents like songwriter Wolf Biermann and chemist Robert Havemann were placed under surveillance and banned from working.

At the beginning of the 1970s, Willy Brandt's 'Ostpolitik' and the Allieds' negotiations made some small progress towards movement between the two Germanies. In 1971, the Federal Republic and the GDR concluded the Transit Agreement, which facilitated visits and travel between West Berlin and the GDR and which, together with the Four Powers Agreement, came into force in 1972.

Nevertheless, the Wall remained a deep fissure through the heart of the city; families were torn apart, friendships destroyed, and West Berlin created an enclave within a dictatorship. Nothing changed until the Wall fell on 9 November 1989.

Durch den Bau der Mauer 1961 werden Familien und Freunde auseinandergerissen.

Families and friends were torn apart by the building of the Wall in 1961.

Ein Loch in der Mauer: Blick durch eine Steinlücke auf einen Ostberliner Grenzposten, Oktober 1961.

A hole in the Wall: Glimpse of an East Berlin frontier post through a gap in the Wall, October 1961.

Oktober 1961: Blick auf die Sperranlagen am Potsdamer Platz. Im Hintergrund links das Brandenburger Tor.

October 1961: View of the frontier barriers in Potsdam Square. In the background on the left is the Brandenburg Gate.

Nach Abschluss der Bauarbeiten an der Mauer werden im November 1961 die Sichtblenden vor dem Brandenburger Tor beseitigt.

After the construction of the Wall was completed, the screens in front of the Brandenburg Gate were removed in November 1961.

Die neu errichtete Mauer in der Bernauer Straße (Bezirk Wedding) im November 1961.

The newly constructed Wall in the Bernauer Straße (Wedding district) in November 1961.

Bei einem Fluchtversuch über die Mauer am 17. August 1962 in der Nähe der Friedrichstraße wird der 18-jährige Bauarbeiter Peter Fechter angeschossen. Weder West- noch Ostberliner Grenzpolizisten greifen ein. Peter Fechter verblutet zwischen den Fronten. Eine Stunde später birgt die Ostberliner Grenzpolizei die Leiche.

On 17 August 1962, an 18-year-old building worker, Peter Fechter, was shot while attempting to escape across the Wall in the Friedrichstraße area. Neither the West nor East Berlin frontier guards went to his aid and Peter Fechter bled to death in No-Man's Land. An hour later, his body was retrieved by East Berlin frontier police.

Der Mauerbau führte dazu, dass die Bernauer Straße zweigeteilt wurde. Die Häuser standen auf der Ostseite, der Bürgersteig gehörte schon zum Westen. Der Kontakt zwischen den Straßennachbarn riss völlig ab. Im Osten wurden die Fenster vermauert, die meisten Bewohner umgesiedelt. Auch auf der Westseite wurde die einst belebte Straße zum Randgebiet.

After the Wall was built, the Bernauer Straße was cut in two. While the houses found themselves in the Eastern sector, the pavement remained on the Western side. Contact between neighbours on the same street came to an abrupt end. In the Eastern zone, windows were bricked up and most of the occupants moved elsewhere. On the Western side, this once bustling street became part of the frontier zone.

CHECKPOINT CHARLIE

Was war er? Wo war er? Wie kam er zu seinem Namen?

Checkpoint Charlie – die in Neonlicht getauchte Verkörperung des Kalten Krieges und Symbol für die Teilung der Stadt. Checkpoint Charlie war der Kontrollübergang zwischen Berlin Mitte und Kreuzberg, zwischen dem amerikanischen und dem sowjetischen Sektor. Hier konnten Angehörige der alliierten Streitkräfte und Diplomaten in Uniform ohne die sonst so strengen Kontrollen passieren. Der Name des Übergangs leitete sich von der militärischen Buchstabiertafel ab und steht für C (Charlie). A (Alpha) war in Helmstedt, B (Bravo) in Dreilinden. Im Gegensatz zu Dreilinden und Helmstedt gelangte Checkpoint Charlie durch zahlreiche Spionage-Thriller zu mystischer Berühmtheit. Der Legende nach saß John le Carré im Café Adler in der Nähe des Checkpoint Charlie und schrieb hier Teile seines Buches »Der Spion, der aus der Kälte kam«.

Im Haus am Checkpoint Charlie existiert schon seit 1963 aufgrund der symbolträchtigen Lage ein Mauermuseum mit einer Sammlung rund um den Mauerbau, bewegenden Zeugnissen von Fluchtgeschichten, Mauerkunst und DDR-Reliquien.

Grenzübergang Friedrichstraße (Checkpoint Charlie) mit neu errichteten Sperren im März 1962.

The Friedrichstraße frontier crossing-point (Checkpoint Charlie) with its newly erected barriers in March 1962.

CHECKPOINT CHARLIE

What was it? Where was it? How did it get its name? Checkpoint Charlie – this starkly floodlit embodiment of the Cold War and symbol of a divided Berlin.

Checkpoint Charlie was the frontier crossing-point between Berlin Mitte and Kreuzberg, linking the American and Russian sectors. Uniformed members of the Allied Forces and diplomats were able to cross the border here without quite such the rigorous controls encountered elsewhere. This border crossing got its nickname from the alphabet code used by the military and stands for 'C' ('Charlie'). 'A' ('Alpha') was in Helmstedt, 'B' ('Bravo') in Dreilinden.

In contrast to Dreilinden and Helmstedt, Checkpoint Charlie acquired its mystical fame as a result of countless spy thrillers. It is said that John le Carré used to sit in the Café Adler near Checkpoint Charlie, writing parts of his book 'The Spy Who Came In From The Cold'.

The Haus am Checkpoint Charlie opened in 1963 as a reflection of its symbolically sensitive location. It houses an exhibition telling the story of the Wall and its construction, displaying poignant reminders of escape stories, Wall art, and GDR memorabilia.

Amerikanische Panzer kurz nach dem Mauerbau am Checkpoint Charlie.

US tanks at Checkpoint Charlie shortly after the Wall was built.

Begrüßungsszenen an einem Sektorenübergang während des Passierscheinabkommens vom 18. Dezember 1965 bis zum 2. Februar 1966. Mehrere Passierscheinabkommen regeln von 1963 bis 1966 Verwandtenbesuche zwischen Ost- und Westberlin. Danach bleibt lediglich eine Passierscheinstelle für dringende Familienangelegenheiten bestehen. Erst mit dem Viermächteabkommen von 1971 können Westberliner wieder regelmäßig den Ostteil der Stadt besuchen.

Reunion scenes at one of the crossing-points during the temporary agreement allowing people with permits to cross the frontier between 18 December 1965 and 2 February 1966. There were several such agreements between 1963 and 1966 regulating the issuing of permits to allow family visits between East and West Berlin. After that, only one frontier-crossing permit point was available in the event of urgent family matters. It was not until the Four-Power Agreement of 1971 that West Berliners were once again allowed to make regular visits to the Eastern sector of the City.

ICH BIN EIN BERLINER

Mit diesen legendären Worten erreichte die Deutschlandreise des amerikanischen Präsidenten John F. Kennedy (1917–1963) im Juni 1963 ihren Höhepunkt. 300.000 Menschen jubelten dem charismatischen Politiker zu, als er auf dem Balkon des Schöneberger Rathauses seine Solidarität mit den Berlinern bekundete. Kennedy war der erste US-Präsident, der Westberlin besuchte. Zwei Jahre nach dem Mauerbau setzte er damit in der geteilten Stadt ein Zeichen für die Freiheit und Demokratie. Gleichzeitig trat er für eine Ostpolitik ein, die sich an den Realitäten des Kalten Krieges orientierte: »Wenn wir für die Zukunft dieser Stadt arbeiten wollen, dann lassen Sie uns mit den Gegebenheiten fertig werden, wie sie tatsächlich sind, nicht (...) wie sie nach unseren Wünschen sein sollten.«

Der jugendlich wirkende Staatsmann begeisterte nicht nur in Berlin eine breite Öffentlichkeit. Seit seiner Wahl zum amerikanischen Präsidenten am 20. Januar 1961 wurde er gerade für die Nachkriegsgeneration zum Hoffnungsträger für eine kooperative Politik gegenüber der Sowjetunion. Nur wenige Monate nach seinem Berlin-Besuch wurde dieser Optimismus brutal zunichte gemacht: Am 22. November 1963 wurde John F. Kennedy in Dallas/Texas erschossen.

Am 26. Juni 1963 jubeln 300.000 Menschen vor dem Rathaus Schöneberg dem Hoffnungsträger John F. Kennedy zu.

On 26 June 1963, John F Kennedy was cheered by a 300,000-strong crowd outside Schöneberg Town Hall.

ICH BIN EIN BERLINER

These legendary words marked the climax of American President John F Kennedy's visit to Germany in June 1963. A crowd of three hundred thousand cheered as, speaking from the balcony of Schöneberg Town Hall, this charismatic politician expressed his solidarity with the people of Berlin. Kennedy (1917-1963) was the first US president to visit West Berlin. By making this visit two years after the building of the Wall, he was pointing the way to the future of freedom and democracy in the divided city. He also favoured a policy towards the Eastern Bloc that showed his awareness of the realities of the Cold War: 'If we wish to work for the future of this city, then let us deal with the situation as it really is, not (...) as we would wish it to be'.

The youthful-looking statesman inspired wide public enthusiasm, not only in Berlin. After his election to the American presidency on 20 January 1961, he became the focus of the postwar generation's hopes for a policy of cooperation towards the Soviet Union. Just a few months after his visit to Berlin, these hopes were brutally shattered. On 22 November 1963, John F Kennedy was shot dead in Dallas, Texas.

Im offenen Wagen durch Berlin: der amerikanische Präsident mit dem Regierenden Bürgermeister von Westberlin, Willy Brandt, und Bundeskanzler Konrad Adenauer.

Tour of Berlin in an open-topped car: the American President with the Governing Mayor of Berlin, Willy Brandt, and Federal Chancellor Konrad Adenauer.

Aufstand gegen die Väter: Die Anti-Schah-Demonstration am 2. Juni 1967 markiert den Beginn der Studentenunruhen in Westdeutschland.

Anti-establishment demonstration: The anti-Shah demonstration on 2 June 1967 marked the start of student unrest in Germany.

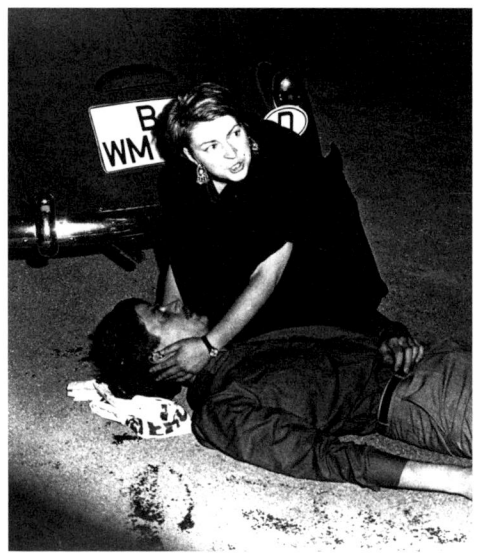

Der Student Benno Ohnesorg wird bei Ausschreitungen während der Anti-Schah-Demonstration von dem Polizisten Karl-Heinz Kurass erschossen. Der Regierende Bürgermeister Heinrich Albertz erklärt einen Tag später: »Die Geduld der Stadt ist am Ende.(...)«

During clashes with police during the anti-Shah demonstration, a student, Benno Ohnesorg, was shot dead by a police officer, Karl-Heinz Kurass. One day later, Berlin's Governing Mayor Heinrich Albertz declared: 'The City's patience is at an end (...)'.

Gegen den Vietnamkrieg: Der Studentenführer Rudi Dutschke (Mitte) mit seiner Frau Gretchen auf einer Demonstration im Februar 1968. Zwei Monate später schießt der 23-jährige Josef Erwin Bachmann Dutschke auf offener Straße nieder. Trotz schwerster Verletzungen überlebt er, stirbt jedoch 1979 an den Folgen des Attentats.

Anti-Vietnam protests: Student leader Rudi Dutschke (centre) with his wife Gretchen at a demonstration in February 1968. Two months later, Dutschke was gunned down in the street by 23-year-old Josef Erwin Bachmann. Despite being seriously injured, he survived, but eventually died in 1979 as a consequence of his injuries.

Rock-Ikone Jimi Hendrix bei einem Konzert im Berliner Sportpalast 1969.

Rock icon Jimi Hendrix at a concert in Berlin's Sportpalast 1969.

»BILD hat mitgeschossen«: Nach dem Attentat auf Rudi Dutschke am 11. April 1968 werfen Studenten Molotowcocktails auf Auslieferungsfahrzeuge des Springer-Verlages in der Kochstraße.

Der Jurist Horst Mahler (Mitte) steht wegen Beteiligung an der gewaltsamen Befreiung Andreas Baaders 1971 vor Gericht. Er wird aus Mangel an Beweisen freigesprochen. Seine Verteidiger sind Christian Ströbele (links) und Otto Schily (rechts).

'BILD magazine's finger on the trigger': In the wake of the attempted murder of Rudi Dutschke on 11 April 1968, students hurl Molotov cocktails at delivery vans belonging to the Springer Verlag in the Kochstraße.

Lawyer Horst Mahler (centre) stands trial charged with having been involved in forcibly freeing Andreas Baader in 1971. He is acquitted due to insufficient evidence. His defence counsels are Christian Ströbele (left) and Otto Schily (right).

EINSTÜRZENDE ALTBAUTEN

Der kleinste, aber am dichtesten besiedelte Bezirk Berlins verdankt seinen Namen dem 66 Meter hohen Kreuzberg. Auf seiner Kuppe steht das Denkmal der Befreiungskriege, das Karl Friedrich Schinkel 1821 errichtete.

Vor allem Migranten haben das traditionelle Arbeiterviertel mit seinen Mietskasernen aus dem frühen 20. Jahrhundert geprägt. Sie wurden gebaut, um den dramatischen Bevölkerungszuwachs der Stadt in den Jahren um 1900 gerecht zu werden. Die Menschen lebten unter schlechten Bedingungen, gewöhnlich teilten sich mehrere Personen einen Raum, es gab weder fließendes Wasser noch Sanitäranlagen.

Das Gebiet wurde im Zweiten Weltkrieg kaum zerstört, und die günstigen Mieten dieser wenig komfortablen Wohnungen lockten in den Wirtschaftswunderjahren zahlreiche türkische Gastarbeiter an. Sie machen heute etwa ein Drittel der Bevölkerung aus.

Doch auch Studenten aus Westdeutschland zog es seit den 60er Jahren in den Stadtteil, dessen Straßenzüge im Osten und Süden abrupt durch die Mauer begrenzt wurden. Das sub-

Vielfältig ist es in Kreuzberg noch immer: Punker haben sich ihr Wohnzimmer auf der Adalbertstraße eingerichtet, türkische Frauen feiern den Geburtstag Mohammeds.

OLD CRUMBLING BUILDINGS

The smallest, yet most densely populated, borough in Berlin owes its name to the Kreuzberg, a hill rising to 66 metres in height at the top of which stands the monument built by Karl Friedrich Schinkel in 1821 to commemorate the war of liberation.

This traditionally working-class area, with its tenement buildings dating from the early twentieth century, is mainly populated by immigrants. These blocks of flats were built in order to cope with the dramatic increase in population experienced by the city around 1900. Living conditions were poor, and it was common for several people to share a room. Running water and sanitary facilities were sadly lacking. The district remained largely undamaged during the Second World War and the cheap rents on this unprepossessing accommodation attracted many Turkish guest workers during the years of the 'economic miracle'. They still make up around one-third of the population.

During the sixties, West German students were also drawn to this area of the city, where the East- and South-leading streets ended abruptly in the Berlin Wall. Subsidized

Kreuzberg has always been a colourful district: Punks have made themselves comfortable on the Adalbertstraße, while Turkish women celebrate the birth of Mohammed.

ventionierte Berlin war ein Refugium für Kriegsdienstverweigerer und wurde zur Hochburg des politischen Widerstands, zu einem Mekka der Alternativen.

In Kreuzberg trieb die Utopie von einem Leben jenseits der bundesrepublikanischen Konvention bunte Blüten – kulturell wie politisch. Die Musik von »Ton, Steine, Scherben«, den »Einstürzenden Neubauten« oder »Ideal«, Studentendemonstrationen gegen die Springerpresse, Hausbesetzer oder die Krawalle der Autonomen Szene am 1. Mai stehen bis heute als Synonym für Kreuzberg und damit für das Westberlin der 70er und 80er Jahre.

»Instandbesetzung«. Der Protest gegen den Leerstand oder den Abriss von Altbauten verlief nicht immer erfolgreich. Räumung des besetzten Hauses Fraenkelufer Nr. 30 und Abriss eines Mietshauses in der Skalitzer Straße. Überall in Kreuzberg laden türkische Imbissbuden zu einem preiswerten Snack ein.

Berlin became a haven for conscientious objectors and a citadel of political opposition, not to mention a mecca for those seeking an alternative lifestyle. In Kreuzberg, the Utopian dream of a life beyond the confines and conventions of the Federal Republic proved very seductive – culturally as well as politically. To this day, music by the rock groups 'Ton, Steine, Scherben', 'Einstürzende Neubauten', and 'Ideal', the student demonstrations against the Springer press, the squatters, and the First of May riots by members of the Autonomous Scene remain synonymous with the name Kreuzberg and, subsequently, with West Berlin of the 70s and 80s.

'Squatters give houses new lease of life': Protests against the policy of leaving old buildings standing empty or demolishing them did not always achieve the desired success. Here, No. 30 Fraenkelufer is being cleared of squatters and a block of rented flats demolished in the Skalitzer Straße. The Kreuzberg district is full of Turkish food stands selling inexpensive snacks.

Der irische Literaturnobelpreisträger Samuel Beckett (1906-1989) inszeniert 1969 am Berliner Schiller-Theater sein Stück »Das letzte Band« mit Martin Held.

The Irish writer, Samuel Beckett (1906-1989), who won the Nobel Prize for Literature, staged his play 'The Last Band', starring Martin Held, at the Schiller-Theater in Berlin.

Die Berliner Philharmoniker feiern zusammen mit ihrem Chefdirigenten Herbert von Karajan, der 1954 Wilhelm Furtwängler ablöste, viele musikalische Erfolge.

The Berlin Philharmonic, with its conductor Herbert von Karajan who took over from Wilhelm Furtwängler in 1954, has enjoyed enormous musical success.

Außenansicht der Berliner Philharmonie in Berlin-Tiergarten. Sie wurde 1960-1963 vom Architekten Hans Scharoun (1893-1972) erbaut.

A view of the Berlin Philharmonic Hall in Berlin-Tiergarten from the outside. It was built between 1960 and 1963 by the architect Hans Scharoun (1893-1972).

Warten an Ostern: Am Grenzübergang Sonnenallee / Baumschulweg bilden sich 1972 nach Inkrafttreten des Transitabkommens, mit dem die Reise- und Besuchsmöglichkeiten für Westberliner verbessert werden, lange Autoschlangen.

Easter queues: In 1972, after the Transit Agreement came into force improving travel and visit opportunities for West Berliners, long traffic jams formed at the Sonnenallee/Baumschulweg frontier crossing-point.

Im November 1974 wird das Richtfest für den Palast der Republik gefeiert. Zwei Jahre später, am 23. April 1976 wird der Bau eröffnet. In dem multifunktionalen Gebäude sitzt die Volkskammer der DDR, aber auch Kulturveranstaltungen finden hier statt. 1990 wird der Palast der Republik wegen Asbestverseuchung geschlossen.

In November 1974, the topping-out ceremony took place at the Palace of the Republic. The new building was opened two years later on 23 April 1976. This multi-purpose building, the seat of the GDR People's Chamber, was also a venue for cultural events. The Palace of the Republic was closed in 1990 due to asbestos pollution.

Hier kommt das Wirtschaftswunder: Im Westen löst seit den 50er Jahren eine Konsumwelle die nächste ab. Das KaDeWe in der Tauentzienstraße gilt als Inbegriff des ungebremsten Kaufrauschs.

The advent of the Economic Miracle: Since the 50s, the West has experienced one wave of consumerism after another. The KaDeWe department store in the Tauentzienstraße is regarded as a cathedral to runaway consumerism.

Das Schlange stehen nach Mangelware gehört zum Alltag der DDR-Bürger. Viele Produkte sind in der DDR nicht oder nur sehr selten zu bekommen.

Queuing for goods in short supply was part of everyday life for GDR citizens. Many products were scarce or not available in the GDR.

AM ALEX

In zentraler Lage Berlins liegt der Alexanderplatz. Er bildet, von Westen kommend, den Abschluss eines städtebaulichen Ensembles, zu dem die Marienkirche, der Neptunbrunnen, das Rote Rathaus und der Fernsehturm gehören. An diesem weithin sichtbaren Wahrzeichen lässt sich der »Alex«, wie ihn die Berliner nennen, überall in der Stadt ausmachen. Nach dem Krieg hatte die DDR-Regierung den völlig zerstörten Platz 1966 neu konzipiert. Das Fußgängerareal mit dem Bahnhof Alexanderplatz, Warenhaus Centrum, dem Interhotel Stadt Berlin, dem Brunnen der Völkerfreundschaft und der Weltzeituhr wurde zum repräsentativen Zentrum Ostberlins. Am 4. November 1989 gab hier eine halbe Million Menschen ihrer Forderung nach Demokratie Ausdruck.

Von den historischen Wurzeln des Alexanderplatzes ist heute allerdings kaum noch etwas zu erahnen. Der ehemalige Exerzierplatz und Viehmarkt wurde 1805 zum Stadtplatz erklärt und verdankt seinen Namen dem Besuch Zar Alexanders I. in Berlin 1808. Seit dem 19. Jahrhundert hatte sich der Platz zum Verkehrsknotenpunkt entwickelt. Gesäumt von Hotels, Geschäftshäusern, Tanzlokalen und Spelunken diente er dem Schriftsteller Alfred Döblin als Schauplatz für seinen berühmten Großstadtroman »Berlin Alexanderplatz«.

Der Alexanderplatz im Wandel der Zeit: Links um 1900 mit Berolina, dem ehemaligen Wahrzeichen der Stadt, und Bahnhof Alexanderplatz. In den 1970er Jahren mit Weltzeituhr, Interhotel Stadt Berlin und Warenhaus Centrum (Mitte) und im heutigen Zustand vom Haus des Lehrers aus gesehen (rechts).

AT THE ALEX

Situated right at the heart of Berlin is the Alexanderplatz. When approached from the west, it forms the final part of a town-planning entity including the Marienkirche, the Neptune Fountain, the Rote Rathaus, and the Television Tower. This symbol, which can be seen from afar, means that no matter where you are in the city you will always be able to make out the exact location of the 'Alex', as the Berliners call it. The square was totally destroyed in the war, but was redesigned in 1966 by the East German government. The pedestrian zone with Alexanderplatz Station, the shopping centre, the Stadt Berlin Interhotel, the Fountain of International Friendship, and the International Clock became the impressive centre of East Berlin. It was here, on 4 November 1989, that half a million people voiced their demand for democracy.

Barely anything remains now, however, to indicate the historic roots of the Alexanderplatz. The former parade ground and cattle market was declared a town square in 1805 and owes its name to Tsar Alexander I who visited Berlin in 1808. From the nineteenth century onwards, the square was a major traffic junction. Lined with hotels, businesses, dance halls, and shady clubs, it provided the author, Alfred Döblin, with the scene for his famous panoramic novel, 'Berlin Alexanderplatz'.

The Alexanderplatz through changing times: On the left, around 1900 with Berolina, once the symbol of the city, and Alexanderplatz Station. In the 70s with the world time clock, the Interhotel Stadt Berlin, and the Warenhaus Centrum (middle) and as it is today, viewed from the Haus des Lehrers (right).

Im Sommer 1973 finden in Ostberlin die 10. Weltfestspiele der Jugend und Studenten statt. Zwei Wochen lang treffen sich 25.000 Jugendliche aus 140 Ländern zu einem Programm aus Politik, Kultur und Sport. Die Veranstaltung wird zur perfekten Inszenierung der seit 1972 offiziell anerkannten DDR, die Polit-Prominenz sitzt auf der Ehrentribüne.

Querdenker: Der Liedermacher Wolf Biermann ist die kritische Stimme der DDR. Schon 1965 wird er mit Berufsverbot belegt, 1976 wird er ausgewiesen. Zu den Unterzeichnern der Protest-Petition gegen Biermanns Ausweisung gehört auch der Schauspieler und Sänger Manfred Krug. Damit endet die Karriere des DDR-Publikumslieblings. 1977 reist er nach Westdeutschland aus.

In the summer of 1973, East Berlin hosted the 10th World Youth and Students' Festival. For two whole weeks, 25,000 young people from 140 countries congregated here for a programme of politics, culture, and sport. The event formed the perfect showpiece for the GDR, which had been formally recognized in 1972. The leading Politbüro members watched from the VIP podium.

Lateral thinkers: Wolf Biermann, though a committed Socialist, criticized the policies of the GDR government in his songs. He was officially barred from working in 1965 and was deported in 1976. One of the signatories of a petition protesting against Biermann's deportation was actor and singer Manfred Krug. This action marked the end of this popular GDR celebrity's career and, in 1977, he left for West Germany.

Auf dem 5. FDJ-Liedersommer 1987 in Berlin-Lichtenberg treffen sich Musiker aus Ost und West. Die DDR-Gruppe »Wacholder« eröffnet das Festival.

The 5th FDJ (Free German Youth) Summer of Songs in 1987 in Berlin-Lichtenberg unites musicians from East and West. The GDR group 'Wacholder' opens the music festival.

»Sonderzug nach Pankow«: Mit diesem Song bittet der westdeutsche Rocksänger Udo Lindenberg Anfang der 1980er Jahre den »Oberindianer« Erich Honecker um einen Auftritt im Osten. Das Lied wurde in der DDR verboten. Erst 1983 durfte Lindenberg vor FDJ-Publikum auftreten, eine geplante DDR-Tour fiel aus.

'Special train to Pankow': This was the title of a song by West German rock singer Udo Lindenberg in the early 1980s asking 'Chief Indian' Erich Honecker for permission to perform in East Germany. The song was banned in the GDR. Lindenberg was not allowed to perform before a FDJ audience until 1983 and a planned GDR tour was cancelled.

REPRÄSENTATION UND WIDERSTAND

Als am 17. Juni 1953 Bauarbeiter gegen Normerhöhung demonstrierten, begann auf der Stalinallee (ehemals Frankfurter Allee) der Arbeiteraufstand, der unter Einsatz von Panzern blutig niedergeschlagen wurde und die DDR in den Grundfesten erschütterte. 1959 erfolgte die Grundsteinlegung zum »ersten sozialistischen Wohnkomplex Karl-Marx-Allee 2«. Neben Herrmann Henselmann waren auch Hartmann, Hopp, Leucht, Paulick und Souradny an den Plänen zur Paradestraße beteiligt. Zwei Jahre später erfolgte die offizielle Umbenennung in Karl-Marx-Allee, und nach sechsjähriger Bauzeit waren die Arbeiten an der in industrieller Großplattenbauweise realisierten Siedlung beendet. Der ehemalige Boulevard des Ostens, der den Alexanderplatz mit dem Stadtteil Friedrichshain verbindet, auf dem verschiedene soziale Schichten zusammen leben sollten, stellt heute Stadtplaner vor die Frage, wie man mit der historisch wertvollen Anlagen umgehen soll.

Im stalinistischen Zuckerbäckerstil gehalten, war die Karl-Marx-Allee (links Anfang der 60er Jahre mit Blick zum Frankfurter Tor, rechts Blick vom Strausberger Platz mit Brunnen und Turmhochhäusern in Richtung Alexanderplatz) als städtebaulicher Boulevard gedacht, auf dem die Mokka-, Milch- und Eisbar, das Kosmos Kino und riesige Nationalitätenrestaurants für Unterhaltung sorgen sollten. Die sieben- bis neungeschossige Bebauung war in Plattenbauweise errichtet worden. Mit ihrer repräsentativen Kulisse diente die auf 90 Meter verbreiterte Straße aber auch für Truppenaufmärsche, Staatsbesuche und Kundgebungen (hier Vorbeimarsch der NVA-Truppen an der Ehrentribüne aus Anlass des 40. Jahrestags der Gründung der DDR am 7. Oktober 1989).

REPRESENTATION AND RESISTANCE

The construction workers' demonstration on 17 June 1953 against a rise in production levels marked the beginning of the workers' uprising on Stalinallee (formerly Frankfurter Allee) that would be so violently suppressed by tanks and which shook the GDR to its very foundations.

In 1959, the foundation stone was laid of the first 'socialist housing complex' Karl-Marx-Allee 2, Alongside Herrmann Henselmann, Hartmann, Hopp, Leucht, Paulick, and Souradny were also involved in the plans for this showpiece parade street. Two years later, its name was changed officially to Karl-Marx-Allee and, after a six-year construction period, work was completed on the settlement built using industrial large panel construction methods. The former Boulevard of the East, which links Alexanderplatz with the Friedrichshain district, where different social classes were intended to live together, now presents town planners with the question of what to do with these historically significant buildings.

Retaining its Stalinist wedding-cake style of architecture, the Karl-Marx-Allee (on the left, in the early 60s looking towards the Frankfurter Tor; on the right, a view from the Strausberger Platz with fountain and high-rise buildings towards the Alexanderplatz) was intended as a municipal boulevard, along which a block of coffee bars and ice-cream parlours, the Kosmos Cinema, and huge ethnic restaurants would provide entertainment. The seven- to nine-storey construction was erected in panels. It served as a representative backdrop to the boulevard, which had been widened to 90 metres to accommodate military parades, state visits, and rallies (pictured here with soldiers of the National People's Army marching past the VIP stand to mark the 40th anniversary of the GDR on 7 October 1989).

In unmittelbarer Nähe liegt das ehemalige Arbeiterviertel Prenzlauer Berg. Aus der bewegten Geschichte dieses Bezirks, der schon in der Weimarer Republik eine Hochburg des Widerstands war, ist uns vor allem die jüngere in Erinnerung. Zu DDR-Zeiten hatte die wachsende Zahl leerstehender Wohnungen einen relativ ungesteuerten Zuzug von jungen Leuten, Intellektuellen und Künstlern ermöglicht , die nach einem anderen, unangepassten Leben suchten. Der Prenzlauer Berg in Berlin wurde Ausgangspunkt für den Aufbruch im Herbst 1989.

Wohnbauten in der Stargarder Straße. Die von Alfred Messel und Paul Kolb um 1900 errichteten Gebäude ließen hinter ihrer repräsentativen Fassade nichts vom Elend der Hinterhöfe erahnen. In unmittelbarer Nähe, in der Gedzehnmaneh-Kirche.

Die Synagoge »Friedenstempel« in der Rykestraße 53 wurde 1903-04 von Johann Hoeniger erbaut und als einzige Synagoge unter der Naziherrschaft nicht zerstört. Blick vom Torbau auf die Hauptfassade zum Hof.

Der Kollwitz-Platz mit dem Kollwitz-Denkmal ist noch immer ein beliebter Treffpunkt für Eltern und Kinder.

Right next door is the former workers' quarter of Prenzlauer Berg. This district has had an eventful history, being a hotbed of resistance even in the Weimar Republic, yet it is primarily the more recent history that we remember. In GDR times, the increasing number of apartments standing empty meant that it was possible for young people, intellectuals and artists, people who were seeking a different, non-conformist way of life to move in, subject to relatively little control. The Prenzlauer Berg in Berlin was the starting point for the uprising in the autumn of 1989.

Housing blocks in the Stargarder Straße: The prestigious exteriors of these buildings, built around 1900 by Alfred Messel and Paul Kolb, gave no hint of the wretched living conditions on the inside. Close by is the Gedzehnmaneh Church. 'Big Brother is watching you': Surveillance camera in the Grand Hotel in East Berlin, 1987.

The Friedenstempel synagogue was built in 1903-1904 by Johann Hoeniger at 53, Rykestraße. It was the only synagogue not to be destroyed by the Nazis. View of the main façade and courtyard from the gatehouse.

Kollwitz Square with the Kollwitz Memorial is still a popular meeting place for parents and children.

Big Brother is watching you: Überwachungskamera im Grand Hotel in Ostberlin 1987.

DDR-Volkspolizisten mit Streifenwagen und Motorrad in Berlin-Mitte 1984.

'Big Brother is watching you': Surveillance camera in the Grand Hotel in East Berlin, 1987.

Members of the People's Police with patrol car and motorcycle in Central Berlin, 1984.

1989 – DIE WELT BLICKT AUF BERLIN

1989 – THE EYES OF THE WORLD ARE ON BERLIN

Als am Abend des 9. November 1989 die Mauer fällt, können es Ost- und Westberliner kaum fassen. Das Wort des Augenblicks: »Wahnsinn, Wahnsinn!«. Die Menschen sind überwältigt. Sie weinen, feiern, liegen sich euphorisch in den Armen. Ganz Deutschland befindet sich im Ausnahmezustand, die Welt blickt auf Berlin.

Der 9. November war der Höhepunkt eines dramatischen Jahres: Als im Mai der Grenzzaun zwischen Ungarn und Österreich nach und nach abgebaut wurde, flohen in den darauffolgenden Monaten Tausende DDR-Bürger in den Westen. Im August kamen auf diese Weise an drei Tagen allein 15.000 Flüchtlinge in die Bundesrepublik. In der Bonner Botschaft in Prag und in der Ständigen Vertretung der Bundesrepublik in Ostberlin hielten sich jeweils mehr als 100 DDR-Bewohner auf, um ihre Ausreise zu erzwingen. Ungarn ließ im gleichen Monat 108 DDR-Bürger aus der Botschaft in Budapest nach Westdeutschland ausreisen. Der Höhepunkt der Flüchtlingsdramen: Am 30. September verkündete der bundesdeutsche Außenminister Hans-Dietrich Genscher nach zähen Verhandlungen die Ausreiseerlaubnis für 6.000 DDR-Bürger in der Prager Botschaft. Sie erhielten westdeutsche Pässe und durften offiziell ausreisen.

Auch innenpolitisch wankte das DDR-System. Nachdem Bürgerrechtsgruppen schon im Mai beim offiziellen Ergebnis der Kommunalwahlen – 98,5 Prozent für die SED -

Seite 308/309: Tanz auf der Mauer: Am 10. November 1989 feiern die Berliner die Öffnung der DDR-Grenzen.

When the Wall came down on the evening of 9 November 1989, East and West Berliners could hardly believe it. Everyone went around saying: 'Amazing, amazing!'. People were overwhelmed. They wept, celebrated, and embraced each other in delight. The whole of Germany was in a state of high excitement; the eyes of the world were on Berlin.

9 November was the climax of a dramatic year; in the months following May, as the border fence between Hungary and Austria was gradually demolished, thousands of East Germans fled to the West. In just three days in August, fifteen thousand refugees arrived in West Germany by this route. More than one hundred East Germans occupied both the West German embassy in Prague and the Permanent Mission in East Berlin, in order to force the authorities to permit them to leave the country. In the same month, Hungary allowed 108 East Germans to leave the embassy in Budapest for West Germany. The climax of the refugee drama came on 30 September when, after delicate negotiations, the West German Foreign Minister Hans Dietrich Genscher announced that six thousand East Germans occupying the embassy in Prague would be given West German passports and officially allowed to leave the country.

The East German internal political system was also tottering. Opposition pressure became stronger than ever after citizens' rights groups declared that the official

Pages 308/309: Dancing on the Wall: Berliners celebrate the opening up of East Germany's borders on 10 November 1989.

Wahlfälschungen nachgewiesen hatten, wurde der Druck der Opposition immer stärker. Inhaltliche Unterstützung erhielten sie dabei vom sowjetischen Staats- und Parteichef Michail Gorbatschow, der im Juni während eines Staatsbesuchs in Bonn verkündete: »Die Mauer kann wieder verschwinden, wenn die Voraussetzungen entfallen, die sie hervorgebracht haben.«

Die DDR-Bürger stimmten mit den Füßen ab. In Leipzig kamen ab September Tausende zu den »Montagsdemonstrationen«. Unter dem Motto »Wir sind das Volk« forderten sie Freiheit und Demokratie. Anfangs versuchten Sicherheitskräfte, die Kundgebungen niederzuschlagen, doch die großen Demonstrationen im Oktober mit über 100.000 Teilnehmern verliefen gewaltfrei. Am 18. Oktober trat Erich Honecker zurück.

Sein Nachfolger als Staatsratsvorsitzender wurde der Reformgegner Egon Krenz. Doch Michail Gorbatschow sollte Recht behalten: »Wer zu spät kommt, den bestraft das Leben.« Am 4. November demonstrierten eine Million DDR-Bürger in Ostberlin friedlich für demokratische Reformen und das Ende der SED-Herrschaft. Die Regierung konnte sich nicht mehr gegen die Realität stemmen: Fünf Tage später erklärte Politbüromitglied Günter Schabowski im DDR-Fernsehen, dass alle Bürger privat ins Ausland reisen dürften.

Mit diesem historischen Tag wurde die Mauer durchlässig. So kündigte sich mit dem größten Volksfest, das Berlin je gesehen hatte, die Wiedervereinigung Deutschlands im Oktober 1990 an.

result of the May local elections – 98.5 per cent for the Socialist Unity Party (SED) – had been rigged. They received support from the words of the Soviet Head of State and Party Leader Mikhail Gorbachov, who announced in June during a state visit to Bonn: 'The Wall can go when the conditions you have created no longer apply'.

The East Germans voted with their feet. From September onwards, thousands came to the 'Monday demonstrations' in Leipzig. With their rallying cry of 'Wir sind das Volk' ('we are the people'), they were demanding freedom and democracy. At first, the security forces tried to suppress the rallies, though the big demonstrations in October with over one hundred thousand participants passed off peacefully. Erich Honecker resigned on 18 October.

His successor as Head of State was Egon Krenz, an opponent of reform. But Mikhail Gorbachov's words were to prove correct: 'Life punishes those who arrive too late'.

On 4 November, a million East Germans held a peaceful demonstration in East Berlin in support of democratic reforms and the end of SED rule. The government was finally forced to face up to reality. Five days later, Günter Schabowski, a member of the Politbüro, announced on East German television that all citizens had permission to travel abroad for private purposes.

This was the historic day when the Wall was opened up. Berlin became the scene of public celebrations of mammoth proportions to mark Germany's reunification in October 1990.

DIE MAUER

Die traurige Bilanz der Mauer: 160 Kilometer innerdeutsche Grenze, 46 davon zwischen Ost- und Westberlin, 116 Wachtürme, 450.000 Quadratmeter Todesstreifen, 10.000 Grenzsoldaten, 5.000 Fluchtversuche und 239 Tote.

Die gewaltsame Teilung Berlins begann am 13. August 1961. Entgegen aller Beteuerungen der DDR-Regierung waren ab jetzt nur noch 13 Übergänge zwischen dem West- und Ostteil der Stadt geöffnet, DDR-Bürger durften nicht mehr im Westen arbeiten. Grenzsoldaten schlossen das symbolträchtige Brandenburger Tor. Schon bald gehörten Todesschüsse auf Flüchtlinge zur Geschichte des »antiimperialistischen Schutzwalls«, wie die Mauer in der Staatsterminologie der DDR genannt wurde.

Über die Jahre wurde die Mauer hochgerüstet: der »Todesstreifen« – ein Stück Niemandsland zwischen Ost und West, Selbstschussanlagen, Beobachtungstürme und Stacheldraht lassen jeden Fluchtversuch aus der DDR fast schon zwangsläufig scheitern.

Erst die Ostpolitik des bundesdeutschen Kanzlers Willy Brandt und später die vom sowjetischen Staatspräsidenten Michail Gorbatschow vorangetriebenen Reformen machten den »Eisernen Vorhang« (Winston Churchill) durchlässiger. Am 9. November 1989 ist es schließlich soweit: die Mauer fällt, die Wiedervereinigung der beiden deutschen Staaten kündigt sich an. Heute kann man nur noch einzelne Mauerstücke und Wachtürme besichtigen

Die Mauer im Wandel der Zeit: 1967 beim Ausbau der Sperranlagen an der Bernauer Straße in Ostberlin, 1989 mit Graffitis besprüht in Kreuzberg und 1990 während der handgreiflichen Demontage durch »Mauerspechte«.

THE WALL

The sorry facts and figures of the Wall: 160 km of internal German border, 46 of them between East and West Berlin; 116 watchtowers; 450,000 square metres of no-man's-land; 10,000 border guards; 5,000 escape attempts; 239 dead.

The forcible division of Berlin began on 13 August 1961. Contrary to everything the East German government claimed, only 13 crossing points between the Western and Eastern parts of the city remained open. East German citizens were no longer allowed to work in the West. Border guards closed the highly symbolic Brandenburg Gate. Shooting to kill refugees soon became part of the history of the 'anti-imperialist protecting wall', as it was known in official East German state terminology.

Over the years, the Wall became heavily armoured; the 'Todesstreifen' (a strip of no-man's-land between East and West), spring-gun emplacements, watchtowers, and barbed wire meant that any attempt to escape from East Germany was almost bound to fail.

First the 'Ostpolitik' of Federal Chancellor Willy Brandt, and later the reforms pushed through by Soviet President Mikhail Gorbachov, made Winston Churchill's 'iron curtain' less watertight. On 9 November 1989, it finally happened. The Wall came down; the reunification of the two German states was near. Now it is only possible to view a few watchtowers and pieces of wall.

Scenes charting the changing times of the Wall's history: In 1967, during the reinforcement of the frontier barriers in the Bernauer Straße in East Berlin; in 1989, sprayed with graffiti in the Kreuzberg district; and, in 1990, being forcibly dismantled by 'Wall-peckers'.

Vier Wochen im Herbst 1989:
Am 7. Oktober präsentieren sich die Spitzenfunktionäre der DDR während der Ehrenparade zum 40. Jahrestag der Staatsgründung auf der Tribüne in der Karl-Marx-Allee den Fotografen.
Am 4. November protestieren rund eine Million Menschen in Ostberlin für mehr Demokratie und Reisefreiheit.

Four weeks in autumn 1989:
On 7 October, leading GDR government officials on the VIP stand in Karl-Marx-Allee face the cameras during the parade of honour to mark the state's 40th anniversary.
On 4 November, around one million East Berliners stage a protest calling for more democracy and the freedom to travel.

Die Mauer wird Geschichte:
Die Mauer zwischen Kreuzberg und Treptow, um 1989.
Am 10. November 1989 besetzen Berliner aus beiden Teilen der Stadt die Mauer.
Am 12. November 1989 wird am Potsdamer Platz ein weiterer Grenzübergang geöffnet. DDR-Grenzsoldaten transportieren Mauersegmente ab.

The Wall becomes history:
The Wall between Kreuzberg and Treptow, around 1989.
On 10 November 1989, Berliners from both sectors of the city occupy the Wall.
On 12 November 1989, another frontier crossing-point is opened in Potsdam Square. GDR frontier soldiers begin removing sections of the Wall.

Am 10. November 1989 begrüßen Westberliner die Besucher aus Potsdam nach Öffnung des Grenzübergangs Glienicker Brücke.

On 10 November 1989, West Berliners welcome visitors from Potsdam following the opening of the Glienicker Brücke crossing-point.

Demonstranten fordern auf Transparenten im Dezember 1989 die Wiedervereinigung Deutschlands.

Demonstrators carrying placards in December 1989 calling for the reunification of Germany.

Die deutsche Einheit zum Greifen nah:
Nach Öffnung des Grenzübergangs am Brandenburger Tor am 22. Dezember 1989 schwingen die Menschen Flaggen von DDR und Bundesrepublik.

German unity almost a reality:
People waving GDR and Federal Republic flags after the opening of the frontier crossing-point at the Brandenburg Gate on 22 December 1989.

DIE NEUE HAUPTSTADT

THE NEW CAPITAL

An sich war es folgerichtig, nach der Wiedervereinigung den Sitz der Hauptstadt von Bonn nach Berlin zu verlagern. Bonn war nach dem Krieg bewusst als Provisorium eingerichtet worden, trotzdem entbrannte bald der Streit, ob nun Bonn Hauptstadt bleiben oder ob Regierung und Ministerien nach Berlin umziehen sollten. Die Wiedervereinigung war geschafft, doch nach der anfänglichen Euphorie traten auch die Probleme der neuen Situation zu Tage. Im Einigungsvertrag hatte man die Hauptstadtfrage noch ausgeklammert. Die Meinungen hierzu waren aber unterschiedlich: Die einen kämpften für Bonn, aus Kostengründen und wegen des föderalistischen Gedankens. Die anderen kämpften für Berlin, aus historischer Perspektive und wegen der Signalwirkung der geografischen Lage, nicht zuletzt im Hinblick auf die neuen Bundesländer. Die endgültige Entscheidung fiel am 20. Juni 1991. Nach fast elfstündiger leidenschaftlicher Debatte beschloss der Deutsche Bundestag mit 338 zu 220 Stimmen die Verlegung des Regierungssitzes nach Berlin.

Die Hauptstadtrolle war für Berlin nicht neu, doch die Kriegs- und Mauerjahre hatten die einst blühende Metropole ausgeblutet. Jetzt brachte ihr die Wende einen gigantischen Boom. Überall war Aufbruchstimmung. Berlin war wieder »in«, besonders bei der Jugend. 1989 zog die

On the whole, it was logical to move the capital from Bonn to Berlin after reunification. When Bonn was set up after the war it was always intended to be a provisional measure but, all the same, arguments soon broke out as to whether Bonn should now remain as the capital or whether the government and ministries should move to Berlin. Reunification had been achieved but, after the early euphoria, the problems of the new situation also surfaced.

In the treaty of union, the question of the capital had been ignored but opinions differed on this matter. Some fought for Bonn for reasons of cost and ideas of federalism. Others fought for Berlin from an historical perspective and because of the symbolic effect of its geographical situation, not least in respect of the former East German states. The final decision was taken on 20 June 1991. After almost eleven hours of passionate debate, the German Bundestag decided by 338 votes to 220 to move the seat of government to Berlin.

The role of capital city was not a new one for Berlin, but the war years and the Wall had sapped the life-blood of the once flourishing metropolis. Now the return brought with it a gigantic boom. Everywhere there was a feeling that it was time for a new departure. Berlin was 'in' again, especially with young people. In 1989, the first Love Parade saw 150 participants marching through the city; in 1996 it was

Seite 322/323: Demokratie im Großformat: Das Bundeskanzleramt erstreckt auf einer Grundstücksfläche von 71.000 Quadratmetern über 335 Meter bis zur Willy-Brandt-Straße im Tiergarten.

Pages 322/323: Democracy on a big scale: On a plot of land measuring 71,000 square metres, the Federal Chancellery extends over 335 metres right up to Willy-Brandt-Straße in the Tiergarten.

erste Love-Parade mit 150 Teilnehmern durch die Stadt, 1996 war sie mit über 750.000 Menschen die größte Party der Welt.

Wer auf sich hielt, ging nach Berlin. Die Prominenz aus Politik, Kultur und Wirtschaft zeigte sich oft und gerne in der Metropole, und große Unternehmen verlegten ihren Hauptsitz in die Hauptstadt. Innerhalb kurzer Zeit wurde Berlin zur größten Baustelle Europas. Ganze Stadtviertel wurden aus dem Boden gestampft. So wurde der Potsdamer Platz zu einem neuen lebendigen City-Quartier. Bedeutende Architekten wie Renzo Piano, Christian Kohlbecker, Richard Rogers, Arata Isozaki, Hans Kollhoff realisierten gigantische Bauprojekte, unter anderem für Daimler-Chrysler, Debis und Sony-Europa. Der Marlene-Dietrich-Platz knüpft heute mit Restaurants, Varieté, Kinos, einem Casino und dem Grand Hyatt Hotel an »goldene« Vorkriegszeiten an.

Ein besonderes Anliegen war Politikern wie Stadtplanern das Zentrum der politischen Macht. Der Bundestag übersiedelte in den Reichstag, der von dem Architekten Norman Foster mit einer neuen gewaltigen Glaskuppel versehen worden war. Das Bundeskanzleramt, an dessen Ausschreibung sich 836 Architekten beteiligt hatten, ging an das Berliner Büro von Axel Schultes und Charlotte Frank, und 1997 kam es zum ersten Spatenstich. 2001 war der Bau fertig, ein Regierungspalast, der Tempo und Erfolg signalisieren sollte. Inzwischen liegt um den Tiergarten ein Regierungs- und Botschaftsviertel mit zahlreichen repräsentativen Bauten bedeutender Architekten.

the biggest party in the world with over 750,000 people.

Everyone who thought they were anyone went to Berlin. Prominent people from the worlds of politics, culture, and economics enjoyed making regular appearances in the capital and large companies moved their head offices there. Within a short time, Berlin became the biggest building site in Europe. Whole districts were razed to the ground. As a result, the Potsdamer Platz became a new, lively, city-centre area, where important architects – Renzo Piano, Christian Kohlbecker, Richard Rogers, Arata Isozaki, Hans Kollhoff – carried out huge building projects for firms such as Daimler-Chrysler, Debis, and Sony Europe. Marlene-Dietrich-Platz, with its restaurants, variety theatres, cinemas, casino, and the Grand Hyatt Hotel, now forms a link with the pre-war 'golden' age.

Of particular concern to both politicians and town-planners was the centre of political power. The Bundestag moved into the Reichstag building, which the architect Norman Foster had furnished with a gigantic new glass cupola. Eight-hundred-and-thirty-six architects tendered for the Bundeskanzleramt (Chancellor's Office); the contract went to the Berlin firm of Axel Schultes and Charlotte Frank, with work beginning in 1997. The building was completed in 2001: a palace of government, intended as a symbol of speed and success. Meanwhile, the area around the Zoo has become an administrative and embassy district, with numerous buildings by major architects.

»Wrapped Reichstag«: Im Juni 1995 verhüllt das Künstlerehepaar Christo und Jeanne-Claude den Reichstag. Die beiden hatten fast 25 Jahre gebraucht, um das Projekt zu realisieren. Schließlich stimmten die verantwortlichen Politiker 1994 den Plänen zu. Der Materialaufwand belief sich auf 100.000 Quadratmeter Polyprophylen-Gewebe und 15.000 Meter Polyprophylen-Seil.
Christo und Jeanne-Claude: Verhüllter Reichstag, Berlin 1971-95. Foto: Wolfgang Volz, © Christo.

'Wrapped Reichstag': In June 1995, the artist-couple Christo and Jeanne-Claude enveloped the Reichstag in fabric. It took the pair of them almost 25 years to realize the project. The politicians in charge finally agreed to the plans in 1994. The project used 100,000 square metres of polypropylene fabric and 15,000 metres of polypropylene rope.
Christo and Jeanne-Claude: Wrapped Reichstag, Berlin 1971-95. Photo: Wolfgang Volz, © Christo.

Auf Betreiben der Großinvestoren wie Daimler-Chrysler, Deutsche Bahn oder Sony unterrichtete die Info-Box am Potsdamer Platz von 1995 bis 2000 mehr als acht Millionen Besucher über die Mega-Baustelle. Ende 2000 wurde sie abgerissen.

From 1995 to 2000, at the instigation of major investors such as Daimler-Chrysler, Deutsche Bahn (German State Railway), and Sony, the Info-Box on Potsdamer Platz informed over eight million visitors about the major construction site. At the end of 2000 it was torn down.

Die erste Loveparade 1989 war eine Geburtagsparty für den DJ Dr. Motte. 150 Teilnehmer zogen auf einem Wagen zu Acid House Music über den Kurfürstendamm. Das Motto: »Friede, Freude, Eierkuchen«.

An der Loveparade 2002 nahmen rund 500.000 Menschen teil. Auf 45 Lovetrucks wurden sie mit einer Million Watt beschallt.

The first 'Love Parade' in 1989 was a birthday party for the DJ, Dr. Motte. The 150 participants wended their way along the Kurfürstendamm to the sound of Acid House Music. Their slogan: 'Friede, Freude, Eierkuchen' ('Peace, Joy, Pancakes').

At least 500,000 people took part in the 2002 Love Parade. They moved through the city on 45 love floats to a megawatt wall of sound.

Berlin bei Nacht: Die junge Szene trifft sich in Berlin-Mitte. Beliebte Treffpunkte sind der Technoclub »Eimer« in der Rosenthaler Straße (links), die Hackeschen Höfe (Mitte) oder die Oranienburger Straße (rechts).

Berlin by night: The young set meets in the centre of Berlin. The Eimer techno club in Rosenthaler Straße (left), the Hackeschen Höfe (centre), and Oranienburger Straße (right) are popular meeting places.

POTSDAMER PLATZ

Die Geschichte des Potsdamer Platzes begann mit dem Bau des Potsdamer Bahnhofs im Jahr 1838. Die beschauliche Straßenkreuzung wuchs in kurzer Zeit zu einem pulsierenden Knotenpunkt des Großstadtlebens. Ab 1900 blühte hier eine lebhafte Vergnügungskultur mit zahlreichen Hotels, Restaurants und Cafés, unter ihnen das »Hotel Esplanade«, das »Weinhaus Huth« und das »Café Josty«, die heute wieder zu den Attraktionen des Potsdamer Platzes gehören.

Der in den Goldenen Zwanziger Jahren verkehrsreichste Platz Europas wurde im Zweiten Weltkrieg zu 80 % zerstört.

In den Folgejahren symbolisierte der Potsdamer Platz den schwierigen Verlauf der deutschen Geschichte. Seine Lage zwischen dem amerikanischen, britischen und russischen Sektor zerstörte die gewachsenen Strukturen. Teilung und Mauerbau machten den Potsdamer Platz zu einem Sperrbezirk in der Mitte Berlins.

Mit dem Fall der Mauer 1989 wurde der Potsdamer Platz zur größten Baustelle Europas. Hier entstand unter der Leitung von Renzo Piano und Christoph Kohlbecker auf 68.000 Quadratmetern ein beeindruckendes Ensemble postmoderner Architektur. Dazu gehört das 2000 eröffnete Sony Center am Kemperplatz, in das der Kaisersaal und das Frühstückszimmer des alten »Hotel Esplanade« integriert wurden. Die Panoramaplattform des Kollhoff-Gebäudes gewährt einen beeindruckenden Blick auf die neue Metropole Berlin.

Ort der Superlative: Vom verkehrsreichsten Platz Europas in den 1920ern zur größten Baustelle in den 1990ern.

POTSDAMER PLATZ

The history of Potsdamer Platz began with the building of Potsdamer Bahnhof in 1838. From a peaceful crossroads it quickly grew into a pulsating nerve centre of metropolitan life. From 1900 onwards, a lively entertainment culture flourished here with numerous hotels, restaurants and cafés, among them the Hotel Esplanade, Weinhaus Huth, and Café Josty which once again feature among the attractions of Potsdamer Platz.

During the Second World War, 80 per cent of what had been the busiest square in Europe in the golden days of the twenties was destroyed. In the years that followed, Potsdamer Platz symbolized the problematic course of German history. Because it was situated between the American, British, and Russian sectors, its organic structure was destroyed. The division of the city and the building of the Wall made Potsdamer Platz a no-go area in the centre of Berlin.

When the Wall came down in 1989, Potsdamer Platz became the biggest building site in Europe. Under the direction of Renzo Piano and Christoph Kohlbecker, an impressive ensemble of post-modernist buildings was created, extending over sixty-eight thousand square metres. One of these is the Sony-Center in the Kemperplatz, opened in 2000, which incorporates the Kaisersaal and the breakfast room of the old Hotel Esplanade. The viewing platform of the Kollhoff building affords a magnificent panorama of the new metropolis of Berlin.

The square of superlatives: From Europe's busiest transit point in the 1920s to the biggest building site in the 1990s.

»Herausragendes Beispiel europäischen Städtebaus«: Auf der internationalen Immobilienmesse in Barcelona erhält das Gesamtprojekt Potsdamer Platz den ersten Preis. Mitte der 1990er Jahre entstand hier aus dem durch den Zweiten Weltkrieg und den Mauerbau verödeten Areal ein neuer Stadtteil.

'An outstanding example of European urban construction': At the international real estate fair in Barcelona, the whole Potsdamer Platz project is awarded first prize. In the mid-1990s, a new part of the city rose up here from the area of desolation left after the Second World War and the construction of the Wall.

Der neue Reichstag: Nach Entwürfen von Sir Norman Foster wurde von 1996 bis 1999 ein Gebäude realisiert, dass mit seiner gläsernen Kuppel die Transparenz der demokratischen Vorgänge symbolisieren soll.

The new Reichstag: Based on designs by Sir Norman Foster, the years between 1996 and 1999 saw the construction of a building that, with its glass cupola, is intended to symbolize the transparency of the democratic process.

Architektur für das 21. Jahrhundert: Das debis-Gebäude am Tiergarten nach Plänen von Renzo Piano (links) und das Sony-Center von Architekt Helmut Jahn. Sein Credo: »Glauben an Fortschritt durch Technologie«.

Architecture for the 21st century: The Debis building in the Tiergarten from plans by Renzo Piano (left) and the Sony-Center by architect Helmut Jahn. His motto: 'Believe in progress through technology'.

Straßenhandel: Auf den so genannten »Polenmärkten« verkauften in den 1980er Jahren eingereiste polnische Bürger Waren aus Ost-Produktion gegen DM, um dann Westwaren einzukaufen. Bis zum Fall der Mauer waren sie Anlass für ausländerfeindliche Ressentiments.

Street trade: In the 1980s, on what are known as 'Polish markets', people who had travelled from Poland to Berlin sold goods made in Eastern Europe in exchange for Deutsch marks, which they then used to buy goods made in the west. Until the Berlin Wall fell, this engendered anti-foreigner resentment.

Das neue Gesicht der Friedrichstraße: ein zentrales Element der »Friedrichstadt-Passagen« bildet die von 1994 bis 1996 errichtete Galéries Lafayette. Das erste französische Kaufhaus Berlins gestaltete der Architekt Jean Nouvel.

The new face of Friedrichstraße: Galéries Lafayette, built between 1994 and 1996, forms a central element of the Friedrichstadt Arcades. The architect Jean Nouvel designed Berlin's first French department store.

Blick auf das Parlaments- und Regierungsviertel am Spreebogen: Axel Schultes und Charlotte Frank konzipieren die Bauten der Bundesregierung als Ost-West-Verbindung über den Spreebogen – es entsteht das »Band des Bundes«.

View of the parliament and government quarter at Spreebogen: Axel Schultes and Charlotte Frank's design conceived the German government buildings as a link between east and west, threading through Spreebogen and giving rise to the 'Band des Bundes' (German Government Row).

REGIERUNGSVIERTEL

Das ehemalige Regierungsviertel um den Tiergarten ist jetzt wieder politisches Zentrum der Bundesrepublik Deutschland. Der von dem britischen Star-Architekten Norman Foster neu gestaltete Reichstag und das 2001 fertiggestellte Bundeskanzleramt der Berliner Architekten Axel Schultes und Charlotte Frank sind nur seine Höhepunkte. Es sind zahlreiche neue Bundesgebäude entstanden, die als »Band des Bundes« über die Spree hinweg angelegt wurden, sozusagen als Sinnbild für die Verbindung von Ost und West, darunter das Paul-Löbe-Haus (Alsenblock) im Spreebogen, das Jakob-Kaiser-Haus (Dorotheenblöcke) und das Marie-Elisabeth-Lüders-Haus (Luisenblock). Die Namen der gigantischen Verwaltungskomplexe erinnern nicht nur an verdiente ehemalige Mitglieder des Reichstages und des Bundestages, sondern auch an die alten Stadtquartiere, die der Neugestaltung weichen mussten.

Schon zur NS-Zeit befand sich am Tiergarten auch das Diplomatenviertel mit zahlreichen repräsentativen Botschaftsgebäuden. Im Krieg wurden viele der Gebäude zerstört. Zu DDR-Zeiten wurden sie als Wohngebäude genutzt oder sind einfach verfallen. Inzwischen ist im Klingelhöferdreieck zwischen Stülerstraße, Klingelhöferstraße und Landwehrkanal ein neues Botschaftsviertel mit eindrucksvollen Bauten renommierter Architekten entstanden.

Die Waschmaschine der Nation: Das Bundeskanzleramt in der Willy-Brandt-Str. 1 wurde nach Plänen von Axel Schultes und Charlotte Frank von 1997 bis 2001 errichtet.

 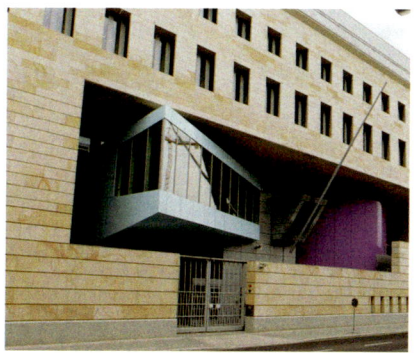

Spreebogen international: Mexikanische Botschaft, erbaut 1997 bis 2000 und Britische Botschaft, erbaut 1998 bis 2000.

International Spreebogen: Mexican Embassy, built between 1997 and 2000, and the British Embassy, built between 1998 and 2000.

THE GOVERNMENT DISTRICT

The old government district around the Tiergarten is now once again the political centre of the Federal Republic of Germany. The new Reichstag building created by the famous British architect Norman Foster and the Federal Chancellor's Office completed in 2001 by Berlin architects Axel Schultes and Charlotte Frank are just two of its crowning glories. Many other new government buildings have sprung up, their layout planned in such a way as to form a 'Band of the Federation' extending across the Spree and symbolizing the joining of East and West. Among these are the Paul-Löbe-Haus (Alsenblock), situated on the bend of the Spree river, the Jakob-Kaiser-Haus (Dorotheen-blocks), and the Marie-Elisabeth-Lüders-Haus (Luisenblock). The names of these huge administrative complexes commemorate not only former members of the Reichstag and Federal Parliament but also old parts of the city, which have had to make way for new buildings.

During the Nazi period, the diplomatic quarter with all its embassies was also situated in the Tiergarten area. During the war, many of the buildings were destroyed. During the days of the GDR, they were turned into apartments or simply left to fall into disrepair. Meanwhile, a new Embassy district has emerged in the Klingelhöfer triangle area between Stülerstraße, Klingelhöferstraße, and Landwehrkanal, boasting impressive buildings designed by famous architects.

The nation's washing machine: The Federal Chancellery at Willy-Brandt-Str. 1 was built to plans by Axel Schultes and Charlotte Frank between 1997 and 2001.

Die Kulturhauptstadt: Frank Castorfs Volksbühne am Rosa-Luxemburg-Platz, das alternative Kulturzentrum »Tacheles« in der Oranienburger Straße und die Hackeschen Höfe.

The Culture Capital: Frank Castorf's Volksbühne theatre at Rosa-Luxemburg-Platz, the Tacheles alternative cultural centre in Oranienburger Straße, and the Hackesche Höfe.

Der amerikanische Architekt Daniel Libeskind sieht in dem von ihm entworfenen Jüdischen Museum ein »Sinnbild der Hoffnung«. Das dekonstruktivistische Gebäude wurde von 1992 bis 1999 in der Kreuzberger Lindenstraße errichtet.

The American architect Daniel Libeskind sees the Jewish Museum he designed as being a 'symbol of hope'. The deconstructionist building was built between 1992 and 1999 in the Kreuzberger Lindenstraße.

DAS WAHRZEICHEN BERLINS

Das Brandenburger Tor gehört seit über zweihundert Jahren zum Stadtbild Berlins. Während dieser Zeit war es Schauplatz und Symbol historischer Ereignisse. Das 1791 fertig gestellte klassizistische Bauwerk war eines von siebzehn Stadttoren in der Zollmauer. Da sein Erbauer Carl Gotthard Langhals der Idee König Friedrich Wilhelm II. Rechnung trug und das Tor als Kopie der Akropolis-Proyläen in Athen baute, blieb es nicht nur als imposanter Zugang zur wichtigsten Stadt Preußens erhalten, sondern auch als beeindruckender Abschluss der Lindenallee. Zwanzig Reliefs in den Bögen zeugten von den Heldentaten Friedrichs. Sie wurden, ebenso wie die Quadriga mit Friedensgöttin von Johann Gottfried Schadow geschaffen. Als Napoleon 1806 im Triumphzug nach Berlin einmarschierte nahm er die Figurengruppe mit. Nach den Befreiungskriegen kam sie 1814 wieder zurück auf ihren Platz. Zuvor wurde die Friedensgöttin von Schinkel noch mit Adlerstab und eisernem Kreuz ausgestattet und zur Siegesgöttin umgedeutet.

Der Naziterror hielt 1933 mit einem Fackelzug durch das Tor in Berlin Einzug. Der sich anschließende Krieg führte zur Teilung Deutschlands. Bis Dezember 1989 verlief hier die

200 Jahre Berliner Markenzeichen: das im klassizistischen Stil erbaute Brandenburger Tor Anfang des 19. Jahrhunderts und in den 1990ern.

THE EMBLEM OF BERLIN

The Brandenburg Gate has been part of Berlin's cityscape for over two hundred years. Throughout this time it was the scene and symbol of many historic events. This neoclassical structure, completed in 1791, was one of seventeen gates in the city wall. When designing the gate, Carl Gotthard Langhals bore in mind King Friedrich Wilhelm II's idea of building the gateway as a replica of the Propylaea, the ceremonial entrance to the Acropolis in Athens. Consequently, it has been preserved ever since, not only as an imposing entrance to Prussia's most important city but also as an impressive terminal point to the Lindenallee. Twenty reliefs in the arches bore witness to Friedrich's heroic exploits. Like the Quadriga with its goddess of peace, they were created by Johann Gottfried Schadow. When in 1806 Napoleon marched in triumphal procession into Berlin, he took the group of figures away with him. After the German Wars of Liberation, the statue was returned to its rightful place in 1814, but not before Schinkel had given the goddess of peace the sword of the German Eagle and the iron cross, thereby transforming her into the goddess of victory.

Two hundred years of the symbol of Berlin: the Brandenburg Gate, built in the neoclassical style, at the beginning of the nineteenth century and in the 1990s.

Grenze zwischen den beiden deutschen Staaten, das Brandenburger Tor wurde zugemauert. Zum Jahreswechsel 1989/1990 erstürmten Deutsche aus Ost und West das Tor. Seitdem ist auch die bekannteste der Berliner Prachtstraßen wieder von Westen her zu erreichen: Unter den Linden. Der große Kurfürst hatte die Allee als bequemen Reitweg von seinem Schloss zum Jagdrevier im Tiergarten anlegen lassen. Sechs Reihen mit Linden- und Nussbäumen säumten die Straße, die ihren Namen daher ableitet. Schon ein Jahrhundert später wurde sie um Oper, Bibliothek, Palais und Kathedrale erweitert und nach den Befreiungskriegen von 1813-1815 mit Standbildern und Monumentalbauten zur »Via Triumphalis« ausgebaut. Lange galt Unter den Linden als die Promeniermeile in Berlin. Der Zweite Weltkrieg hinterließ auch hier eine Schneise der Zerstörung. In den 50er und 60er Jahren wurden die Fassaden der Monumentalbauten wieder hergerichtet.

Aufmarsch von rechts und links: Die Prachtstraße Unter den Linden war für Nationalsozialisten wie Kommunisten ideal für ihre Paraden.

Marching from right to left: Both the National Socialists and the Communists found the monumental street of Unter den Linden the perfect place for their parades.

In 1933, a torch-lit procession through the Brandenburg Gate brought the terror of Nazi rule to Berlin. The subsequent war led to the division of Germany. Until December 1989, the border between the two German states ran through here, with the Brandenburg Gate being sealed off. At the end of 1989 and beginning of 1990, both East and West Germans stormed the Quadriga, thus reopening the western entrance to Berlin's best-known boulevard: Unter den Linden. Friedrich Wilhelm, known as the Great Elector, had had the boulevard laid out as a bridle path connecting his castle to the hunting ground in Tiergarten park. Six rows of nut and linden trees line the street, giving it its name. Just a century later, the opera house, library, palace, and cathedral were added to the avenue and, after the German Wars of Liberation from 1813-1815, it was developed into a 'Via Triumphalis' with statues and grand buildings.

For a long time, Unter den Linden was thought of as Berlin's mile-long promenade. Here, too, the Second World War left a swathe of destruction, the façades of the grand buildings being restored in the 1950s and 60s.

Mega-Marathon: 1992 laufen rund 18.000 Menschen durchs Brandenburger Tor.

Mega-Marathon: In 1992, at least 18,000 people ran through the Brandenburg Gate.

CHRONIK

1237	erste urkundliche Erwähnung der Siedlung Cölln; offizielles Gründungsdatum Berlins.
1244	Berlin erstmals urkundlich aufgeführt.
1307	20. März: Markgraf Hermann bestätigt die Union zwischen Berlin und Cölln.
1432	Zusammenschluss Berlins und Cöllns zu einer Stadt.
1451	Friedrich II. ruft Berlin/Cölln als kurfürstliche Residenz aus.
1616-48	Berlin und Brandenburg leiden unter dem 30jährigen Krieg. Als Folge von Pest und Hungersnöten hat Berlin/Cölln am Ende des Krieges nur noch 6.000 Einwohner.
1685	Friedrich Wilhelm I. nimmt nach der Aufhebung des Ediktes von Nantes in Frankreich verfolgte Hugenotten auf (Edikt von Potsdam).
1700	Gottfried Wilhelm Leibniz erster Präsident der neu gegründeten Akademie der Wissenschaften.
1701	Kurfürst Friedrich III.: Krönung zum König in Preußen als Friedrich I.; Grundsteinlegung des Deutschen und des Französischen Doms.
1735	Die Einwohnerzahl steigt auf ca. 90.000 an.
1747	Grundsteinlegung zum Dombau am Lustgarten.
ab 1780	Am Französischen und Deutschen Dom auf dem Gendarmenmarkt werden Turmbauten unter der Leitung von Karl von Gontard durchgeführt.
1788-91	Belvedere im Schlosspark Charlottenburg wird durch Carl Gotthard Langhans gebaut; ebenso das Brandenburger Tor, das Johann Gottfried Schadow mit der Quadriga krönt.
1806	Napoleon zieht mit seinem Heer in Berlin ein. Ende des Heiligen Römischen Reichs Deutscher Nation.

CHRONOLOGY

1237	Cölln first mentioned in written records; official date of Berlin's founding.
1244	First mention of Berlin in written records.
1307	20 March, Margrave Hermann acknowledges union between Berlin and Cölln.
1432	Amalgamation of Berlin and Cölln into a single town.
1451	Friedrich II designates Berlin/Cölln a royal seat.
1616-48	Berlin and Brandenburg suffer the effects of the 30 Years' War. By the end of the war, there are only 6,000 people left in Berlin/Cölln as a result of the ravages of plague and starvation.
1685	Friedrich Wilhelm I offers refuge to persecuted Huguenots following France's revocation of the Edict of Nantes (Edict of Potsdam).
1700	Gottfried Wilhelm Leibniz becomes first president of the newly established Academy of Sciences.
1701	Elector Friedrich III: Coronation as Friedrich I, King of Prussia; Lays the foundation stones of the German and French Cathedrals.
1735	Number of inhabitants rises to almost 90,000.
1747	The foundation stones of the Dom building at the Lustgarten are laid.
From 1780	Building work begins on tower structures of the German and French Cathedrals in Gendarmenmarkt Square, under the supervision of Karl von Gontard.
1788-91	Belvedere in Schlosspark Charlottenburg is built by Carl Gotthard Langhans; also the Brandenburg Gate, which Johann Gottfried Schadow crowned with the Quadriga.
1806	Napoleon and his troops march into Berlin. End of the Holy Roman Empire's German nation.

1809	Die Selbstverwaltung der Städte wird durch Heinrich Friedrich Karl Reichsfreiherr vom und zum Stein reformiert.	1809	Reforms of the city's self-government are implemented by Heinrich Friedrich Karl Reichsfreiherr vom und zum Stein.
1810	Wilhelm von Humboldt gründet die Friedrich-Wilhelms-Universität.	1810	Friedrich Wilhelms University founded by Wilhelm von Humboldt.
1848	Blutige Auseinandersetzungen zwischen Bürgern und Militär während der Märzrevolution.	1848	Bloody battles between workers and militia occur during the March Revolution.
1856	Erstes Wasserwerk und städtische Wasserleitungen.	1856	First waterworks and municipal water supply system are built.
1861	Vergrößerung Berlins durch Eingemeindung von Wedding, Tempelhof, Gesundbrunnen, dem nördlichen Teil von Moabit und Schöneberg	1861	Berlin increases in size after the incorporation of Wedding, Tempelhof, Gesundbrunnen, and the northern part of Moabit and Schöneberg.
1871	Wilhelm I. wird deutscher Kaiser (Proklamation in Versailles) mit Bismarck als Reichskanzler; Berlin wird Reichshauptstadt.	1871	Wilhelm I is proclaimed German Emperor (Proclamation in Versailles) with Bismarck as Reichskanzler (Imperial Chancellor); Berlin becomes the capital of the Empire.
1877	Erstmals liegt die Einwohnerzahl Berlin über einer Million.	1877	The number of residents in Berlin tops one million for the first time.
1883	Gründung der »Allgemeinen Electrizitätgesellschaft« (AEG) durch Emil Rathenau.	1883	Emil Rathenau forms the Allgemeine Elektrizitätsgesellschaft (General Electric Company) (AEG).
1894	Einweihung des Reichstagsgebäudes von Paul Wallot.	1894	Opening of the Reichstag building by Paul Wallot.
1907	Das KaDeWe (Kaufhaus des Westens) und das Hotel Adlon werden eröffnet.	1907	The KaDeWe (Kaufhaus des Westens) and Hotel Adlon open their doors.
1914-18	Erster Weltkrieg, der durch die Revolution und die Abdankung des Kaisers am 9. November 1918 beendet wird.	1914-18	First World War, which ends in revolution and the abdication of the Kaiser on 9 November 1918.
1919	Spartakusaufstand. Ermordung von Rosa Luxemburg und Karl Liebknecht. Aufhebung des Dreiklassenwahlrechts am 24. Januar; Versailler Vertrag; Ende des Ersten Weltkriegs am 28. Juni.	1919	Spartacus revolt; Murder of Rosa Luxemburg and Karl Liebknecht.
1920	Kapp-Putsch.	1920	Kapp putsch.
1923	Höhepunkt und Ende der Inflation; Erste Rundfunksendungen.	1923	Inflation reaches its peak and ends; First radio broadcasts.
1924	Bau des Flughafens Tempelhof.Erste Funkausstellung.	1924	First radio exhibition; Building of Tempelhof airport.

1926	Eröffnung des Funkturms; Goebbels wird Gauleiter der NSDAP in Berlin-Brandenburg.	1926	Opening of the radio tower; Goebbels appointed NSDAP Gauleiter of Berlin-Brandenburg.
1932	Die letzten freien Reichstagswahlen führen am 6. November zur Absetzung der preußischen Regierung.	1932	The last free German elections on 6 November lead to the demise of the Prussian Government.
1933	Am 30. Januar ernennt Reichspräsident Hindenburg Hitler zum Reichskanzler; Fackelzug der SA durch das Brandenburger Tor. 10 Mai: Bücherverbrennung auf dem Platz vor der Berliner Universität.	1933	On 30 January, President Hindenburg appoints Hitler Chancellor of the German Reich; SA marches through the Brandenburg Gate in a torchlight procession; 10 May: Burning of books in the square in front of Berlin University.
1934	Hitler lässt in Berlin unter der Leitung von Joseph Goebbels SA-Konkurrenten ermorden (»Röhm-Putsch«).	1934	Hitler has Joseph Goebbels organize the murder of SA rivals ('Röhm putsch').
1936	XI. Olympischen Sommerspiele im Berliner Olympiastadion.	1936	Berlin hosts the 11th Olympic Summer Games at the Olympic Stadium.
1937	Albert Speer wird von Hitler zum »Generalbauinspektor für die Reichshauptstadt Berlin« ernannt und mit der Neugestaltung Berlins beauftragt.	1937	Albert Speer is appointed 'General Building Inspector of the Reich's capital, Berlin' and as the international capital of 'Germania'.
1938	9./10 November: Pogromnacht, Zerstörung von Synagogen und jüdischen Geschäften.	1938	9/10 November: Mobs destroy synagogues and Jewish businesses.
1939	Beginn des Zweiten Weltkrieges mit dem Einmarsch in Polen.	1939	Start of World War 2 after German invasion of Poland.
1940	Berlin wird Ziel erster britischer Luftangriffe.	1940	Berlin becomes the target of British bombs.
1943	Goebbels ruft nach der Niederlage von Stalingrad im Berliner Sportpalast den »totalen Krieg« aus.	1943	Following the defeat at Stalingrad, Goebbels, in a speech at Berlin's Sport Palace, calls for 'total war'.
1944	20. Juli: missglücktes Attentat auf Hitler. Die Anführer der Widerstandsgruppe um Oberst Graf von Stauffenberg werden erschossen.	1944	20 July: Assassination attempt on Hitler fails; ringleaders of the attempted coup, led by Count von Stauffenberg, are executed.
1945	Am 2. Mai erobert die Sowjetarmee Berlin; am 8. Mai im sowjetischen Hauptquartier in Berlin-Karlshorst kapituliert die Wehrmacht; am 5. Juni beziehen die Kommandaturen ihre Quartiere in den vier Besatzungszonen.	1945	On 2 May, the Soviet Army enters Berlin; the Wehrmacht surrenders on 8 May at the Soviet headquarters in Berlin-Karlshorst; on 5 June, the Allied Commanders occupy their headquarters in the four occupation zones.
1948	18. Juni: Währungsreform in Westdeutschland; in der Nacht zum 24. Juni wird die einzige Schienenverbindung zwischen Helmstedt und Berlin durch die Sowjetische Militäradministration unterbrochen; Beginn der sowjetischen Blockade Berlins,	1948	18 June: Currency reform in West Germany; during the night of 23/24 June, the Soviet military authorities close the only rail link between Helmstedt and Berlin; start of the Soviet blockade: Western Allies set up the air

	Einrichtung der Luftbrücke durch die Westalliierten; 24. Juni: Auch in den Westsektoren Berlins wird die West-mark eingeführt.		bridge; 24 June: The West mark is extended to include the Western sectors of Berlin.
1949	23. Mai: Die Sowjets brechen die Blockade ab. Bonn wird Hauptstadt der am 23. Mai gegründeten Bundesrepublik Deutschland; das Grundgesetz wird unter Einbeziehung von »Groß-Berlin« als Verfassung in Kraft gesetzt; Ostberlin wird am 7. Oktober Hauptstadt der Deutschen Demokratischen Republik.	1949	23 May: The Soviets end the blockade. Bonn becomes the capital of the newly formed Federal Republic of German; the Basic Law comes into force as the country's Constitution, also incorporating 'Greater Berlin'; Democratic Republic (GDR).
1953	17. Juni: Volksaufstand in der DDR, wird durch sowjetische Truppen blutig niedergeschlagen.	1953	17 June: Popular uprising in the GDR is quashed by Soviet forces in bloody battles.
1956	Marienfelde ist Notaufnahme-/Durchgangslager für über 1 Mio. Flüchtlinge aus der DDR.	1956	Marienfelde becomes an emergency transitcamp for over one million refugees fleeing the GDR.
1961	Am 13. August beginnt die Nationale Volksarmee und die Volkspolizei mit dem Mauerbau in Berlin und der Abriegelung der Demarkationslinie durch Stacheldrahtzäune und Minenfelder.	1961	On 13 August, the National People's Army and People's Police start building the Berlin Wall and seal off the demarcation lines of the occupation zones with barbed wire fences and minefields.
1963	US-Präsident John F. Kennedy besucht Westberlin.	1963	US President John F Kennedy visits West Berlin.
1967	Erste Studentenunruhen; 2. Juni: Benno Ohnesorg wird von einem Polizisten bei einer Demonstration erschossen.	1967	Beginnings of student unrest, 2 June: Benno Ohnesorg shot dead by a policeman during a demonstration.
1968	11. April: Attentat auf Rudi Dutschke, den führenden Kopf des Sozialistischen Deutschen Studentenbundes.	1968	11 April: Rudi Dutschke, leader of the Socialist German Student League, assassinated.
1971/72	Besuchsregelungen für Westberliner nach Ostberlin und in die DDR werden gelockert; das Vier-Mächte-Abkommen bringt deutliche Verbesserungen im Transitverkehr zwischen der Bundesrepublik und Westberlin.	1971/72	Relaxation of travel regulations for West Berliners visiting East Berlin and the GDR; the Four-Power Agreement leads to distinct improvements in transit traffic between the Federal Republic and West Berlin.
1976	Palast der Republik wird eröffnet; Wolf Biermann wird während einer Tournee durch die BRD ausgebürgert.	1976	Palace of the Republic opened; Wolf Biermann is banned from returning home while on a tour of the Federal Republic.
1989	22. Dezember: Öffnung des Brandenburger Tores.	1989	22 December: Opening of the Brandenburg Gate.
1990	3. Oktober: Wiedervereinigung Deutschlands.	1990	3 October: Reunification of Germany.
1999	Am 12. Juli zieht der Deutsche Bundestag in das umgebaute Reichstagsgebäude.	1999	On 12 July, the German Bundestag moves to the restored Reichstag building.
2001	Einweihung des Bundeskanzleramtes am 2. Mai.	2001	Inauguration of the Federal Chancellor's Office on 2 May.

**How Did We
Find Out About
Lasers?**

The "HOW DID WE FIND OUT—?" series
by *Isaac Asimov*

HOW DID WE FIND OUT

The Earth Is Round?
About Electricity?
About Numbers?
About Dinosaurs?
About Germs?
About Vitamins?
About Comets?
About Energy?
About Atoms?
About Nuclear Power?
About Outer Space
About Earthquakes?
About Black Holes?
About Our Human Roots?
About Antarctica?
About Oil?
About Coal?

About Solar Power?
About Volcanoes?
About Life in the Deep Sea?
About the Beginning of Life?
About the Universe?
About Genes?
About Computers?
About Robots?
About the Atmosphere?
About DNA?
About the Speed of Light?
About Blood?
About Sunshine?
About the Brain?
About Superconductivity?
About Microwaves?
About Photosynthesis?

About Lasers?

How Did We Find Out About Lasers?

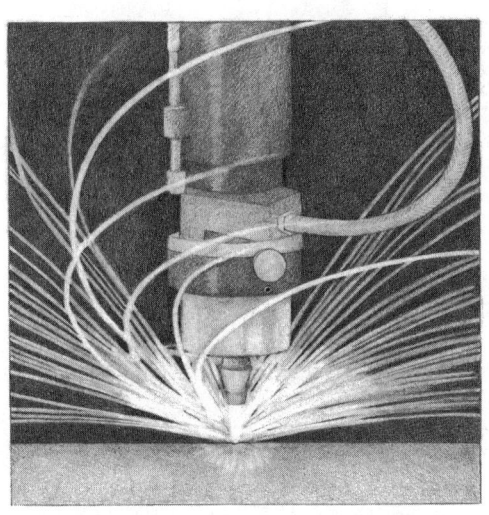

Isaac Asimov

Illustrated by Erika Kors

Walker and Company
New York

Copyright © 1990 by Isaac Asimov

All rights reserved. No part of this book may be
reproduced or transmitted in any form or by any means,
electronic or mechanical, including photocopying,
recording, or by any information storage and retrieval
system, without permission in writing from the Publisher.

First published in the United States of America in 1990
by the Walker Publishing Company, Inc.

Published simultaneously in Canada by Thomas Allen & Son
Canada, Limited, Markham, Ontario.

Library of Congress Cataloging-in-Publication Data

Asimov, Isaac
   How did we find out about lasers? / Isaac Asimov; illustrated by
Erika Kors.
     p.   cm.—(The "How did we find out—?" series)
   Summary: Discusses lasers, how they work, and their many uses.
   ISBN 0-8027-6935-7.—ISBN 0-8027-6936-5 (lib. bdg.)
   1. Lasers—Juvenile literature. [1. Lasers.] I. Kors, Erika
W., ill. II. Title. III. Series: Asimov, Isaac, 1920– How did we
find out—series.
TA1682.A85   1990
621.36'6—dc20   89-21515
                                                                         CIP
                                                                           AC

Printed in the United States of America

10 9 8 7 6 5 4 3 2 1

Dedicated to the memory of:
Nicholas Repanes (1918–1989)
Harold C. Horsley (1918–1989)

Contents

1	Waves	9
2	Radiation and Energy	17
3	Masers	25
4	Lasers	37
5	The Uses of Lasers	47
	Index	61

1
Waves

THE LIGHT WE see consists of a stream of tiny waves. It takes about fifty thousand of these *light waves* to stretch across the distance of an inch. That means that each wave is about 1/50,000 of an inch long. This is a *wavelength*.

Before we go any further, let's describe the wavelengths without using inches. We use inches here in the United States, but everywhere else in the world, *meters* (MEE-terz) are used. Scientists everywhere, even in the United States, use meters.

One meter is equal to 39.37 inches, or about 3¼ feet. That is a pretty long distance, but meters can be divided into smaller units, just as we can divide yards into feet and feet into inches. A yard is divided into three feet, and a foot is divided into twelve inches. A meter, though, is always divided by even numbers such as ten, or a hundred, or a thousand. That is what makes the *metric system* (MET-rik) more sensible than the one we use.

So we have:

1 *centimeter* (SENT-ih-MEE-ter) = 1/100 of a meter, or about 2/5 of an inch.

1 *millimeter* (MIL-ih-MEE-ter) = 1/1000 of a meter, or about 1/25 of an inch.

1 *micrometer* (MIKE-roh-MEE-ter) = 1/1000 of a millimeter, or 1 millionth of a meter.

1 *nanometer* (NAN-oh-MEE-ter) = 1/1000 of a micrometer, or 1 billionth of a meter.

A light wave is about 500 nanometers long. That's the same as saying 1/50,000 of an inch, but scientists all over the world prefer to use nanometers.

Of course, not all light waves have the same length. Some are a little longer, some a little shorter. We can tell the difference just by looking, because light waves of different lengths produce light that seems of different colors to our eyes.

The longest wavelengths that we see look deep red to us. Those wavelengths are 780 nanometers. The shortest wavelengths we see look deep violet to us, and those are 390 nanometers. In between are the other colors: orange, yellow, green, and blue.

Each color has a small spread of wavelengths and, as the wavelengths change, the colors fade into one another. There are no sharp divisions. If we make a

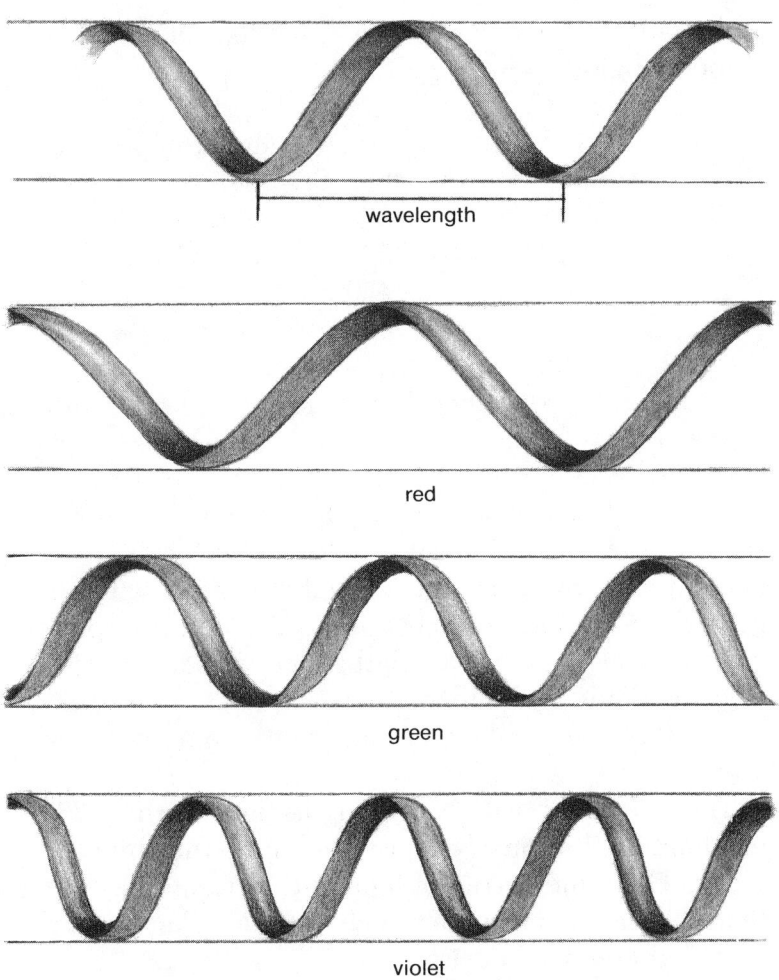

Differences in wavelengths

little table of the average wavelengths of different colors of light, it looks like this:

red	700 nanometers
orange	600 nanometers
yellow	580 nanometers
green	520 nanometers
blue	450 nanometers
violet	410 nanometers

Light bends slightly when it passes from air into water or glass. The shorter the wavelength, the more it bends. Sunlight is a mixture of all wavelengths, all colors, but when it passes into tiny drops of water in the air, the different wavelengths bend by different amounts and the colors all separate. That's what happens when we see a rainbow in the air. Water droplets have separated the wavelengths, and we see bands of color blending into one another.

But those are only the wavelengths our eyes can see.

There is light with wavelengths longer than 780 nanometers, but our eyes just don't have the ability to see it. The same is true of light with wavelengths less than 390 nanometers. Yet such extra-long and extra-short light waves do exist.

In 1800, the extra-long light waves were discovered by a German-born, British scientist, named William Herschel (HER-shel, 1738–1822). Those extra-long light waves are called *infrared rays* (IN-fruh-red, meaning "below the red"). Infrared rays can have wavelengths of from 780 nanometers all the way up to

Light bending as it passes from air to water

10 million nanometers, or 1 centimeter, which is the same thing.

In 1801, the extra-short light waves were discovered by a German scientist named Johann Wilhelm Ritter (RIT-er, 1776–1810). Those extra-short waves are *ultraviolet rays* (UL-truh-VY-oh-let, meaning "beyond the violet"). Such ultraviolet rays have wavelengths of from 390 nanometers down to about 10 nanometers.

But where does it stop? How short can the waves get? How long?

In 1873, a British scientist, James Clerk Maxwell (1831–1879), showed that electricity and magnetism were different ways of dealing with the same thing. The combination is called *electromagnetism* (ee-LEK-troh-MAG-neh-tiz-um).

Objects that carry electricity or objects that are magnetic produce an *electromagnetic field* that fills the space around them. This electromagnetic field can produce waves of *electromagnetic radiation* (RAY-dee-AY-shun). The kind of light we see, as well as infrared rays and ultraviolet rays that we don't see, are all examples of such electromagnetic radiation.

Maxwell argued that such radiations could come in any wavelength from thousands of meters down to tiny fractions of a nanometer.

In 1888, a German scientist, Heinrich Rudolf Hertz (HURTS, 1857–1894), discovered very-long-wave radiation. These waves came to be called *radio waves*, and some of them are indeed thousands of meters long. In American measurements, it means that some radio waves have wavelengths of miles.

The shortest radio waves, those that are just a little

longer than the longest infrared rays, are *microwaves* (MIKE-roh-wavez). The wavelengths of microwaves are anywhere from 1 millimeter long to 150 millimeters. (In inches, that would be anywhere from 1/25th of an inch to 6¼ inches.)

In 1895, another German scientist, Wilhelm Konrad Roentgen (ROINT-gen, 1845–1923), discovered very-short-wave electromagnetic radiation. He called it *X rays*, and its wavelengths turned out to be anywhere from 10 nanometers down to about 1/1000 of a nanometer.

The next year, a French scientist, Antoine Henri Becquerel (beh-KREL, 1852–1908), found that certain elements, like *uranium* (yoo-RAY-nee-um), were constantly giving off radiation. Another French scientist, Paul Ulrich Villard (vee-YARD, 1860–1934), found that among the radiations given off by uranium was a kind of electromagnetic radiation with wavelengths even shorter than those of X rays. The new radiation are the *gamma rays* (GAM-uh), which have wavelengths all the way down to 1/100,000th of a nanometer, or less.

Here, then, is a list of the different kinds of electromagnetic radiation, from the longest waves down to the shortest:

radio waves
microwaves
infrared rays
visible light
ultraviolet rays
X rays
gamma rays

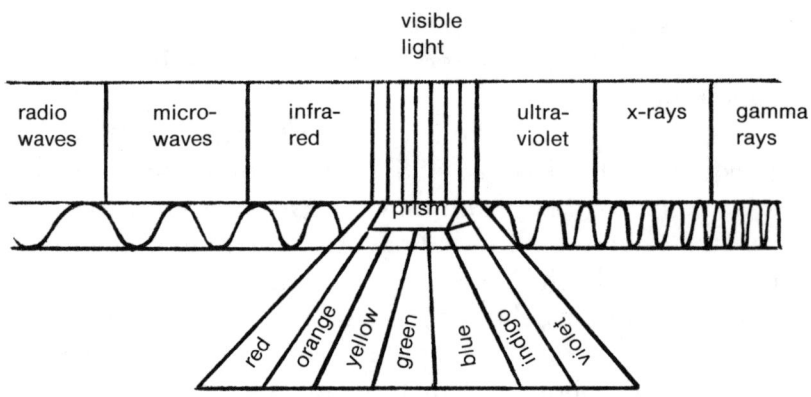

Different kinds of electromagnetic radiation from longest to shortest

2
Radiation and Energy

LIGHT IS A form of *energy* (EN-ur-jee). Energy is anything that can do work, and light can do work.

A beam of light seems to pour out energy continuously, just as though it were a stream of water. The energy might seem as though it could be broken up into smaller and smaller bits forever. The stream of water looks like that, too, but we know that water is made up of tiny atoms that are far too small to see, and that atoms are the smallest bits of ordinary matter.

If water looks as though it pours out in a steady stream but is really made up of tiny atoms, is it possible that energy is really made up of tiny chunks of some kind, too?

A German scientist, Max Karl Ernst Ludwig Planck (1858–1947), was wondering about that in 1900. He was trying to work out the way in which hot objects give off electromagnetic radiation of different wavelengths. Why do they give off more of one kind of wavelength than of another kind?

A number of scientists had tried to work out an explanation and to use that as a way of describing how the wavelengths ought to come off. However, their descriptions never fit what was really so, and a scientific explanation that doesn't match reality is useless.

All the other scientists, however, had tried to work things out by supposing that energy just poured out continuously and didn't consist of little chunks. Planck thought: What if those little chunks are there?

He put that possibility into his thinking and found that he was able to work up a description of how hot objects produced radiation of different wavelengths. His description matched what was really so.

Planck wondered just how much energy there was in each little chunk, so what he worked out is called *quantum theory* (KWAN-tum, from a Latin word meaning "how much?"). Planck found that the amount of energy in each chunk was extremely tiny. That's why it took so long for scientists to realize those chunks were there.

In 1918, Planck received a Nobel Prize for this work.

Eventually, each little chunk was called a *photon* (FOH-ton). One very important thing that Planck found out was that the amount of energy carried by a photon was different for electromagnetic radiation of

Max Planck in his study

different wavelengths. The shorter the wavelength, the greater the energy of the photon.

For instance, violet light has a wavelength about half that of red light. This means that a violet-light photon has twice the energy of a red-light photon. For this reason, violet light can do more work. Even though a particular beam of red light and another of violet light might have the same total energy, the violet light comes in larger photons, and that's what counts.

Suppose, for example, someone threw a pound of powder at you. You wouldn't feel a thing. If he threw a pound of pebbles at you, you would feel each pebble. If he threw a one-pound piece of rock at you, he might hurt you very badly.

One of the kinds of work light does is to darken the chemical on photographic film, so that you can form a picture on it. The red-light photons are so small that, with ordinary film, nothing happens to the chemicals. That's why films are often developed under red light. You can see what you're doing and the film isn't affected. With shorter-wavelength light, the film would be darkened at once.

Naturally, wavelengths that are longer than red light carry still less energy. Infrared rays have less energy than visible light. Microwaves have still less energy, and radio waves have the least energy.

It works the other way at the other end of the spectrum. Ultraviolet rays, with shorter wavelengths than visible light, have more energy. X rays have still more energy, and gamma rays have the most energy.

We can feel the increase in energy as wavelengths

grow shorter. Radio waves are all about us because radio and television stations broadcast them, but they are too low in energy to harm us. Sunlight, on the other hand, darkens our skin. If we have very fair skin, sunlight might even burn our skin.

Exposure to sunlight over a considerable period, especially to the shorter wavelengths of sunlight, can cause skin cancer. There are ultraviolet rays in sunlight, and those do most of the damage.

X rays and gamma rays are even more dangerous. Doctors and dentists use X rays to study the situation in tissues inside your body. However, they expose you as briefly as possible. Gamma rays are even more dangerous.

Whenever any object is surrounded by material that is cooler than it is, the object gives off electromagnetic radiation that cools it down. When an object is surrounded by materials that are warmer than it is, the object absorbs the electromagnetic radiation being given off by the other material, and it warms up. Electromagnetic radiation always goes from a warmer place to a cooler place, evening out the temperature.

So everywhere in the universe, photons are flying from one object to another. Some are being given off all the time, and this is called *emission of radiation*.

Objects giving off photons give them off in a variety of wavelengths, but some wavelengths come off in greater quantities than others. Usually, there is some intermediate wavelength that comes off in greatest amounts. Wavelengths that are longer or shorter come off less frequently. Wavelengths that are much shorter or much longer hardly appear at all. This was all explained by the quantum theory.

Suppose an object gets hotter and hotter. Naturally, as it does so, it gives off more and more photons. What's more, as it gets hotter and hotter, the photons it produces have more and more energy, on the average. That means that the intermediate-wavelength photons that are given off most frequently are of shorter wavelength in hot objects than in cold objects.

Thus, very cold objects give off only photons of radio waves and microwaves. By the time an object is as warm as the human body, it is giving off mostly infrared rays.

A kettle of boiling water gives off a great deal of infrared rays, and if you put your hand near the kettle (not on it, of course), you can feel the rays as heat. Your hand is cooler than the kettle, so it absorbs the infrared-ray photons, and that warms your hand.

If you were to heat something very strongly, then, eventually some photons of visible light would begin to be given off. Mostly there would be the longer light waves, so the object would be *red hot*. If it were heated further and further, more and more visible-light photons of shorter and shorter wavelength would come off and the object would be *white hot*.

The surface of the sun is white hot. If you build a bonfire, that fire is not as hot as the sun's surface, and the flames seem to be yellowish or even orange.

In any object, the various atoms and combinations of atoms contain energy, and they are always moving around and jostling each other. The jostling transfers

Emission of photons as an object becomes hotter

photons from atom to atom and sends some into the outside world.

Generally, each atom gives off a photon of some particular wavelength in such a way that it is moving in some particular direction. Another atom may give off a photon of a different wavelength in a different direction.

This means that in any object, we have photons spraying outward in all directions and over a whole range of different wavelengths. This is true of sunlight, of bonfires, of candles, of electric lights, of hot kettles, of everything. You wouldn't think there was any other way in which photons could be given off.

3
Masers

IN 1917, A German scientist, Albert Einstein (1879–1955), thought about the way photons are given off. It seemed to him that a particular type of atom or group of atoms could pick up a photon of just the right size to send it to a higher level of energy, one that would just fit its structure. The atom or group of atoms would then be *excited* and, sooner or later, it would give up the extra energy and would produce a photon of just the size that had excited it. Different atoms would give up those photons at different times and in different directions.

But suppose you could get all the atoms in a given material excited. All of them would have this extra energy. And suppose that a photon would now come along of just the right size to excite them. It would hit an atom, but it wouldn't excite it because that atom was already excited. Instead, the photon would cause the atom to give up its own extra photon at the moment it was hit. The photon it gave off would be exactly the size of the photon striking it, and the second photon would move off in exactly the same direction as the first.

Now there would be two photons of the right size, and they would hit two other atoms and produce two more photons. Then the four would hit four other atoms and there would be eight, and so on, and so on. All this would happen very quickly so that, before you could blink your eyes, billions and billions of photons would be produced, all of the same wavelength and all moving in the same direction.

This is not the ordinary kind of emission of radiation that you see in a bonfire or in the sun, where the photons fly off every which way and at every wavelength. It is the kind of emission that happens when excited atoms are struck by a photon of just the right size. The atoms are *stimulated* by the photon, so this kind of emission is called *stimulated emission of radiation*.

What's more, though you start off with a single photon, you end up with countless numbers. You might not detect the single photon to begin with, but the vast numbers of photons you produce are easy to detect. The original photon has been magnified or *amplified* into a much larger display of energy. When this happens, you can speak of *amplification by stimulated emission of radiation*.

Ordinary radiation, with its photons moving in every which way on every which wavelength, doesn't stick together. It tends to spread out. Even if you use a curved mirror so that all the rays of light are reflected in the same direction, as in a flashlight or in an automobile light, the light still spreads out quickly. Such light is *incoherent* (in-koh-HEER-ent), meaning "doesn't stick together." It is also *polychromatic* (POL-ee-kroh-MAT-ik), meaning "in many colors" or "in many wavelengths."

Stimulated emission of radiation, however, has all the same wavelength. It is *monochromatic* (MON-oh-kroh-MAT-ik), meaning "one color" or "one wavelength." Also, since all the photons are moving in the same direction, the light hardly spreads out at all. It is *coherent* (koh-HEER-ent), meaning it "sticks together."

Einstein was a theoretical physicist. That means he tried to work out in his mind and on paper what ought to happen if Planck's quantum theory was correct. But suppose Planck's quantum theory wasn't completely correct. We should set up an experiment and see if we actually do get stimulated emission of radiation. We have to see if reality matches the theory.

In 1924, experiments were conducted that showed there could indeed be stimulated emission of radiation

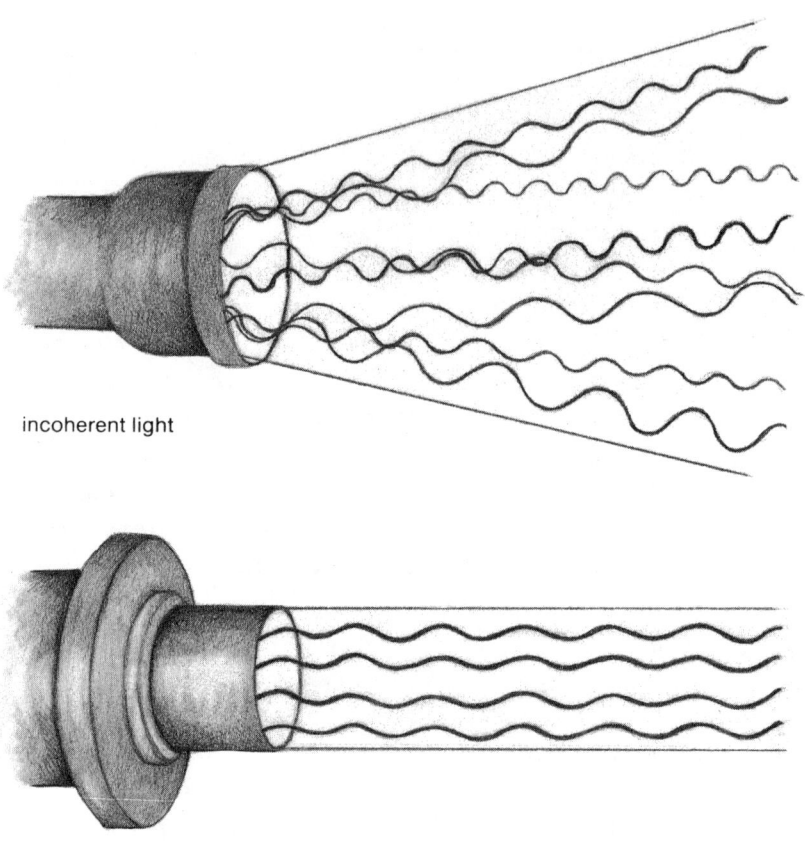

Comparison of coherent and incoherent light

and that such radiation would indeed be coherent and monochromatic.

But how could you produce real quantities of such coherent radiation? It doesn't sound as though it would be easy. After all, there is a great deal of radiation in the universe about us, but it is all incoherent. That makes it look as though ordinary emission is easy to produce and stimulated emission is hard.

The reason stimulated emission is hard to create is that once you stimulate atoms to absorb particular photons, they don't hang on to those photons very long. You can't seem to get enough atoms excited and keep them excited long enough to stimulate them.

This seemed so clear that, for a long time after scientists knew that stimulated emission of radiation was possible, no one tried to bring it about in an important way.

But then, in 1951, an American scientist, Charles Hard Townes (b. 1915) was trying to figure out a way of producing a strong beam of microwaves. It occurred to him that the molecule of a gas called "ammonia" would absorb a microwave photon of just the size he was interested in. If enough ammonia molecules could be excited and if they could be stimulated, he would get a strong beam of microwaves.

Townes realized that it wouldn't be possible to excite all the ammonia atoms and keep them excited just by heating them. Other methods would have to be used. An electric current might do it, or a beam of light, or a chemical reaction. If he could do it, then he could stimulate the excited ammonia and get his large beam of microwaves.

Charles H. Townes explaining his ammonia maser

Not until December 1953 were Townes and his students able to devise a successful instrument. Inside it, the ammonia molecules could all be excited and made to hang on to their extra photons till a photon of the right size was sent in to make them all let go at once. That was amplification by stimulated emission of radiation, but since it involved microwaves, it was *microwave amplification by stimulated emission of radiation*.

Even scientists don't like to say all that every time they want to talk about the device, so Townes took the initial letters of the long words: m–a–s–e–r. He called it a *maser* (MAYZ-er).

At about the same time, two scientists in the Soviet Union were also working on schemes for setting up a maser. One was Alexander M. Prokhorov (proh-HOR-ov, b. 1916) and the other was Nikolai G. Basov (BAS-ov, b. 1922). In 1964, a Nobel Prize was shared by all three—Townes, Prokhorov, and Basov—for their work on the maser.

The first masers that were built gave off only brief pulses of microwaves. Once the atoms or molecules were excited and then stimulated, all the extra photons would be emitted and, in a fraction of a second, there would be no more excited atoms or molecules in the maser. The molecules would have to be excited again before they could be made to emit radiation again.

But in 1956, a Dutch-American scientist, Nicolaas Bloembergen (BLOOM-ber-gen, b. 1920), got the idea of using a molecule that would have three energy levels. There would be the ordinary level at the bottom, then an excited level above that, and then a still more excited level above that.

If you have such a three-level maser, you can pump the molecules from levels one to level three. A photon of the proper size will drop the molecule from level three to level two, releasing a flash of microwaves. The molecules would then drop from level two to level one but would be immediately pumped up to three again. One kind of photon could do the pumping and another kind could do the stimulation. They could work together, without interfering with each other, so that the maser stays excited and continues to emit.

Bloembergen was the first to build a "continuous maser," and, in 1981, he was given a share of the Nobel Prize for this.

Remember that masers are amplifiers. Suppose a maser is exposed to radiation from space. If a photon happens to come along that is at the proper energy level, it will excite a beam of microwaves from the maser. Scientists would find it much easier to detect the beam than the original photon. This makes a maser a very sensitive *detector* and helps astronomers learn more about what goes on in space.

Of course, a particular maser might detect only photons of a certain energy, but different kinds of masers were quickly manufactured. Some made use of one gas or another. Some made use of solid materials. Actually, then, microwaves of a great many different wavelengths can be detected by one type of maser or another.

Remember, too, that the microwave beams produced by masers are coherent. They don't spread out very much even over long distances. A beam of such microwaves, aimed in the right direction, can travel all the way to Venus without spreading much. It will hit Venus and be reflected, and the *microwave echo* can then be detected when it returns to earth.

Microwaves travel at the speed of light, and we know the speed of light very exactly. The time between the emission of the beam and the detection of the echo is the time it takes the microwaves to go to Venus and back at the speed of light. (It's only a matter of minutes!) That tells us exactly how far away Venus was at the moment the microwaves struck its stuface.

In fact, measuring astronomical distances by microwave beams is the best way of doing it that we have yet discovered. Astronomers now know the orbits of the planets more exactly than ever before.

Venus has a thick layer of clouds that covers the entire planet at all times. We can't see through the clouds, even with the best telescopes, so until recent years no one had any idea what the solid surface of Venus was like. They couldn't even tell how fast Venus was turning or in which direction.

Microwaves, however, can pass right through Venus's clouds and hit the solid surface. There they are reflected and pass through the clouds again so that the echo reaches us.

A beam sent out by a maser is monochromatic and is all the same wavelength. If Venus's surface were perfectly smooth and motionless, the beam would be reflected with no change in its wavelength. However, if the planet is turning, the surface is moving, and that produces a change in the wavelength. The faster it is moving, the greater the change. Through studying microwave echoes, scientists were able, in 1962, to calculate the exact way and speed in which Venus was rotating. They never knew that before.

Then, too, if the surface of Venus is uneven, if it has mountains and ravines, that also affects the microwave echo. Such beams have actually been used to locate those unevennesses. In 1978, a probe was put into orbit around Venus, and it worked out a map of Venus's surface by microwave echoes.

Microwave beams have reached farther than Venus. They have touched Mercury, Mars, the sun, Jupiter, and so on. In 1989, microwave echoes were detected after a microwave beam was bounced off Titan, a large satellite of the planet Saturn, which is thirty-five times as far from Earth as Venus when Venus is closest to us.

Titan is the only satellite that has an atmosphere, and that atmosphere is so thick and hazy that even a probe wasn't able to tell us anything about its surface.

The microwave beam, taking about $2\frac{1}{3}$ hours to go to Titan and back, could pass through the clouds and give us information about the surface. It was sent out on three different days, hitting different parts of Titan's surface each day, since the satellite turns. The echo on the first and third days was very weak, as though it had hit liquid. On the second day, it was strong, as though it had hit solid material.

It may be, then, that Titan, like Earth, has both oceans and continents. But, of course, the materials making up Titan's oceans and continents are surely far different from those making up Earth's surface.

4
Lasers

IF YOU CAN prepare masers that produce beams of microwaves of one wavelength or another, then why can't you produce beams of electromagnetic radiation that are not microwaves at all? If you choose your materials carefully, you may get energy levels that are far enough apart to produce unusually energetic radiation. That would be radiation with unusually short wavelengths. Perhaps you could produce a beam of infrared waves, or even of visible light.

Townes was already thinking about that in 1958 and

trying to work out what materials might be needed in a maser to produce a beam of light instead of microwaves. A light-producing maser would be an *optical maser*.

That's not what scientists decided to call it, however. A maser is *microwave amplification by stimulated emission of radiation*. If a light beam were produced instead, that would be *light amplification by stimulated emission of radiation*. The initials of that, as you can see, are l–a–s–e–r, so the device is called a *laser* (LAYZ-er).

You can tell by the first letter. A maser produces a coherent, monochromatic beam of microwaves; a laser produces a coherent, monochromatic beam of light.

The first successful laser was put together in 1960 by an American scientist, Theodore Harold Maiman (MAY-man, b. 1927). He used a rod of synthetic ruby, which consists of a material called aluminum oxide to which a small amount of chromium oxide is added. It is the chromium atoms that give the material a red color and make it a ruby.

The chromium atoms can be pumped up to an excited state, and, when they fall to a lower level, they produce enough energy to emit photons of a wavelength that is seen as red light. After the rod has been excited, a photon of the correct wavelength is sent into the rod. Then it begins to produce additional photons of that same wavelength. These flash out of the ruby bar to form a deep red beam of coherent, monochromatic light.

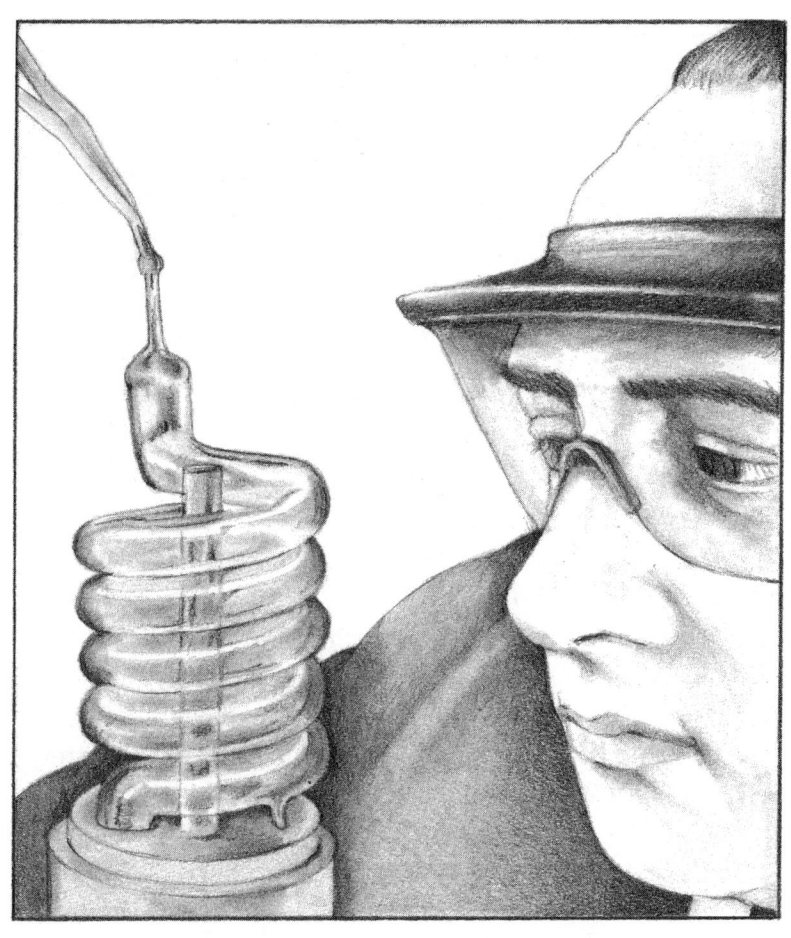

Theodore Maiman contemplating the first ruby laser

The first laser was intermittent. It produced a flash of light, and it had to be excited again before it could produce another. However, before 1960 was over, an Iranian-born scientist, Ali Javan, used a gas mixture of neon and helium and produced a continuous laser.

Before 1960, scientists had never seen coherent, monochromatic light. All the light that reached them from ordinary Earth sources, from the sun, and from the stars was incoherent and polychromatic.

Since 1960, however, coherent light has been detected from astronomical objects. There are clouds of thin gas in places between the stars, and they are called *interstellar clouds* (IN-ter-STEL-er). The atoms in these gases are, in a few cases, stimulated by light from nearby stars, and they can produce beams of coherent microwaves as a result. Such clouds are called *cosmic masers*.

Something similar happens in the atmospheres of Mars and Venus. The atmosphere on each of these planets is mostly carbon dioxide. The carbon dioxide in the upper heights of those atmospheres is excited by sunlight and produces coherent beams of infrared rays. In fact, carbon dioxide lasers have been designed here on Earth that produce radiation very much like that produced naturally by the upper atmospheres of Mars and of Venus.

Cosmis masers and lasers, however, are not nearly as effective as the devices we build on Earth. The coherent beams of radiation produced in space form bundles that go off in different directions. That's what

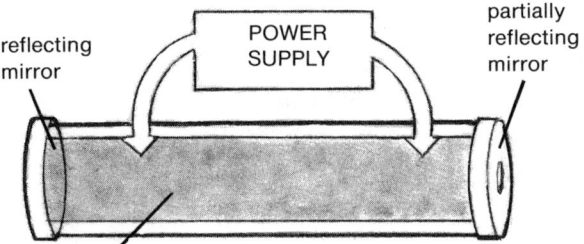

Material (solid, liquid, or gas) which produces the laser beam

Initial burst of light excites the atoms inside the tube. Photons fly out in all directions.

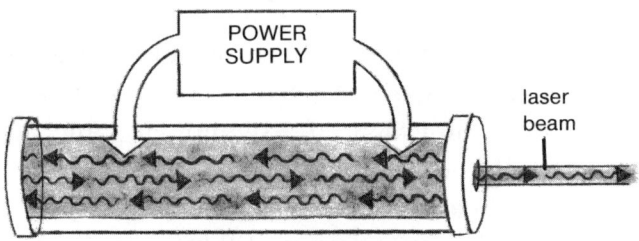

The excited atoms bounce back and forth between the mirrors until they build up enough energy to burst through the partial mirror and produce a beam of light.

made them so difficult to detect until scientists knew what they were looking for.

In lasers designed on Earth, the natural tendency for coherent light to move in the same direction is increased by the use of mirrors, which, of course, don't exist in interstellar clouds or in planetary atmospheres. The two ends of the tube in which the laser beams are formed are accurately polished and made into mirror surfaces. The photons in the beam then bounce back and forth in an exact straight path, gathering more photons and more total energy with each pass.

Any photon that happens to be moving in a direction that is the slightest bit different from the rest reaches one side of the bar in a tiny fraction of a second and is absorbed or leaks out. Any photon that happens to get into the bar from outside and is moving in the wrong direction passes through the bar and out the other side.

Eventually, the laser beam is very tightly focused. One of the mirrors is partly transparent, and when the laser beam grows intense enough (which is almost at once), it blasts through that end of the rod.

A laser beam can be focused so tightly that it can travel a million meters and still hit something as small as a pot and heat the coffee in it. In 1962, a laser beam reached the moon, which is about 383 million meters away, and even at that distance it had only spread out about two miles. We can do better now. In 1969 astronauts left a mirror on the moon and laser beams began bouncing back to earth, allowing scientists to

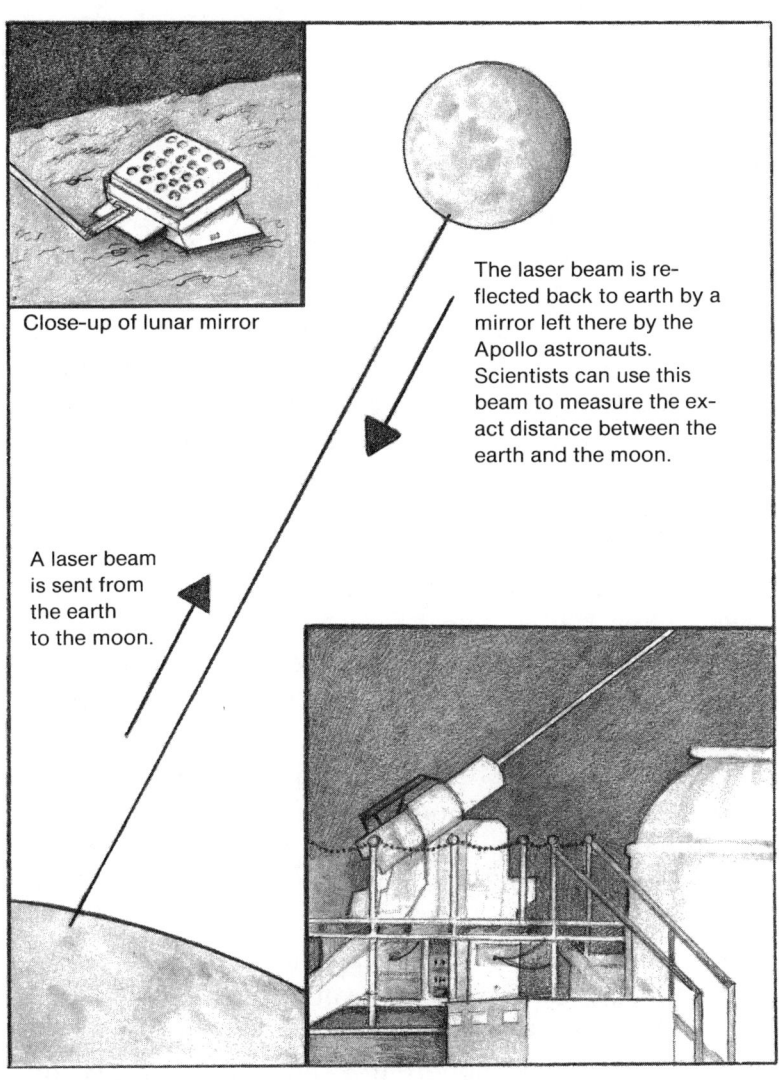

Use of the laser beam in astronomy

measure the distance between the moon and earth with new accuracy.

In 1964, the first *chemical laser* was devised by an American scientist, Jerome V. V. Kasper. In such a laser, the source of the energy is a chemical reaction. The energy produced by this chemical reaction excites the molecules in the laser and produces the coherent light.

An ordinary laser is like an electric device that has to be plugged into a socket so that energy can reach it from the outside to make it work. In a chemical laser, the energy source is part of the laser. It is like an electric device that includes a battery so that electricity runs it without the need for a socket.

Of course, a battery runs down eventually, and so do the chemical reactions in a chemical laser. However, while the chemical laser is running, it is more efficient than an ordinary laser. More of the energy in a chemical laser is turned into coherent light than in an ordinary laser.

Organic lasers were first developed in 1966 by John R. Lankard and Peter Sorokin. They make use of what are called *organic molecules*. Such molecules are built up of many atoms, including a number of carbon atoms.

Because organic molecules are so complicated, they can gain energy at various levels as one part of the molecule or another is excited. That means an organic laser can produce coherent beams in a variety of wavelengths, and there are ways of tuning it so that it will produce one particular wavelength on one occasion and a different wavelength on another occasion.

Nowadays, the most common types of lasers are *semiconductor lasers* (SEM-ee-kon-DUK-ter). They use small devices made of the same materials we find in computers, the so-called "chips." Such a laser can be no larger than a grain of salt. An electric current passes through it and causes it to emit tiny rays of coherent light.

5
The Uses of Lasers

WHEN MASERS AND lasers were first invented, it seemed they might be suitable for scientists, but many people wondered if they would ever have any uses in the ordinary world around us. It turned out that there are many such uses.

In the first place, lasers can produce coherent light in all sorts of amounts, and they are all useful. Semiconductor chips that produce very tiny laser beams can be used to read the bar codes on the objects you buy in the supermarket so that the price can be recorded. The beam is so feeble that it is not even noticeable. Its power is less than a thousandth of a watt, thousands of times weaker than the smallest night-light.

It is also possible, however, to build a large laser and arrange it so that the energy in it piles up to incredible heights and is then released all at once. In that case, an enormous amount of energy can be produced, but it all gets used up almost at once so that the beam lasts only for a short while.

There are lasers that can produce a flash of coherent light of more than 2 million watts, but it lasts only for a few seconds. There is even one that can flash at 100 million million watts, which is a hundred thousand times as much energy as a large nuclear reactor can produce. However, such a flash can last only less than a billionth of a second. These giant lasers are only used for scientific work, or for possible weapons. They are not for supermarkets.

Actually, lasers use up a lot more energy than they produce. Of all the energy that goes to excite the molecules, only a part can come out as a flash of laser light—perhaps twenty percent at most. The rest is just turned into heat.

You might wonder what good it is to have a laser beam if you have to waste eighty percent or more of the energy used to produce it. The answer is that the laser beam can be put to use to do things that other forms of energy cannot do. That more than makes up for the energy that is lost.

For instance, because the laser beam is coherent, it can be concentrated and made to come to a very fine point. Ordinary light won't do that because its waves go every which way and can't be brought to an exact point. A laser beam can easily be focused into a tiny spot only 1,000 nanometers across, and that is only

A carbon dioxide laser cutting through metal.
The flashes are incandescent specks of metal.

twice as wide as a light wave. All the energy of the laser beam is concentrated into that tiny spot, and the temperature at that spot goes way up.

If the laser is very weak, it can be used to cut paper and rubber. A stronger laser can be used to cut and drill plastic or wood. If you concentrate the beam very tightly, you can make it hot enough to melt its way through metal.

A concentrated laser beam can cut through metal more quickly and far more neatly than a torch or a saw can. It can also cut metal with the use of less energy altogether, even if eighty percent or more of the energy producing the laser beam is wasted.

The laser can also be used to do very delicate work, if the flash comes and goes in just a tiny fraction of a second. While it is on, the temperature is very high at the exact point where the beam is concentrated, but then the flash goes off again before the heat has time to spread.

For instance, a laser-eraser was invented that produces enough heat to burn off the typewriter ink and does it so quickly that it doesn't have time to scorch the paper. Naturally, it would be silly to use a laser when an ordinary eraser, or a bit of whitener, would do the trick, but the process shows what lasers can do.

Lasers can be used in this way in the human body. For instance, if the retina of the eye should show signs of coming loose, that could lead to blindness. A quick flash of laser light through the pupil can pin the retina tightly to the back of the eye, forming so small a spot that it doesn't interfere with vision. The laser does

The use of the laser in eye surgery

this so quickly that the heat has no chance to harm anything around the spots. Laser light can also be used to remove warts, freckles, tattoos, corns, wine marks, and even for simple operations.

Lasers can also be used for printing. Early word processors have printers that slam letters against a ribbon onto the paper. That makes considerable noise. In a laser printer, the laser prints the letters on the page, does it very quickly and very silently. All word processors will eventually have laser printers, even mine.

The most common use of lasers right now, though, is in reproducing sound. Until recently, recordings were made on flat disks. A groove is formed by a vibrating needle. The needle vibrates to the complicated sound waves of speech and music. Later, when the record has been hardened, another needle can follow the groove and is made to vibrate in exactly the same way the original needle did. That means the original sound waves are formed again. These are amplified and you can hear speech and music.

In this arrangement, the needle slowly wears out and has to be replaced. There is often a faint scraping sound.

But now there are records in which the sound waves are converted into a pattern of tiny dark spots on a shiny surface. The dots are invisible to the eye. A very weak infrared beam from a tiny semiconductor laser scans the surface and changes the pattern into sound waves.

There is no actual touch of metal against record, so there is no scratching of any kind. The sound reproduction is completely pure and without noise. What's more, more sound can be squeezed onto a record of a given size in the form of tiny dark spots than as a wavering groove. For this reason, since the new laser records are smaller and more compact, they are called *compact disks,* or *CD recordings.* CD recordings are rapidly replacing all others.

Another important use for lasers involves sending messages. For years, people have been using radio waves to communicate. Different radio or television stations can send out programs at the same time, because each one uses a different wavelength. On your radio set or television set, you can adjust the wavelength that is being received by turning a knob. In that way, you get only the station or the channel you want and the rest can be ignored.

Radio and television stations, however, must leave gaps between the wavelengths they use so that there is no overlap and confusion between two nearly alike wavelengths. This means that only a certain number of stations and channels can be found on your sets.

The shorter the wavelength, the more different messages can be squeezed into a given range. For instance, light waves are only about a millionth as long as radio waves, so that you might be able to fit a million times as many stations or channels into a range of light waves as into the same range of radio waves.

There is a catch, though. Radio waves can travel through rain, fog, clouds, trees, walls, and so on. Light can't do that. Radio waves bounce off regions in the upper atmosphere so that they can follow the curve of the Earth and reach long distances. Light travels in a straight line and quickly moves off the curve of the Earth.

But suppose we're talking about satellites in space. In space, there is no interfering weather, nothing solid to block the light, no curve of the Earth that has to be followed. Someday, when we have many people in space, they will be able to communicate with each other by means of laser beams along millions of different wavelengths.

We can do it on Earth, too, but not for radio and television, where the radiation beams go through the air. What about telephones, though?

We speak on telephones because an electric current races along copper wires. Many different messages can be carried by cable, but suppose we send light beams on long thin glass fibers. If we use a laser beam, we can squeeze hundreds, or even thousands, of different messages into these *optical fibers*.

Glass is much cheaper than copper, and coherent light will carry more messages than an electric current will. Right now fiber-optic telephone links run between many cities. Toward the end of 1988, a fiber-optic link was laid across the bottom of the Atlantic Ocean.

Fiber optics can guide light to where we want it to go inside the human body.

In 1989, doctors are experimenting with the use of laser beams to treat some kinds of cancer. First, a patient is given a *photosensitive drug* (FOH-toh-SEN-sih-tev), one that absorbs light. After two or three days, when the drug has gone all through the body, a thin optical fiber is inserted into the body and pushed

 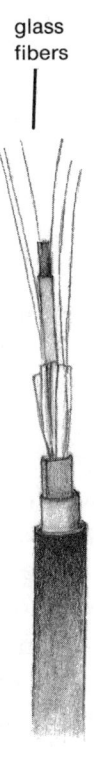

A comparison of ordinary telephone cable and new fiber-optic cable

into the tumor. A laser flash goes through the fiber and into the tumor. The drug absorbs the light and produces energetic atoms and molecules that kill the cells in the immediate neighborhood. In this way, the tumor might be destroyed, while normal cells outside the tumor aren't touched.

Laser beams have also shown their usefulness in photography. In ordinary photography, a beam of ordinary light is reflected from an object and falls on a photographic film. Where a lot of light is reflected, the film is darkened; where little light is reflected, the film isn't darkened. A dark-and-light pattern is produced, and when the film is developed, you have a photograph. The photograph, however, is flat. You don't see anything in three dimensions.

Instead, suppose a beam of light is split in two. One part of the beam strikes the objects being photographed and is reflected, while the second part strikes a mirror and is reflected. The two beams are then allowed to cross each other. They mix and form a jumble because one beam has been scattered by reflecting from an object while the other has not changed.

If you let the jumble where the two beams cross strike a photographic film, you get only a gray fog that doesn't look like anything at all. However, if you then allow light to shine through the foggy film, the light takes on all the wave forms of the two reflected beams and forms an image in the air. It is a three-dimensional image that looks very real, and it is called a *holograph* (HOH-loh-graf).

The theory of this was worked out in 1947 by the

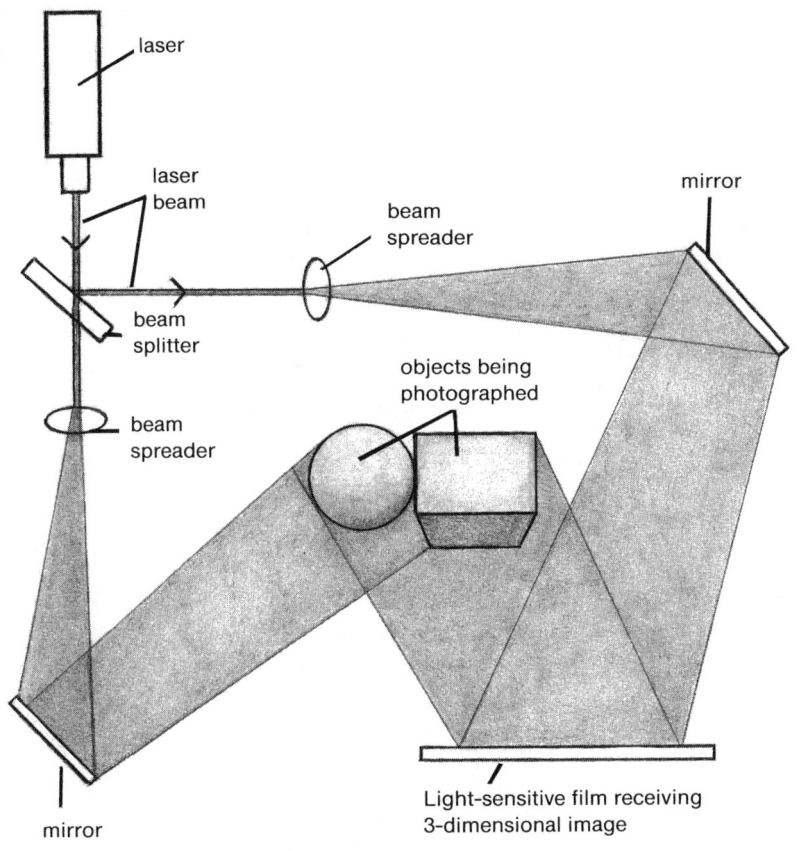

Diagram of the production of a holograph.

The image of an object is reflected onto photographic film from two different angles.

Hungarian-born British scientist Dennis Gabor (1900–1979), and in 1971, twenty-four years later, he received a Nobel Prize for the holograph.

The reason it took so long was that at first no holographs could be taken, because ordinary light doesn't give a sufficiently neat jumble. Once lasers were invented, however, holographs could be taken. In 1965, the first holograph was produced by two Americans, Emmet N. Leith and Juris Upatnieks.

Holographs are still not entirely practical, but some say we may be watching three-dimensional television on a table top. You will see football games or listen to orchestras, in miniature, that will look entirely real, except that you will be able to put your hand through them, for they will be only radiation.

Some things are still further off in the future. Scientists are trying to find ways to produce energy by making hydrogen atoms fuse to helium atoms. Such *fusion reactors* (FYOO-zhen) would produce far more energy than ordinary nuclear reactors do. Fusion reactors might also produce very little radioactivity and would be less likely to have dangerous accidents. In addition, the atoms used in fusion are much more common than those used in ordinary nuclear reactors so that the fusion fuel would last us for billions of years.

The catch is that hydrogen won't undergo fusion unless it is heated up to very high temperatures and kept in one place long enough at those temperatures for the fusion to start. Scientists have been trying to do this for nearly forty years, and so far they haven't succeeded.

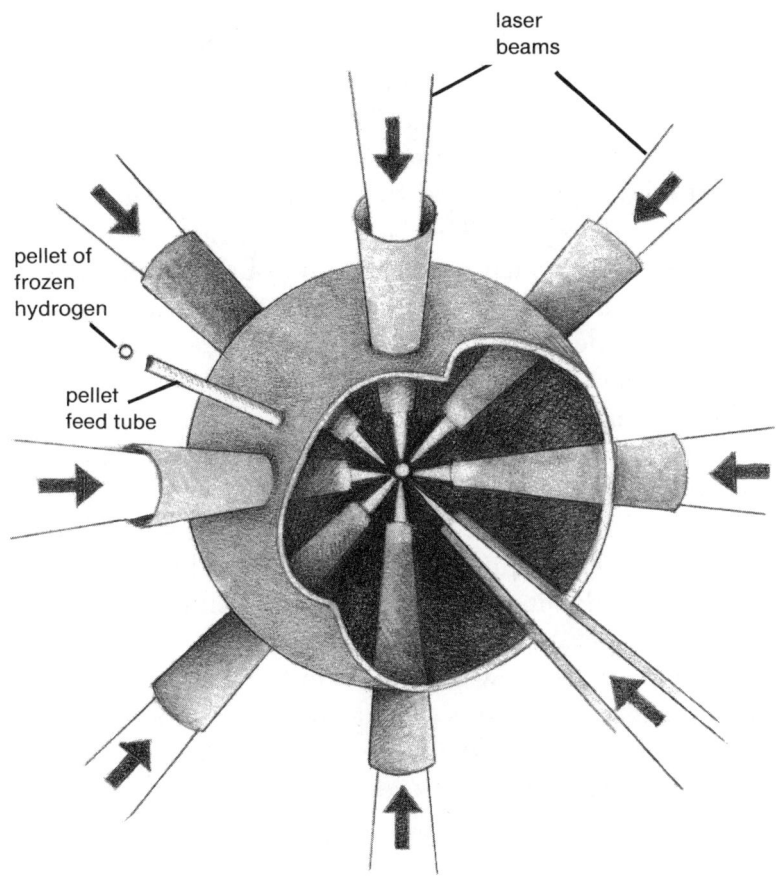

In an experimental fusion reactor, laser beams are focused on a pellet of frozen hydrogen, heating it to millions of degrees.

One of the possible ways of creating fusion is to start with frozen hydrogen. A tiny pellet of frozen hydrogen would be hit simultaneously from various directions by laser beams. That would raise its temperature to hundreds of millions of degrees. Ordinarily, the hot hydrogen gas that is produced would just expand and escape. The lasers would heat it to that temperature in such a tiny fraction of a second, however, that the hydrogen wouldn't have time to escape. It would undergo fusion instead.

This hasn't been done yet. We need stronger lasers, and scientists are working on the problem.

They are also working on systems whereby lasers in space can shoot down enemy missiles carrying nuclear bombs. This may or may not work, but missiles travel through space so quickly that only a laser beam aimed by a very advanced computer can possibly be quick enough to put a missile out of action.

Isn't it amazing, when you stop to think of it! Look at all the things lasers can do and how many more things they might do in the future. Yet only thirty years ago, lasers had not even been heard of.

Index

Ammonia, 29, 31
Amplification by stimulated emission of radiation, definition of, 27
Amplification by stimulated emission of radiation, light. *See* Lasers
Amplification by stimulated emission of radiation, microwave. *See* Masers
Astronomical distances and bodies, measurement of, 33–35, 42, 44

Basov, Nikolai, G., 31
Becquerel, Antoine Henri, 15
Bloembergen, Nicolaas, 31–32

Cancer treatment, lasers in, 54, 56
Centimeter, definition of, 10
Chemical lasers, 44
Clouds, interstellar, 40
Coherent, definition of, 27
Colors, of visible light waves, 10, 12, 20
  monochromatic, definition of, 27
  polychromatic, definition of, 27
  red hot, 22
  white hot, 22
Communications, lasers in, 53–54
Compact disks (CDs), 53
Cosmic lasers, 40
Cosmic masers, 40
Cutting tools, lasers as, 50, 52

Detectors, masers as, 32–34
Drugs, photosensitive, 54, 56

Echo, microwave
  definition of, 33
  uses of, 33–35
Einstein, Albert, 25, 27
Electromagnetic field, definition of, 14
Electromagnetic radiation
  definition of, 14
  emission of radiation, 21, 26–27, 29, 31–35
  list of different kinds of, 15
  wavelengths of, 9–10, 12, 14–15, 18, 20–22, 24
Electromagnetism, definition of, 14
Emission of radiation
  definition of, 21
  stimulated, 26–27, 29, 31–35

Energy
  definition of, 17
  relationship between wavelengths and heat, 18, 20–22, 24
Excitation, definition of, 25–26

Fiber optics, 54
Fusion reactors, 58

Gabor, Dennis, 58
Gamma rays
  discovery of, 15
  energy of, 21
  length of, 15

Heat energy, relationship between wavelengths and, 18, 20–22, 24
Herschel, William, 12
Hertz, Heinrich Rudolf, 14
Holographs, lasers and, 56, 58
Hydrogen and helium, fusion of, 58

Incoherent, definition of, 27
Infrared waves
  discovery of, 12
  energy of, 20 lengths of, 12, 14
Interstellar clouds, 40

Javan, Ali, 40
Jupiter, microwave-echo measurement of, 34

Kasper, Jerome, V. V., 44

Lankard, John R., 44
Lasers (light amplification by stimulated emission of radiation)
  in cancer treatment, 54, 56
  chemical, 44
  in communications, 53–54
  cosmic, 40
  as cutting tools, 50, 52
  definition of, 38
  discovery of, 38, 40
  focus of, 42
  holographs and, 56, 58
  organic, 44
  in photography, 56, 58
  powerful, 48
  in printing, 52
  ruby, 38, 40
  semiconductor, 45
  in sound reproduction, 52–53
  in supermarket scanners, 47
  in surgery, 50, 52
  uses of, 40, 42, 44–45, 47–48, 50, 52–54, 56, 58
  weak, 47
  in weapons, 48
Leith, Emmet N., 58
Lengths of waves. *See* Wavelengths
Light amplification by stimulated emission of radiation. *See* Lasers
Light waves, visible. *See* Visible light waves

Maiman, Theodore Harold, 38
Mars
  atmosphere of, 40

microwave-echo measurement of, 34
Masers (microwave amplification by stimulated emission of radiation)
  continuous, 32
  cosmic, 40
  definition of, 31, 38
  as detectors, 32–34
  discovery of, 31
  optical, 38
  uses of, 31–35
Maxwell, James Clerk, 14
Mercury (planet), microwave-echo measurement of, 34
Meter, definition of, 9
Metric system measurements, 9–10
Micrometer, definition of, 10
Microwave amplification by stimulated emission of radiation. See Masers
Microwaves
  echoes of, 33–35
  energy of, 20
  length of, 15
Millimeter, definition of, 10
Molecules, organic, 44
Monochromatic, definition of, 27
Moon, laser-beam measurement of the, 42, 44

Nanometer, definition of, 10
Nobel Prize
  for Basov, 31
  for Bloembergen, 32
  for Gabor, 58
  for Planck, 18
  for Prokhorov, 31
  for Townes, 31

Optical fibers, 54
Optical masers, 38
Organic lasers, 44
Organic molecules, 44

Photography, lasers in, 56, 58
Photosensitive drugs, 54, 56
Phototons
  definition of, 18
  relationship between wavelengths and heat energy, 18, 20–22, 24
Planck, Max Karl Ernst Ludwig, 18, 20, 27
Polychromatic, definition of, 27
Printing, lasers in, 52
Prokhorov, Alexander M., 31

Quantum theory, 18, 27

Radiation, electromagnetic. See Electromagnetic radiation
Radio waves
  discovery of, 14
  energy of, 20, 21
  length of, 14–15
Red hot, 22
Ritter, Johann Wilhelm, 14

Roentgen, Wilhelm Konrad, 15
Ruby lasers, 38, 40

Saturn, microwave-echo measurement of, 34
Semiconductor lasers, 45
Sorokin, Peter, 44
Sound reproduction, lasers in, 52–53
Stimulated emission of radiation, definition of, 26
  See also Amplification by stimulated emission of radiation
Stimulation, definition of, 26
Sun, the
  microwave-echo measurement of, 34
  temperature of, 22
Supermarket scanners, lasers in, 47
Surgery, lasers in, 50, 52

Titan, microwave-echo measurement of, 34–35
Townes, Charles Hard, 29, 31, 37–38

Ultraviolet waves
  discovery of, 14
  energy of, 20, 21
  length of, 14
Upatnieks, Juris, 58
Uranium, 15

Venus
  atmosphere of, 40
  microwave-echo measurement of, 33–34
Villard, Paul Ulrich, 15
Visible light waves
  colors of, 10, 12, 20, 22, 27
  definition of, 9
  energy of, 20, 21
  lengths of, 10, 12

Wavelength(s)
  definition of, 9
  of infrared waves, 12, 14
  metric system for measuring, 9–10
  of microwaves, 15
  of radio waves, 14–15
  relationship between heat energy and, 18, 20–22, 24
  of ultraviolet waves, 14
  of visible light waves, 10, 12
  of X-rays, 15
Waves
  gamma, 15, 21
  infrared, 12, 14, 20
  micro-, 15, 20
  radio, 14–15, 20, 21
  ultraviolet, 14, 20, 21
  visible-light, 9–10, 12, 20–22, 27
  X-ray, 15, 20, 21
Weapons, lasers in, 48
White hot, 22

X-rays
  discovery of, 15
  energy of, 20, 21
  length of, 15